顾家北 2.0版

顾家北◎编著

手把手教你雅思词伙

提高作文和口语水平

包括最新雅思教学成果，紧随剑桥最新考试动态

中国人民大学出版社
· 北京 ·

词伙的力量

非常感谢顾家北老师为雅思培训行业率先引入了词伙概念。在经过数十万考生反复实践的基础上，顾家北和雅思词伙，已经完全画上了等号。在上一个版本问世后的第一周，有数万考生第一时间使用本书，提供了大量鲜活的实践经验。在各种教学研讨会上，本书亦成为焦点。本次修订，基于考生的大量练习结果、同行们的教学感悟和语言专家的理论探讨。

词伙不是单词，而是流畅自然的表达。积累词伙，是跨文化交流中非常重要的一环，有助于克服中式英语，促进交流的有效性。

在雅思培训行业中引入词伙概念，让整个培训行业的有效性得到实质性提升，也让英语培训变得更加有趣和有意义。

当然，仅仅一个概念是不够的。理论与实际相结合建立在数十万考生经验积累的基础上，建立在大量的写作口语高分培训的基础上，也建立在顾家北老师数次亲临考场、自身实践的基础上。这才有了完整的雅思词伙教学。不仅仅是理论，而且是实战型教学法。

词伙的来源是大量的语言使用材料，你可以去读，可以去听；词伙的输出具有广泛的适用性，你可以去说，可以去写。

英语不难，但是方法须正确。

这本书，不仅仅是讲理论、讲教学，还讲口语和写作题库，还有考生的种种克服障碍的过程。

跟着本书的脚步，让顾家北老师手把手教你雅思词伙，让顾家北老师手把手提高你的雅思写作成绩。

吕蕾公众微信号：lvlei1973

吕蕾微博：http://weibo.com/lvlei1973

吕蕾博客：http://blog.sina.com.cn/wonderfullei

一直播：76304044

群号：572129683

吕蕾

序 言

我最先计划写有关词伙的书，大概还是在五年前。作为一个从事雅思培训十多年的老师，我非常清楚中国考生在写作和口语考试上分数很低的原因：没观点、不扣题、有观点却没有地道的表达，导致考官看不懂或者听不懂。

第一个版本我大概写了 200 页，类似于词典的方式，将一个个词伙和例句罗列出来。我越写越觉得不对劲，因为感觉学生怎么可能有耐心一个个地背这些词伙。终于，有一天早上，我痛苦地将这个文档丢进电脑的垃圾箱里。

第二个版本我大概写了 100 多页，思路是写一个类似于作文题库的东西。我将历史上考过的作文真题找出来，然后写范文，把范文里的词伙抽出来，一一讲解。因为作文是老本行，我出手很快。但是到了中间，我的直觉告诉我，这种思路也不行。一来，学生看到一篇篇范文，琢磨起来很花时间；二来，学生即便分析了范文，也只是知道这些题目的文章怎么写，题目一变又抓狂。中国学生的特点是“喜欢考试，怕学习”，你让他们学习那么多，才能去考试，他们会和你拼了。因此，我又放弃了。

来回这么一折腾，三年过去了。期间，我的微博和微信粉丝数量刷刷地涨着，学生各种提分反馈。越来越多的雅思考生相信我的方法，因此也催促我早点写完有关词伙的书。有些同学说：“老顾，我上课的时候你就说写词伙书，现在我都毕业回国了，你还没写完。”

我不是拖延症，我也不是不喜欢出书赚钱，而是我在写书上有自己的追求。一本没有创新、没有实用价值的书，一本学生觉得不好用的书，写来有什么用呢?

行内的人会觉得我很傻，马上就可以将自己名声变现卖书赚钱，却迟迟没有脱稿，真够“傻”。

所谓“傻人有傻福”。

2015 年有一天洗澡，我一边在身上抹肥皂，一边任凭思绪飞扬，突然琢磨出了一种新的思路：

(1) 挑选口语和写作比较重合的话题；

(2) 按照话题分类；

(3) 总结出一些常见的思路和观点；

(4) 给出对应词伙；

(5) 让学生大声说（而不是写）。简而言之，就是将写作和口语的 Part 3 结合到一起。

这是我记忆中时间最长的一次洗澡，越洗越兴奋。

这个思路后来经我不断打磨，渐渐有了目前的版本。

这种写作和口语结合练习词伙的思路有几个优点：

(1) 学生更加愿意练习，因为他们利用碎片时间就可以进行口语练习，不需要坐下来提笔写。

(2) 非常实惠。学生不仅复习了写作，也复习了口语。

(3) 摆脱了特定题目的约束，因为我们主要关注的是不同常见话题下的常见观点。如果考试中遇到新题目，调整观点扣题就可以。

(4) 学生在练习中记忆词伙，更加容易记住；通过对照答案，学生也能更深入了解词伙使用的语境。这样比枯燥地背词伙和例句要好。

我十多年前出国的时候，看过国内的一些语言培训资料，with the development of society, social harmony, social stability, social economy, every coin has two sides, physically and mentally, effectively and efficiently, vivid images 这些表达（要么是陈词滥调，要么是中式）基本上每个学生都写，而我后来回

国，看到很多学生还是在写这些。

我们国家经济迅速发展，而我们的作文教育还是停留在 20 世纪 90 年代的水平，这是很可悲的。可能在那个年代，大家能说英文已经不错了。而现在，我们越来越多的同学去海外不只是为了留学，还为了工作和移民，每天都和当地人交流，只是“说英文”是不够的，还要“说好英文”。这决定了我们在外国是不是轻松、自信和体面地活着。

这本书不管是在用词上，还是在学习方法上，都会给大家一个新的角度。

本书在编写过程中，陈业基、黄玉珠、黄忠武、黄玉英、黄欣、张靖娴、吕依儒、陈志爽、贾红梅、杨志、张美荣、贾玉梅也参与了资料的搜集和部分整理工作，在此一并表示感谢。

顾家北

本书使用指南

这本书主要是介绍雅思写作和口语的词伙。因为《顾家北手把手教你写作》已经系统和详细地给了很多范文，告诉学生怎么在作文中使用词伙了，所以本书更多地使用雅思口语考试的题目来告诉学生怎么使用词伙。

词伙学习贵在应用。大家可以遵循下表的学习步骤来阅读和使用本书。

进程	学习内容	页数	自我监督 完成打（√）
Day 1	阅读第 1 章 阅读第 2 章 2.1 和 2.2.1		
Day 2	练习 2.2.2 的常见问题类型 1：现状		
Day 3	练习 2.2.2 的常见问题类型 2：喜好		
Day 4	练习 2.2.2 的常见问题类型 3：看法，原因		
Day 5	练习 2.2.2 的常见问题类型 4：时间和频率		
Day 6	练习 2.2.2 的常见问题类型 5：现在和以后		
Day 7	练习 2.2.2 的常见问题类型 6：具体信息		
Day 8	练习 2.2.2 的特殊题目 阅读 2.2.3 内容		
Day 9	阅读 2.3.1 内容 练习 2.3.2 双拼法的练习		
Day 10	练习 2.3.3 双拼法的要点		
Day 11	练习 2.3.4		
Day 12	练习 2.3.5 避免雷同 阅读 2.3.6 和 2.4 内容		
Day 13	阅读 3.1, 3.2, 3.3 的内容 练习百搭观点 1 ～5		
Day 14	练习百搭观点 6 ～10		
Day 15	练习百搭观点 11 ～15		
Day 16	练习百搭观点 16 ～20		
Day 17	练习百搭观点 21 ～25		
Day 18	练习百搭观点 26 ～30		
Day 19	练习百搭观点 31 ～35		
Day 20	练习百搭观点 36 ～40		
Day 21	练习百搭观点 41 ～45		
Day 22	练习百搭观点 46 ～50		

Day 23	练习百搭观点 51 ～55		
Day 24	练习百搭观点 56 ～60		
Day 25	练习百搭观点 61 ～65		
Day 26	练习百搭观点 66 ～70		
Day 27	练习百搭观点 71 ～75 阅读 3.6 和 3.7 内容		
Day 28	阅读附录 4，5 口译附录 3		

注：备考 G 类的同学可以自己安排时间阅读第 4 章，考 A 类的同学可以不用阅读这个部分。

本书 Part 1 和 Part 2 都有中文思路，大家可以看了中文思路，自己说一次，对照范例再说一次，记忆词伙。

本书第 3 章篇幅很长，主要是 75 个作文和口语百搭观点的对应口语 Part 3 练习，每个百搭观点都有对应的一些话题词伙，而题目后面有中文思路、词伙、答案。

这些题目是方便读者练习词伙和熟悉话题观点的。建议读者按照下面的步骤练习：

第一步（熟悉百搭观点 + 思考观点）

看到 Part 3 题目之后，首先可以看一下题目之前的百搭观点，自己想想有什么观点，然后按照这个观点大声回答这个题目。

第二步（对比思路，检验自己的已有词汇量）

按照 Part 3 题目之后的中文思路，用自己的已有词汇大声说出来（注：不要看答案，因为只有自己先说出来，才会知道自己的表达有什么问题）。

第三步（使用和练习词伙）

使用 Part 3 题目之后的词伙，按照中文思路再说一次（在这个过程中，大家不仅会知道自己用词的问题，也会开始对词伙进行第一轮记忆）。

第四步（对比答案，加深对思路和词伙的记忆）

最后，看一下参考的回答，再说一次（这样不仅能对词伙进行第二轮记忆，而且还可以看一下词伙在句子中出现的位置，同时还能学习句子的连接。）

这种练习的设置是因为学生在应用词伙中要完成两个任务：

任务 *1*：学生遇到一个题目，首先能够想到观点，要知道说什么。

任务 *2*：学生想到观点的时候，大脑里马上要出现一些相关的词伙，也就是知道怎么说。

例如，口语中，考官可能会问 Do you think it is important for children to read books?（你认为阅读对小孩来说重要吗？）

那么你要马上想到一个观点：阅读书籍可以增加知识，提高竞争力等。如果你连观点都没有，你在考场上只会不断重复问题，或者只能说一两句话，而不能具体解释。

当你的大脑里有中文观点时，剩下的就是表达的问题。对应观点的英文你马上应该能够想到 increase knowledge, gain knowledge 等，提高竞争力你可以说 at an advantage, stand competition, survive in a competitive world 等。

注意事项

注意 1. 不要死记硬背词伙

如果大家只是记忆这些词伙，到了考场上可能有三个问题：① 不知道在哪里用；② 观点想出来却不知道用哪个词伙；③ 词伙想到了，但是用不准确。

按照上面的步骤学习是最好的，会有一个对词伙加深理解的过程：① 想词伙；② 用词伙；③ 检查词伙是否用对。

注意 2. 不要写，而要说

本书的内容很多，对于很多希望在一个月之内就通过雅思的同学来说，如果每个练习都要写出来那就太慢了；而且很容易变成哑巴英文的学习。

如果是用嘴巴写作文，大声说，复习一个题目的速度会大大加快，这样口语和写作可以同时练习到。

特别是那些参加了我网络课程的同学，他们的作业更多，如果要提高效率，最好的办法就是用嘴巴写作文！

在口语 Part 3 练习之后，我会讲解如何将词伙应用到口语 Part 1 和 Part 2 的备考中。Part 1 和 Part 2 提供的练习也是（中文—词伙—答案）的组合，考生可以按照思路练习，说到顺口为止，这样对词伙会更加熟悉。

最后我也会说一下怎么将词伙用到书信写作里，对于考移民类雅思的同学来说，会帮他们解决平时不知道该怎么准备雅思的问题。

目 录

第 1 章

词伙的介绍

1.1 什么是词伙

词伙（collocations）对于准备雅思写作的同学是很重要的，尤其是对希望获得 7 分的同学来说，因为剑桥雅思公布的官方评分标准（不管口语还是写作）明确指明考生需要展示词伙的能力。

Collocations 在朗文词典的定义是 the ways in which some words are normally used together。有一些国内的同行会认为这就是大家常说的“搭配”，质疑为什么要用一个新名字——“词伙”。在我眼里，“词伙”和“搭配”有以下一些不同。

特点 1：词伙要和话题相关（topic specific）

有些搭配如 demand for, positive effect, significant impact 我们经常学习，但是在雅思考试里，这些只是基础的表达，却不是重要的词伙，因为这些词在不同话题的作文或者口语题目中都可以用到，在考官眼里不是可以体现考生词汇量的“词伙”。

反之，demand for housing（对房屋的需求），impact on the environment（对环境的影响）就是词伙，前者可以用在雅思建筑类话题里，后者可以用在雅思环境类话题里。

特点 2：词伙很多时候不只是 2 个单词，可以是多个单词

词伙的学习主要意义在于可以很自然地将词伙用在写作和口语的表达中，能够很好地讲出我们经常想说的一些东西。这也就意味着词伙有时候可能会由多个单词组成，而这些单词会形成句子的主体。

如在犯罪类话题里，我们说一个东西有震慑力，词伙是 act as a deterrent。如果你说“搭配”，a deterrent 不是一个搭配，as a deterrent 也不算一个有意义的搭配，而只有 act as a deterrent 4 个单词在一起，这个词伙才有存在的意义。有些时候，为了增加变化，你可以说 act as an effective deterrent，这样，这个词伙就是 5 个单词组成的了。而我相信，很少有老师会叫学生关注有 5 个单词的“搭配”。

又如在城市类话题里，我们说移居城市，大家要学习 move to cities, migrate to cities, flock to cities，而你去查词典，词典里不会说 move to 后面一定要加 cities，migrate to 后面一定要加 cities，但是在学习中，只有把这三个单词当作一个词伙一起去记忆和使用才有意义。

特点 3：词伙学习要注意单复数、句子的位置和其他使用的特点

我们很多同学以前学习“搭配”都是死记硬背，如背记 public transport，但是在词伙学习中，这样远远不够。

首先你要知道 transport 不可数，不能加复数；其次，你要知道怎么用在作文或者口语里：

比如使用公共交通，你要记住是“use public transport”，这个词伙出现在句末比较多。又如“公共交通过于拥挤”，你要记住是“public transport systems are overcrowded”，这个词伙出现在句首的可能性更大。

这些词伙在很多词典里可能都不会收录，但是不管是雅思考试中，还是在我们和外国人交流时，都是很有用的，因为这些表达外国人也经常使用。

1.2 词伙的分类

类别 1：动词和名词的搭配

例子：raise awareness, adopt measures, take steps, adopt approaches

类别 2：形容词和名词的搭配

例子：compelling reason, ample evidence, harsh punishment

类别 3：名词词组

例子：environmental awareness, coverage of crime, health effect

类别 4：介宾短语的搭配

例子： in the media, on the internet, on television, in newspapers

类别 5：名词和介词的搭配

例子：demand for, awareness of, reason for, passion for, affection for

类别 6：形容词和介词的搭配

例子：essential/vital to, aware of, likely to, conscious of, sensitive to

类别 7：其他

除了这些比较简单的词伙之外，还有一些表示某个特定意思的习惯搭配，这些词伙往往比较多变（可能由形容词、动词、名词连在一起），也是学生在雅思备考中最应该注意的。

例子： lead a fulfilling life, close the rich/poor gap, discriminate between right and wrong

1.3 词伙的重要性

1.3.1 减少中国式英文

所谓的中国式英文，就是字字翻译中文，而最后翻译出来的英文是一些别扭的表达，这些表达外国人不认可或者是看不明白。学习词伙主要的目的就是避免学生按照中文的语感和表达创造词组搭配，减少中国式英文：

例如学习知识，很多同学觉得学习是 learn，知识是 knowledge，两者一合并，就是 learn knowledge。但是这个表达在英文里并不地道，常见的表达是 gain/increase/acquire knowledge。

另外一个例子是接受教育，很多同学认为接受是 accept，教育是 education，那么接受教育就是 accept education。但是这个表达也是不恰当的，常见的说法是 receive education。

很多时候，学生的中文也有问题。

又如有些学生说 “improve the problem”（提升问题），问题怎么可能是提升呢？应该是解决问题（solve the problem or improve the situation）。

建立起“词伙”的概念和意识可以督促大家在学习英文的过程中关注更加地道的表达。当你意识到直接翻译中文外国人看不懂的时候，你就会更加愿意去阅读英文原版的书籍，英文的媒体资料（如 BBC）。在写作和口语中，我们有些东西经常说，但是拿不准是否地道，那么通过阅读外国人写的东西，可以记住相应的表达，从而避免中式英文。

例如雅思作文媒体类话题经常说“接触暴力”，很多人会写成 contact with violence，如果我们阅读过 BBC 的文章，就会发现外国人比较喜欢的表达是 exposure to violence，那么就记住。

又如针对儿童的广告，有人喜欢写成 advertisements about children, 但是如果我们阅读过相关的书籍，就会发现 native speakers 常用的表达是 advertisements aimed at children。

又如政府类题目下的“政府的宣传”，很多同学说 government propaganda, 事实上常用的说法是 awareness campaigns。

1.3.2 辨析单词

我在微博上经常遇到的问题都是关于一些单词的辨析的。很多同学分不清楚一些近义词或者是形近词的区别，原因主要有两个：① 盯着单词的中文意思或者是单词的拼写，而不通过英文词典上的例句来学习单词的用法；② 不关注词伙。

单词辨析方法 1：查英文词典，看单词的用法

很多同学说分不清楚 prompt, promote 这两个词，主要是因为它们长得比较像，但是查一下词典的英文解释和英文例子，你就知道两个词根本没有可比性。

prompt：一般可以说 prompt somebody to do something，就是促使某人做某事

promote：不能说 promote somebody to do something，promote 有“推广”的意思，如推广产品，promote a product，还有“促进、提升”的意思，如 promote trade。

单词辨析方法 2：注意词伙

有些单词的意思相近，词性一样，用法差不多，区分主要靠词伙。

例如，大家比较纠结的 electric, electrical，如果你真要讲清楚两个单词的区别，估计比较难，但是如果记住词伙，electric cars（电力驱动汽车），electrical equipment（电器），然后多说几次、多写几次就熟悉二者的差异了。

还有 influence, impact, effect 这些单词，很多同学要么随便替换，要么不知道怎么替换。他们搞不清楚是不是替换词。最好的办法也是用词伙来辨析。

我们可以说 destructive effect, damaging effect, harmful effect，但是很少会将这些形容词和其他两个词搭配使用。

同理，我们会说 environmental effect/impact，却很少会说 environmental influence。

我们会说 huge influence，但是很少说 huge effect。

还有 consequence, result, outcome 这三个词，你一看中文词典就晕了，三个词都是表示“后果，结果”，你可能一辈子都分不清楚。

但是如果你知道 dire consequences, environmental consequences, unintended consequences 这些词伙，你就可能知道 consequence 经常是指不好的结果。

如果你知道 exam results, test results，你就可能知道 result 经常是指考试或者测试的结果。

如果你知道 learning outcome, achieve outcomes 等，你就可能知道 outcomes 经常是指达到的成果。

只有通过掌握这些词伙和阅读例句，你才可以慢慢熟悉这些单词的区别，然后多练习，最后就可以比较自然和准确地运用它们。

我们学英文的时候喜欢用眼睛学习，并且只看中文词典，这是不好的习惯。除了多看英文词典和材料，我们还要多用耳朵和嘴巴，多听一些单词在什么地方出现，学了一个词伙之后自己马上找机会使用一下，这样就会比较轻松地提升语言水平。

你光靠死记一些单词，并且以为它们是替换词，是很难做到表达地道的。在同胞面前用词不地道没什么，因为这是通病。如果和外国人交流，你可能会发现他们有时候会觉得你用词有点儿怪。

1.3.3 使表达更加简洁

很多同学在看我的文章的时候，经常有的一个感慨就是：老顾，我一句话都描述不了的东西，你几个单词就搞定了。

其实，这也是使用词伙带来的差异。我在表达一个事情的时候，一般都不会翻译我大脑里的中文，而是问自己，有没有什么词伙可以表达这个想法。

例如，有同学会写“在全球化的背景下，很多国家的有钱人跑去发展中国家投资”。在这个句子里，有两个表达很难翻译，一个是“背景下”，一个是“跑去”。如果你直接翻译，句子不仅很长，而且很别扭。而我问自己有没有词伙，如果有，就围绕词伙去表达。

In a globalised economy, investors from rich countries have flocked to the developing world in search of business opportunities.

你会发现在这个句子里我使用了 a globalised economy, rich countries, flock to, developing world, business opportunities 这些我比较熟悉的词伙。英文的句子和中文的句子不是字字对应，但是读起来通顺地道，而且非常简洁，这就是词伙的力量。

又如，有同学想表达“文凭代表着学生各方面的综合能力得到提高，以后在工作单位如鱼得水”。这个句子里有一些我们中文比较常见的表达“综合能力”，还有成语“如鱼得水”，如果字字翻译不仅啰唆，而且别扭。

我会写：Students can **expand their skills set** at university and these well-rounded graduates can complete their tasks with ease.

我使用的词伙是：

expand skills set（增加不同的技能）

well-rounded graduates（全面发展的毕业生）

complete tasks（完成任务）

这样的表达可能没有原文那么文学化，但是外国人阅读和理解都没问题，还会感觉非常地道和流畅。

这就是词伙的魅力。

1.4 词伙使用的注意事项

词伙的使用一定要注意准确性和合理性，不能看到一个词伙比较新颖就不惜一切代价地使用，这样只会让考官觉得你不懂得这些词伙的具体意思和使用特点。

常见问题 1：词伙使用的语境

有些词伙可能只用于描述某些特定的人，如 good manners, good behaviour, behavoural problems 一般来说用于描述小孩，较少用于描述成年人。

常见问题 2：词伙的正式或者非正式

有一些词伙，如 recharge batteries, let off steam, add spice to your life 多用于口语，用在书面语中就不是很好。

常见问题 3：太过极端和夸张的词伙

如 intractable problems（不可解决的问题）很多同学很喜欢用，一个问题都解决不了，那说来又有什么用呢？可以说 seemingly intractable problems。

很多同学喜欢说压力导致精神问题，会用 mental health problems, mental diseases 这两个词伙，这两个词伙事实上指的是 psychological problems“精神病”，是比较严重的心理问题，而我们生活中情绪的波动和精神压抑远远达不到这个级别。

contract a disease 很多同学以为是“生病，身体不舒服”的意思，但 disease 一般是指传染病，如果是轻微的头疼、感冒、没有胃口等，说 fall ill, suffer poor health 就可以。

常见问题 4：词伙的正确理解

很多同学学习词伙的时候比较喜欢看中文表达，而不注意其例句和英文解释，往往导致理解出现偏差。

recharge batteries 充电，不是指我们接受培训，而是表示人们去度假或者休闲。

basic necessities 表示生活必需品，不是生活用品，如住房、医疗服务、能源和水都是 basic necessities，而不是我们生活中使用的一些产品 essentials, household goods。

field work 是科学家或者做研究的人去现场进行勘察，实地做实验，而不是在实验室做工作。很多同学以为这是在公司里实习（internships or work placements）的意思。

第 2 章

词伙在口语中的应用

2.1 雅思口语考试的步骤

雅思口语考试一般来说是 10～12 分钟。主要分 4 个部分。

第一部分：Introduction

考官会先让你坐下，然后问这个问题：Do you have any electronic devices on you, like a cell phone, MP3 or a recorder?（你身上有没有任何电子设备，比如手机、MP3 或者是录音器？）

你的回答是 No（因为进入考场之前，一般都会全身检查，确保你没有携带这些电子设备）。

在确认了这一点之后考官会问你的名字（full name），然后说：Can I see your ID please?（可否把身份证给我看一下？）看了身份证之后考官会说一大段话，大概意思是考试的日期、考试中心号码、考试人的信息（比如考号、他自己的名字以及监考人号码等一大堆），之后他会说 OK。然后考试正式开始。

第二部分：Part 1

这一部分一般是问一些比较简单的问题，主要是关于考生个人的，时间是 3～4 分钟。我们会在以后的章节详细说一下 Part 1 怎么应付。

第三部分：Part 2

这一部分需要考生就一道题目做 2 分钟左右的小演讲。这一部分我会在口语 Part 2 考试备考攻略中解释。

第四部分：Part 3

这一部分考官会问大概 4～5 个问题，每个问题考官都希望你能够详细地回答。

这一部分非常像雅思大作文。相似点如下：

- 每个问题都有点像大作文的题目，虽然略微简单一点。
- 每个问题的回答都要注意扣题，体现在题目关键词的不断出现。
- 回答需要拓展，很多同学的回答很空洞，不断重复一两句话，很难获得好的分数。拓展的方法包括解释、举例、拓展结果等，这些都在《顾家北手把手教你雅思写作》中有具体的阐述。
- 回答过程要注意连贯性和逻辑性，不能天南地北胡说一气。

2.2 口语 Part 1 考试备考攻略

2.2.1 Part 1 考试注意事项

口语 Part 1 考试一般会问 5～10 个问题，时间大概是 3～4 分钟。

有时候考官可能会缩短这部分的时间，如果他们觉得考生可能“准备得很充分”，回答很模式。他们会尽快进入 Part 2 和 Part 3 部分，这两部分可以更加容易检查学生的表达能力。

在口语 Part 1 的考试中，注意以下 10 点：

(1) 回答一般要简单，由 2 句话组成，不要超过 3 句话。

(2) 第一句话要直接回答题目，最好出现题目关键词。

(3) 不要过分使用模板和套路化的语言，如 well, to be honest, it depends。

(4) 要增加自己的反应能力，能够做到迅速回答问题，平时要多积累常见的句子。

(5)Part 1 不要用太正式的语言或者大词，否则考官可能会觉得你在背答案，或者你没听懂问题，这样会影响分数。

(6) 不要追求复杂的句式或语法，关键是能够回答问题，句子结构不要残缺，句子要有逻辑。

(7) 不要只说 yes, no，要解释原因，说自己的感受，或者是适当延伸，给出例子等。

(8) 听完考官问题后不能迟迟不回答，不能保持沉默，也不能让考官换题，更不能说 I don't know, I don't know how to put it in English, I don't know the answers, I don't know how to answer these questions 这些表达。只要听懂题目，尽量说出自己的看法和想法就可以了。

(9) 语速自然，不需要蓄意加快速度，发音要清晰，不要担心自己的口音问题，雅思口语不关心口音 (不管英国口音，还是美国口音，或是亚洲口音都不重要)。

(10) 尽量保持流利性，雅思考试允许考生想不到观点的时候有所迟疑或者是语速变慢，但是如果考生在某些表达上 (如词伙) 吞吞吐吐，迟迟说不出一个单词，考官会认为考生的语言能力有问题。

Part 1 的很多题目都比较个人化，包括吃、穿、住、行、个人爱好、家乡、学校、学习、工作、娱乐、运动、媒体、网络、送礼等。

不难发现，这些题目和口语 Part 3 有很多相同之处，唯一的区别就是：Part 3 回答要非常详细和具体，而 Part 1 比较简洁 (一般就 2 句话)。

在备考 Part 1 的过程中，学生主要是关注 3 点：① 常用的句子；② 观点；③ 词伙。

首先，口语问题的问法比较类似，一般就是 where, when, how, how often, what 等。

也有一些观点类的问题，如 do you think..., is it important... 等。

在问答这些问题的时候，会用到一些常用的句子，只要平时多加练习就可以应对。

雅思口语考试 Part 1 的备考难点主要是：

难点 1: 开口难，或者使用套句。

难点 2: 内容空洞或者重复。

难点 3: 用词怪异或者中式。

解决这三个问题的方法分别是：

方法 1: 熟悉 Part 1 的常见问题类型，练习相应的句子表达。

方法 2: 熟悉 Part 1 的常见话题，思考相应的观点。

方法 3: 熟悉相关的词伙。

一般来说，Part 1 的回答由两部分组成。

第一部分：直接回答题目。

第二部分：简单说一下原因，或者是自己的个人感受。

口语 Part 1 一般都是考衣食住行、工作、娱乐、购物、休闲活动等事情，当我们给出自己的个人看法的时候，千万不要只是简单地说 yes，no，要给出解释。一般来说，可以用于解释的原因如下：

有关金钱的考虑	① 是不是贵，是不是便宜
	② 是不是提高收入，是不是对工作有帮助
	③ 是不是节省时间，是不是能够增加效率
	④ 是不是对学习有帮助，是不是对以后的择业有帮助
	⑤ 是不是对我的健康有利，是不是能减少疾病
有关快乐的考虑	① 是不是对家庭生活、家人有影响
	② 是不是对社交有影响
	③ 是不是能减压，让自己更加轻松
	④ 是不是能体现自己的个性、身份、喜好、目标
	⑤ 是不是能够丰富我的生活，提高我的生活标准
	⑥ 是不是让我们的环境更好，是不是能减少环境问题
	⑦ 是不是对我们的传统、文化有好处

2.2.2 Part 1 常见问题分类和练习

常见问题类型 1：现状

常见问法：Do you...?

Do you ever...?

Are there...?

Is...popular in...?

特点：这种题目一般是问你的个人情况（包括你的习惯），或者是社会的一个现状（包括一样东西是否常见和流行）。

回答可用句型：No, I don't, because...

Yes, I do, because...

I'm currently...

Not really...

Yes, it's true that...

Yes, we have seen...

例 1：Do you do housework at home?

直接回答题目	是的
原因或者感受	因为我觉得做家务是一种运动，对我的健康好

英文句子 *1*：Yes, I do, because I think it is a good physical activity which is beneficial to my health.

或者说：Yes, I do, because it is a kind of physical exercise, which can help me stay healthy.

直接回答题目	不是
原因或者感受	因为我学习很忙，有很多作业要做，没时间

英文句子 *2*：No, I don't have time to do housework, because I am busy with my studies. I have a lot of assignments to do.

或者说：No, I don't have a lot of free time to do household chores because I have to focus on my assignments.

例 2：Do you live in a house or a flat?

直接回答题目	住 flat
原因或者感受	因为中国城市拥挤，一般人买不起房子，只能住 flat

英文句子 *3*：I'm currently living in a small flat, because cities in China are very crowded and most people are not able to afford a house. They have to live in apartment buildings.

或者说：At the moment, I live in a small flat, because cities are densely populated in China and buying a house is unaffordable. They have to live in apartment blocks.

直接回答题目	住 flat
原因或者感受	因为我在大城市里工作，和同事合租一个房子

英文句子 *4*：I'm living in a flat, since I work in a large city. I don't live with my parents and I rent a flat with my colleagues.

或者说：I live in a flat. I share a studio with my colleagues to save money. The cost of living is rather high in this city.

例 3：Are there many advertisements in your country?

直接回答题目	很多
原因或者感受	因为中国人收入提高，有很多钱买东西

英文句子 *5*：Yes, there are many advertisements. People's income has increased significantly, and they have a lot of money to buy things.

或者说：Yes, we can see advertisements nearly everywhere. Chinese people have become better off, and they have spare money to buy whatever they like.

例 4：Do you have many books at home?

直接回答题目	很多
原因或者感受	因为我觉得读书让我很博学，对我的职业发展有帮助

英文句子 *6*：Yes, I have a lot of books at home, because I think reading can make me knowledgeable and help me advance my career.

或者说：Yes, I have heaps of books at home. I strongly believe books are a source of knowledge and can contribute to my career advancement.

直接回答题目	没有多少
原因或者感受	因为现在网络上有很多电子书，都是免费的

英文句子 *7*：Not really, because there are many e-books online, and you can read them for free. It's not necessary to buy books.

或者说：No, I don't buy books. There are many digital books available on the Internet. They are free.

例 5：Is chocolate popular in China?

直接回答题目	是的
原因或者感受	因为这已经成为惯例，年轻人买巧克力给女朋友

英文句子 *8*：Yes, chocolate has become increasingly popular in China, and it's customary for many young people to buy chocolate for their girlfriends.

或者说：Yes, many people today love to buy chocolate on special occasions, such as Valentine's Day. It's the custom to do so.

直接回答题目	不是
原因或者感受	巧克力很不健康，吃巧克力和其他糖果会导致肥胖、蛀牙

英文句子 *9*：No, I don't think so. Chocolate is unhealthy. Eating chocolate and other sweets can cause obesity and tooth decay.

或者说：Not really. We all know that chocolate is not healthy. We can become overweight and have bad teeth.

例 6：Are you close to your family?

直接回答题目	不是
原因或者感受	因为我忙于工作，很少和父母聊天

英文句子 *10*：No. I am too busy with my work so I hardly spend time talking to my parents.

或者说：No. Most of the time, I have a tight timetable, so it's difficult for me to make time to talk to my parents.

常见问题类型 2：喜好

常见问法：Do you like...?

Do you prefer...?

What do you like about...?

Is there anything you dislike...?

What...do you like?

特点：这种题目一般是问你喜欢什么（或者不喜欢什么），或者人们喜欢什么（或者不喜欢什么）。

回答可用句型：I like...

I love...

I prefer...

It depends on...

例 1：Do you like where you live?

直接回答题目	是
原因或者感受	因为交通便利，每天可以走路去公车站

英文句子 *1*：Yes, I do, because it's easy to get around. I can walk to the bus station every day.

或者说：Yes, it's a nice place. There are many forms of transport available. The bus station is within the walking distance.

直接回答题目	不是
原因或者感受	因为挺吵的，我的邻居喜欢聚会，音乐声开得很大，非常烦人

英文句子 *2*：No, not at all, because it's rather noisy. My neighbours love partying. They play loud music from time to time. It's really annoying.

或者说：No, I'd possibly move to a new place shortly. Nobody likes living next to rowdy neighbours. They play loud music when they have parties. It's really annoying.

例 2：Do you prefer to speak to people by phone or by writing emails?

直接回答题目	看情况
原因或者感受	如果我赶时间，我会打电话。如果我希望把事情说得更清楚，会写邮件

英文句子 *3*：It depends on the situation. If I am in a hurry, I'd like to make phone calls. If I want to talk about things in detail, I'd love to write emails.

或者说：It's hard to say, but I would call somebody on the phone, if I want to save time. If I want others to understand me clearly, I might choose to send emails.

例 3：Is there anything you dislike about your hometown?

直接回答题目	不喜欢
原因或者感受	环境不好，人们乱扔垃圾

英文句子 4：I don't like the ways people manage waste. They don't protect our environment well. Many people drop litter. Streets are awash with rubbish.

或者说：Waste management is the main problem. People in my hometown don't pay attention to their responsibility to community. They drop litter. It's not easy to clean up waste.

例 4：Do you like cooking? Why/Why not?

直接回答题目	有时候喜欢
原因或者感受	对健康好，食材比较新鲜

英文句子 5：Sometimes. I like cooking a meal at home, which is healthy, since I can choose fresh ingredients.

或者说：Yes, as long as I have free time. I think home-cooked meals are healthy, since I can buy fresh ingredients.

例 5：Do you prefer to write by hand or on a computer?

直接回答题目	看情况
原因或者感受	大部分时候喜欢用电脑，因为比较快。如果我需要做笔记，就用手写

英文句子 6：It depends on what I'm doing. I'd like to use the computer most of the time because it's faster, but I'd like to write things by hand if I want to make notes.

或者说：It really depends on what I write. I would prefer the computer for most things, but I'd like to make notes by hand.

例 6：Do you like to send expensive gifts?

直接回答题目	喜欢
原因或者感受	因为我喜欢看到家人和朋友收到礼物的样子，他们知道我很在意他们

英文句子 7：Yes, I do. It's a nice feeling when I see my family or friends receive gifts. They know I care about them.

或者说：Yes, I do. It's a great feeling to see my parents or friends open presents. They know I care about them.

例 7：What outdoor sports do you like?

直接回答题目	没有特别喜欢的
原因或者感受	但是喜欢跑步，适度的运动，可以和朋友一起跑，也可以认识新朋友

英文句子 8：I don't have any favourite sport, but I like jogging, gentle exercise. Running with friends is nice, and it's also a good way to meet new friends.

或者说：I don't have a great liking for any sport, but I normally go for a jog with my friends. I can handle this kind of gentle exercise, and it's also a good way to make new friends.

例 8：Do you like to be a leader?

直接回答题目	不喜欢
原因或者感受	因为这不是我擅长的，我不知道怎么鼓励人们去努力工作

英文句子 *9*：No, definitely not. Because it's not something I'm good at. I don't know how to motivate others to work hard.

或者说：No, that would be the last thing I'd like to do. I am not good at leading others. I have no idea how to encourage others to work hard.

例 9：Do you prefer to study alone or with others? Why?

直接回答题目	喜欢一个人学习
原因或者感受	因为这样比较有效率，更加专注，不容易分心

英文句子 *10*：I prefer to study alone, because I'd be more productive. It's easier to concentrate on my work. I won't get distracted.

或者说：I think I prefer to study alone, because I could achieve more. It's easier to stay focused. There are fewer distractions.

常见问题类型 3：看法，原因

常见问法：Is...important?

Do you think...?

Do you think...should...?

Why...?

特点：这种题目一般是问你对某个东西的看法，为什么这么看，这个东西是不是重要，你觉得为什么这个事情会发生。这种题目的特点就是要说原因，你可以直接陈述原因，也可以加上 because, since, it's because, the main reason is that 这样的表达来引导原因。

如果题目是以 why 起头的问句，你不需要回答 yes，直接说原因就好。

如果你不是很清楚原因，也可以用 to be honest, I'm not sure 这样的表达，但是尽量说出原因，而不只是重复题目。

回答可用句型：It's important to...

It's necessary to...

It is easy to...

It's difficult to...

It's enjoyable to...

从这个类型起，我们一个问题给 2 个回答，帮助大家拓展思路。

例 1：Do you think the clothes we wear say something about who we are?

直接回答题目	可能是的
原因或者感受	如果我们穿得很正式，说明我们很在意工作，在大公司工作有严格的着装要求

英文句子 *1*：Probably. If we wear formal dress, it means that we care about our work, and we possibly work for large companies, which have a strict dress code.

直接回答题目	可能是的
原因或者感受	如果我们买很贵的衣服，我们可能是为了展现自己的地位和品位

英文句子 *2*：Yes, possibly. If we buy expensive clothes, we may want to show our wealth or status. We possibly want to show others we have good taste.

例 2：Do you think children should be taught cookery at school?

直接回答题目	是的
原因或者感受	这样他们会更加注重饮食健康，少吃快餐

英文句子 *3*：Yes, I think it's important for children to learn how to cook meals, so they would pay more attention to healthy eating. They would eat less fast food.

直接回答题目	不需要
原因或者感受	这样会影响他们的学习，他们可以在家里学习怎么做饭

英文句子 *4*：No, I don't think so. This would interfere with their studies. Actually, they can learn how to cook at home.

例 3：Do you think walking is important?

直接回答题目	重要
原因或者感受	这样对环境好，不会产生尾气

英文句子 *5*：Yes, I think it is very important to us. It should be promoted. This mode of travel is environmentally friendly. It doesn't create car emissions.

直接回答题目	重要
原因或者感受	这样对健康好，这是一种运动

英文句子 *6*：Yes, I think we should promote walking. It's a physical activity we can do every day. It can help us stay healthy.

例 4：Do you think children should be encouraged to do more sport?

直接回答题目	重要
原因或者感受	通过体育他们可以认识朋友，提高社会能力

英文句子 *7*：Yes, I think it's necessary for children to play sport. They can make friends through playing sport, such as soccer, and improve social skills.

直接回答题目	重要
原因或者感受	通过体育他们可以知道团队的重要性，以后在工作中也会懂得怎么在团队工作

英文句子 *8*：Yes, I believe it's important. Sport can help them realise the importance of teamwork. They will know how to work in a team in the future.

例 5：Do you think it's important that children read regularly?

直接回答题目	重要
原因或者感受	阅读可以增加词汇量，提高写作能力，对学习有帮助

英文句子 *9*：Yes, I believe reading is a good activity to children. It can improve vocabulary as well as writing skills, which can lead to good school performance.

直接回答题目	重要
原因或者感受	阅读可以开阔视野，让孩子熟悉不同科目，对以后择业有帮助

英文句子 *10*：Yes, there are many advantages to reading. It can broaden children's minds, enable children to get familiar with different subjects. This can broaden their career horizons in the future.

例 6：Why are parks an important part of many towns and cities?

直接回答题目	重要
原因或者感受	公园是人们跑步，散步的地方，可以放松

英文句子 *11*：I think the main reason is that parks are where people go for a jog, or take a walk. They can do activities for relaxation.

直接回答题目	重要
原因或者感受	公园里面有很多树，可以吸收城市的灰尘，提高空气质量

英文句子 *12*：Yes, parks are the lung of a city. There are many trees which can absorb dust and improve air quality.

例 7：Why did you study this subject?

直接回答题目	
原因或者感受	在中国很容易找到工作，这个行业发展很快

英文句子 *13*：Because it is easy to find a job in China, if you specialise in this subject. This is a fast-growing industry.

直接回答题目	
原因或者感受	这是我父母的选择，他们觉得我在这方面比较有优势

英文句子 *14*：It's a choice made by my parents. They both think I'm good at this subject.

例 8：Why do you think some people like to have a painting or other artworks at home?

直接回答题目	
原因或者感受	可以让家更加漂亮，心情更好

英文句子 *15*：I suppose the main reason is that they want to make their homes beautiful. They want to have a happy mood when they get home.

直接回答题目	
原因或者感受	艺术品可以展示一个人的品位，朋友来了也是一个话题

英文句子 *16*：I think people purchase artworks in order to show their taste. Artworks also make good conversation starters when their friends pay a visit.

例 9：In what ways are your friends important to you?

直接回答题目	
原因或者感受	朋友可以和我交流，当我不开心的时候，帮助我解压

英文句子 *17*：Friends play an important role in my life. They can talk to me, when I am unhappy or upset. Their encouragement or advice can help me cope with stress.

直接回答题目	
原因或者感受	朋友可以给我意见，让我知道怎么解决工作或者学习上的问题

英文句子 *18*：Friends can have a vital role to play on some occasions. They can give me advice, telling me how to solve problems at school or in the workplace.

例 10：Why do some people like water sport?

直接回答题目	不是很清楚
原因或者感受	可能这种体育让他们很兴奋，可以解压

英文句子 *19*：I don't know the exact reason. But I suppose this kind of sport can give them a sense of excitement. It's also a stress reliever.

英文句子 *20*：To be honest, I'm not sure. But I suppose it's different from the sports we are familiar with such as basketball. People may regard it as a unique, special experience.

常见问题类型 4：时间和频率

常见问法：How often...?

Do you often...?

How long...?

When...?

How much time do you...?

特点：这种题目一般是问你的一个习惯，做什么多久了，什么时候去做什么，花多少时间在一件事情上等。准备这种题目的关键是你要熟悉一些表示时间和频率的词。

同时，你要注意时态：如果问一个事情发生多久，用一般现在时；如果问事情发生多久了，用现在完成时；如果这个事情过去发生，现在不发生，那么用一般过去时。

回答可用句型：every day/on a daily basis 每天

every other day 隔天

every couple of days 每隔两天

twice a week 一周 2 次

a few times a week 一周几次

every week 每周

during the week 周中

at weekends 周末

every month 每个月

hardly 几乎不

in/during the daytime 白天

in the evenings/during the evening 晚上

on holiday 度假的时候

when I have free time 当我有空的时候

例 1：How long have you been living in your hometown?

直接回答题目	我住在那里差不多 20 年了
原因或者感受	读大学，我去了其他城市

英文句子 *1*：I lived there for about 20 years, before I went to college. I went to another city for my undergraduate education.

直接回答题目	我一直住在那里
原因或者感受	我很享受和父母生活在一起，享受家庭生活

英文句子 *2*：I have been living there since I was born. I enjoy living together with my parents and enjoy family life.

例 2：When do you listen to music?

直接回答题目	当我心情不好的时候
原因或者感受	音乐可以减轻压力，可以减少生活的烦闷

英文句子 *3*：When I am upset. Music is a stress reducer, and it can also make life less boring and alleviate boredom.

直接回答题目	很少
原因或者感受	音乐会让我分心，让我很难专注工作

英文句子 *4*：I hardly listen to music, because I can get distracted, if I wear headphones.

例 3：Do you often read newspapers?

直接回答题目	每一天
原因或者感受	因为看报纸可以让我知道世界上发生了什么事情，让我思维更开阔。

英文句子 *5*：Every day, because reading newspapers allows me to keep up to date with what's happening throughout the world, broadening my mind.

直接回答题目	很少
原因或者感受	因为手机上可以看新闻，更加方便、更加及时

英文句子 *6*：No, I hardly read newspapers because I can read news on my phone. It's convenient and I can get information in real time.

例 4：How often do you write an email or a letter?

直接回答题目	每天都要写
原因或者感受	这是和朋友、同事交流的最好的方式，非常省时

英文句子 *7*：I write emails every day. It's the best way to communicate with my friends and colleagues. It saves time.

直接回答题目	很少写
原因或者感受	因为我可以用手机发信息，或者通过一些手机 APP 和他人交流

英文句子 *8*：I hardly write emails because I prefer to send text messages or use mobile phone apps to communicate with others.

例 5：How much time do you spend outdoors every week?

直接回答题目	看我有没有时间
原因或者感受	有时候如果我要写作业、备考，就没有时间去

英文句子 *9*：It really depends on whether I have free time. Sometimes, I have to do assignments and revise for exams, so I have no time for outdoor pursuits.

直接回答题目	一般每周都有几次
原因或者感受	我喜欢去跑步，否则，我会觉得自己变胖了

英文句子 *10*：A few times a week. I love running, and I try to make time for that. Otherwise, I'd feel I am gaining weight.

例 6：When do your friends visit your home?

直接回答题目	周末的时候
原因或者感受	我会邀请他们来聚餐，这是联络感情的好方法

英文句子 *11*：At weekends. I'll invite them to my home to eat a meal together. It's a good way to do some catching up.

直接回答题目	很少
原因或者感受	我住的地方很小，容不下那么多人，我们一般都出去玩

英文句子 *12*：No, I hardly invite them to visit my home, because it's too small. It cannot accommodate many people, so we normally hang out somewhere else.

例 7：When do you usually go out, in the daytime or in the evening?

直接回答题目	都要
原因或者感受	白天我要去上课，晚上在图书馆里学习

英文句子 *13*：Both. I need to attend lectures during the daytime, and need to go to the library to do homework.

直接回答题目	取决于做什么
原因或者感受	白天一般要去上班，晚上有时候会出去买东西

英文句子 *14*：It depends. I need to work in the daytime. Sometimes, I need to do some shopping at night.

例 8：Do you often travel by bus or taxi?

直接回答题目	不
原因或者感受	附近没有 bus，而且人太多了

英文句子 *15*：No, I don't take a bus. There is no bus station nearby and it's normally overcrowded.

直接回答题目	每天都要
原因或者感受	每天我坐 bus 上下班，比较省钱

英文句子 *16*：Yes, on a daily basis. I travel to work by bus. It saves money.

例 9：How often do you communicate with parents?

直接回答题目	每天
原因或者感受	我们会打电话，父母很在乎我每天的生活

英文句子 *17*：Nearly every day. We make phone calls. My parents want to know whether everything goes well with me.

直接回答题目	很少
原因或者感受	我每天都要加班，回到家很累，不想说话

英文句子 *18*：I hardly have time to talk to my parents. Every day I have to work overtime. When I get home, I'm too tired to talk.

例 10：How much time do you spend at home?

直接回答题目	很少
原因或者感受	我只有放假才回家，我在其他城市读大学

英文句子 *19*：I hardly stay at home. I normally go home when the semester ends. I study in a different city for the degree.

直接回答题目	晚上
原因或者感受	要回家睡觉，白天工作比较忙，不回家

英文句子 *20*：I normally sleep at home. I'm busy with work during the day, so I don't go home.

常见问题类型 5：现在和以后

常见问法：...now compared to 10 years ago?

Do you think...one day...?

Did you...when you were a child?

Do you think...in the future?

Would you like to...in the future?

When was the last time...?

At what age did you...?

特点：这种题目一般是问你过去是怎么样的，你觉得以后是怎么样的，现在和过去有什么不同等。这种题目往往会出现一些动词的过去时，或者是将来时。

你回答时也要非常注意时态，如果是过去发生的事，用一般过去时；如果是将来发生的事，用一般将来时。

回答可用句型：At some point, ...

When I get older, ...

When I was young, ...

When I was a kid, ...

As I grew older, ...

I cannot exactly remember, ...

As far as I can remember, ...

If I remember rightly, ...

例 1：Do you wear the same styles of clothes now compared to 10 years ago?

直接回答题目	没什么改变
原因或者感受	我不喜欢赶潮流，时装一般比较贵

英文句子 *1*：No, I have basically dressed in a similar way in the last 10 years, because I don't like to follow fashion. Famous brands are normally expensive.

直接回答题目	我穿着更加正式
原因或者感受	毕竟已经开始工作，需要经常见客户

英文句子2：I think I tend to dress formally now because I have started working, and I need to meet clients from time to time. Formal dress can make me look professional.

例2：Are you willing to live in the countryside in the future?

直接回答题目	不想
原因或者感受	那里的设施不是很好，你生病的话，很难找到药店或者是医院

英文句子3：Not really, because rural areas don't have facilities to meet our daily needs. If I fall ill, I cannot find a pharmacy or a hospital easily.

直接回答题目	可能
原因或者感受	那里的空气很好，也可以吃到新鲜的蔬菜和水果，对身体好

英文句子4：Possibly, because it's where you can breathe fresh air and also eat fresh fruit and vegetables. This can benefit your well-being.

例3：Do you often watch television when you were a child?

直接回答题目	是的
原因或者感受	因为我父母工作很忙，很少陪我，我只能看电视

英文句子5：Yes, when I was young, my parents led a busy life. They could hardly spend time with me, so I had little choice but to watch TV.

直接回答题目	不是
原因或者感受	我父母限制看电视的时间，他们希望我多读书，做作业

英文句子6：Not really, my parents restricted my screen time. They wanted me to spend more time reading books and doing homework.

例4：Do you think computers might one day replace handwriting?

直接回答题目	是的
原因或者感受	因为发电邮和使用网络交流工具更加方便，手写东西太慢

英文句子7：Yes, because sending emails and using online communication tools are much faster than writing something by hand.

直接回答题目	不一定
原因或者感受	因为有时当我们做笔记的时候，更加喜欢用纸和笔

英文句子8：I'm not sure because sometimes when we make notes, we tend to put pen to paper.

例5：When was the last time you worked in a team?

直接回答题目	做大学作业的时候
原因或者感受	我们需要做一个演讲，需要一起做调查

英文句子 *9*：It was a university assignment. We did a presentation together. It's based on the findings of the research we did together.

直接回答题目	我实习的时候
原因或者感受	我们需要做一个项目，整个团队的人需要一起工作去完成一些任务

英文句子 *10*：It's when I worked as an intern. We completed a team project together. We should work closely as a team to complete some tasks.

例 6：Would you like to ride a bike to work in the future?

直接回答题目	有可能
原因或者感受	骑车很健康，我希望可以降低体重

英文句子 *11*：Possibly, because cycling is a good physical activity. I hope that I can lose some weight by doing that.

直接回答题目	不会
原因或者感受	因为街上到处都是车，没有专门的自行车道，骑车太危险

英文句子 *12*：No, it's unlikely to happen, because cars are everywhere. Many city roads don't have bike lanes. It's dangerous to ride a bike.

例 7：Do you think you will travel more in the future?

直接回答题目	肯定会
原因或者感受	可能我有足够的收入，我不需要担心柴米油盐，这个时候我会更多度假

英文句子 *13*：Definitely. Perhaps I can make good money at some point in the future, and I don't have to worry about basic needs. So I'll possibly go for a holiday whenever possible.

直接回答题目	可能会
原因或者感受	因为我觉得为了工作我很少陪家人，我觉得很内疚

英文句子 *14*：Possibly, because I have hardly made time for my family. I spend too much time on my career. I feel guilty from time to time.

例 8：Is there any sport you would like to try in the future?

直接回答题目	golf
原因或者感受	我知道很多商人都喜欢玩这个。我觉得这样可以帮助我拓展人脉

英文句子 *15*：Golf. I know many businesspeople play golf. I think it can help me build up a network of contacts.

直接回答题目	滑雪
原因或者感受	我希望可以看到雪山，欣赏那里的美景

英文句子 ***16***：Possibly skiing. I hope that I can see snowy mountains, appreciate the breathtaking views there.

例 9：At what age did you start studying mathematics?

直接回答题目	记不清楚了
原因或者感受	可能是小学，因为在中国数学是必修课，中国老师认为数学是一项基本技能

英文句子 ***17***：I can't exactly remember, but possibly at primary school, because it's a required course in China. Teachers in my country regard maths as a basic skill.

直接回答题目	可能是 7 岁
原因或者感受	到了上学的年龄的时候，我们从简单的计算学起，如加和减

英文句子 ***18***：Possibly 7, when I reached the school age. We learned simple calculation, addition and subtraction at that age.

例 10：What indoor games did you play when you were a child?

直接回答题目	下棋
原因或者感受	我父母教我，他们觉得这样可以提高我的智力，对我学习有帮助

英文句子 ***19***：As far as I can remember, my parents taught me how to play chess. They believe it can make me smart and benefit my schooling.

直接回答题目	大富翁
原因或者感受	和我的兄弟姐妹玩，这个游戏可以提高我的理财能力，让我们知道管理财产的重要

英文句子 ***20***：If I remember rightly, I played Monopoly with my cousins. This game improved our financial skills, allowed us to understand the importance of managing properties.

常见问题类型 6：具体信息

常见问法：What...?

Which...?

How do you...?

How well/easy/difficult do you...?

How do you feel...?

Who...?

Where...?

特点：这种题目主要是问地点、人物、方式、感受等问题，非常具体。一般来说，直接回答即可，后面加上原因还有感受。

回答可用句型：It's where...

I am happy, upset, nervous, anxious, not comfortable...

It's good/a great feeling to...

例 1：Which part of your home do you like the most?

直接回答题目	起居室
原因或者感受	那里我可以看电视，和家人吃饭，聊天

英文句子 *1*：The sitting room. That's where I can watch TV, have a dinner with my parents, and have a chat.

直接回答题目	没有特别喜欢的地方，可能是书房
原因或者感受	那里我可以看书，打游戏，听音乐

英文句子 *2*：I don't actually have any favourite room, but if I had to choose, possibly the study, where I can read books, play games, and stream music online.

例 2：Which do you prefer to read, magazines or newspapers?

直接回答题目	杂志
原因或者感受	因为有很多图片，特别是看时尚杂志，让我看到很多明星

英文句子 *3*：Magazines, because they have many pictures, especially fashion magazines. I can see many glamorous celebrities who wear stylish clothes.

直接回答题目	报纸
原因或者感受	因为有很多严肃的新闻，是专栏人士写的，能让我深入了解时事

英文句子 *4*：I like reading newspapers because they report hard news. Many articles are written by columnists, giving me insight into current affairs.

例 3：What kinds of teachers do you like?

直接回答题目	比较风趣的
原因或者感受	这些老师会让课堂比较活泼，可以让我集中注意力，对学习有热情

英文句子 *5*：I like those teachers who have a sense of humour. These teachers can make a class lively, which can hold my attention and maintain my enthusiasm.

直接回答题目	会使用各种教具的
原因或者感受	这些老师会用视频、电脑等物品，让课程更加生动，也更有启发

英文句子 *6*：I like teachers who know how to use different teaching aids. They can use videos and computers to bring subjects to life. They can make every lesson stimulating.

例 4：How do you feel about advertisements?

直接回答题目	广告比较烦人
原因或者感受	它们无处不在，当你看电视剧的时候，常常被打断

英文句子 *7*：Advertisements are annoying. They are everywhere. When you watch TV series, you're interrupted frequently.

直接回答题目	不可信
原因或者感受	公司会夸大产品的功效，事实上，产品没那么好

英文句子 *8*：Advertisements are not trustworthy. Companies tend to exaggerate the outcomes of using their products, but in reality, these products are not as good as expected.

例 5：Who do you think is the most important member in your family?

直接回答题目	我的父亲
原因或者感受	他是家庭的经济支柱，他的收入让我们衣食无忧

英文句子 *9*：I suppose my father is the most important person. He's the breadwinner and his income enables us to live comfortably.

直接回答题目	我的母亲
原因或者感受	她不仅全职工作，而且还做了很多家务，她让我们的家干净、整洁、温馨

英文句子 *10*：I have to say my mum. Not only does she have a full-time job, but she also does a lot of housework. It's her hard work that makes our home clean, tidy and cosy.

例 6：Where do Chinese like to go swimming?

直接回答题目	一般是游泳池
原因或者感受	最好是离家很近，这样比较方便，特别是上班族没有那么多时间

英文句子 *11*：Normally swimming pools. The best choice is the pool close to where we live. It's convenient, especially for those who are busy with work.

直接回答题目	一般是体育中心
原因或者感受	政府建造，设施完备，除了游泳，还可以健身

英文句子 *12*：They like to go to the fitness centre or sports centre, which is normally built by the government. It's well-equipped. Apart from swimming, you can also work out.

例 7：How well do you know your next-door neighbours?

直接回答题目	不熟悉
原因或者感受	我不是很喜欢社交，所以很少和邻居交流，而且邻居总是搬家

英文句子 *13*：I am not very familiar with them. I am not very sociable. I hardly communicate with neighbours. Sometimes, people move in, and sometimes, they move out.

直接回答题目	非常熟悉
原因或者感受	我们是很好的朋友，经常在一起吃饭，当他们出差的时候，我帮他们拿快递

英文句子 *14*：Yes, I know them well, because we're close friends. We eat outside a lot. I take a delivery for them when they are on business trips.

例 8：How do you keep your photos?

直接回答题目	在我手机里
原因或者感受	我喜欢用手机拍照，比较方便，也可以很容易上传到电脑中，然后放到不同的文件夹里

英文句子 *15*：I normally put them in my phone. I love taking photos with my phone. It's convenient, and I can upload them to my computer and save them in different files.

直接回答题目	放在相册里
原因或者感受	照片能够记录很多特别的时刻，如和父母的聚餐，一起去旅游的经历，和朋友的派对

英文句子 *16*：I normally put them in photo albums. Pictures capture many special moments, such as family dinners with parents, trips we made together, and parties with friends.

例 9：How do you feel when you listen to music?

直接回答题目	我会觉得很放松
原因或者感受	特别是我心情烦躁的时候，听点钢琴曲有助于睡眠

英文句子 *17*：I'd feel relaxed. Especially when I am anxious, listening to piano music can really make me sleep well.

直接回答题目	看情况
原因或者感受	如果饭店的音乐很大声，我会很烦躁

英文句子 *18*：It depends. If a restaurant plays loud music, I'd become restless and irritable.

例 10：What kinds of TV programmes do you like most?

直接回答题目	我喜欢看新闻
原因或者感受	因为我会知道很多事情，如汇率、房价、外国的政策等，对我做决定有帮助

英文句子 *19*：I normally watch news programmes because I can keep pace with many changes such as currency, housing prices and the policies of foreign countries. All are helpful when I make decisions.

直接回答题目	我喜欢看肥皂剧
原因或者感受	这些节目可以让我大笑，可以让我忘记我的工作

英文句子 ***20***：Soap operas are my favourite. They can make me laugh and take my work off mind for a while.

特殊题目

雅思口语考试每年的 1、5、9 月都会改变考试的题库。如 1 月到 4 月的题目（包括 Part 1、Part 2 和 Part 3）到了 5 月就会有一部分不再使用，被新题取代。

我们之前六天所练习的 Part 1 题目大部分都是关于工作、学习、日常生活、家人和朋友、旅游和休闲等内容，这些题目属于常规题目，都比较简单，一般来说全年都有可能考到。然而，除了这些常规题目之外，Part 1 也会出现一些非常规题目，这些题目有时候不是特别生活化，或者不是我们日常生活中经常会讨论的话题。这些题目需要另外准备。

如 2017 年 1 月就出现了 dreams, robots, handwriting, video games, toys 这样的新题。备考时，你首先可以按照我们之前六天的题目类型，自己写一些可能出现的题目。以 dreams 为例，你可以使用下面这个表格设计一些问题。

看法	Do you think it is necessary to interpret dreams?	回答：没必要，没有证据表明梦和我们生活有关系，还不如认真学习和工作
时间和频率	Do you often have dreams at night?	回答：有时候会有，特别是我比较忙的时候，会有噩梦，梦见自己没考过
过去和现在	What was the strangest dream you had?	回答：梦见自己在养老院工作，照顾父母
具体信息	What do you normally dream about? Who do you normally dream about? How do you feel when you have bad dreams?	回答：我经常梦见和家人在一起吃饭，因为我不和父母住在一起 回答：我经常梦见父母，有时候我想家 回答：我会有点紧张，不知道是不是不好的兆头

下面是相应的英文回答（大家可以先自己按照中文思路说一下，然后对照英文再说一次）：

- No, I don't think we should take dreams seriously. There is no evidence showing that it has relevance to our lives. I'd rather focus on something more important.
- Sometimes, I do dream at night, especially when I'm overwhelmed with my work. I have nightmares. I dream that I don't pass some important tests or I fail to finish things before the deadline.
- Perhaps the strangest dream I had was about how I work for a nursing home, and take care of my parents.
- I dream about my family a lot, having a dinner together, perhaps because I don't live with them. I miss them from time to time.
- I dream about my family, because I am homesick sometimes.
- I'd possibly be nervous, because I am not sure whether they are bad signs.

在练习的时候，多想例子，并且总结相关的词伙。例如梦一般是梦见一些自己生活中没有取得成功，或者担心发生的事情，如迟到、考试没通过、没有赶上飞机、溺水等。例子想得多，在考场上就会有足够丰富的东西说。

下面我们再用玩具的话题，想一些 Part 1 的题目。我们还要想想玩具一般来说有什么例子？如 doll, jigsaw puzzles, lego, toy car, toy gun, teddy bears 等。

现状	Do you buy toys now?	回答：买，给朋友的小孩，我的朋友会觉得我非常体贴
喜好	Do you like to buy toys as gifts for children?	回答：是的，有些玩具，如 Lego，对小孩的智力好，有很高的教育价值
看法，原因	Do you think parents should buy many toys for children?	回答：不是，因为玩具很贵，会让孩子变得很物质
时间和频率	When do people normally buy toys for children?	回答：庆祝生日的时候，或者小孩成绩好的时候作为奖励
过去和现在	Did you have many toys when you were a child?	回答：是的，我父母很忙，他们总是给我买很多礼物，让我开心
具体信息	Who would normally buy toys for you? What kind of toy do you think is the best for children?	回答：我的父母。他们总是尝试满足我所有对物质的需要 回答：可能是一些教育类的玩具，如 Jigsaw puzzles, 可以提高小孩处理问题的能力

下面是相应的英文回答（大家可以先自己按照中文思路说一下，然后对照英文再说一次）：

- Yes, I normally buy toys for children of my friends. My friends would think I'm very kind and considerate.
- Yes, some toys such as Legos are beneficial to children's brain development. They are of educational value.
- No, because toys are very expensive. Possessing many toys would make children materialistic.
- We buy gifts when we celebrate a child's birthday or it's a kind of prize when children perform well at school.
- Yes, my parents were terribly busy, and they bought me many presents to make me happy.
- My parents. They always tried to satisfy all my needs of material things.
- Perhaps some educational toys, such as jigsaw puzzles, can improve children's problem solving skills.

2.2.3 Part 1 学生常问问题解答

学生常问问题 1：如果我的回答和别人重复怎么办？

很多同学可能会担心，如果我看了这本词伙书，我用的一些句子差不多怎么办？我说的观点差不多怎么办？我用的词差不多怎么办？

方法 1：一些常用的句子和表达可以找替换

表示原因除了用 because, since，你还可以说 it's because, the main reason is that 等。

表示结果除了 so，你还可以说 for this reason, that's why 等。

如果你的句子本身已经有很强的逻辑关系了，甚至可以不用这些连接词。

方法 2：加入个人的例子和情况

如你的观点可能是很忙，那么你未必一定说忙于学习或者工作，你可以具体化：

I am busy with a big project at the moment.

I have to finish some reports from time to time.

I have a part-time job, so I don't have much time.

方法 3：加入个人的感受和看法

如你的观点是健康，那么你可以说一下自己对健康的看法和感受：

I'm not very comfortable with my body shape. I want to be fit.

I feel great when I am in good shape.

I'm confident if I have a healthy weight.

总的来说，在雅思口语考试中，你的表达越自然、越随意、越轻松、越灵活，分数就越高。背诵和练习的目的不是让你在考场上原封不动地把学过的东西一字不漏地说出来，而是让你熟练后，随意说出，"左右逢源"。

学生常问问题 2：如何在口语考试不让考官觉得你是在背答案？

大部分同学在准备雅思口语的过程中，都是选择背一些答案。原因之一，他们不相信自己的回答比背的材料更好。原因之二，他们的老师就是这么教，他们也只能这么做了。

当然，也有一些同学问老师：毕竟考官是人，难道听不出来我是背的？

他们的老师会说：你有时候要故意放慢速度，不要背得很流利；你要懂得保持微笑，和考官保持眼神接触，让考官觉得你很自信，就知道你不是背的。

很多学生就以为考场上"演戏"，假装自己是一个会说英文的人，就能骗过"笨笨的"考官。

然而，演技并不能够掩盖一切，这只是掩耳盗铃，考官会从你的回答中的很多地方听出你是在背答案。我下面会说说演技派学生的一些常见问题：

演技派问题 1：过分依赖套句

很多同学背不少句子，所以遇到生疏问题的时候，可以不断拖时间。如 Well, I don't know the answer to this question.

To be honest, I have no idea. I am not an expert on...

考官要么已经听过很多学生说这些话了，要么就是你在一次考试中用这样的表达高达 2～3 次。考官会知道，你是准备好怎么说自己不懂，而不是去真正回答问题的。

解决的方法就是尽量少用这些套句，多注意题目，多给具体的回答。

演技派问题 2：说话前后矛盾

口语考试很多题目是关于你自己的现状、习惯、家人等。有些时候可能为了回答问题，你要"说谎"，但是要注意，"说谎"要保持一致。

例如，在 Part 1 部分，考官问你专业，你说这个专业很容易找工作，那么在 Part 2 的时候，如果是描述一个痛苦的决定，你说自己选专业的时候特别纠结，不清楚是不是好找工作，那就是前后矛盾。考官会问自己：难道我刚才听到的是一个假的你，现在才是真的你？

又如，在 Part 1 部分，考官问你 shopping，你说自己经常和父母去 shopping，其乐融融的样子，但是到了 Part 2 的时候，如果是描述一个引以为豪的家人，你说自己的父亲事业很忙，经常不在家，很少见到他。考官真想问：你有几个爸爸？

解决的方法是不要尝试背所有的答案，而是懂得合理利用资料里的一些词伙回答问题，不断练习，这样你的回答会更加符合你自己的个人情况，你描述自己的时候也会更加熟练、更加真实。

有时候，如果中间说到一些内容是之前提到过的，可以通过 as I mentioned earlier, as I said before，来让人觉得内容一致。

演技派问题 3：回答和题目不符

背答案的同学有时候会背错答案，或者忘记了答案，也有一些题目他们是没有背到答案的。这个时候，他们很有可能硬着头皮去说一些和题目无关或者是关系不大的东西。这种回答很别扭，让别人觉得很懵。

例如，题目是 What robots would you like to have? 考官可能非常关心机器人的功能。

有些同学可能根本没准备过机器人的话题，这个时候硬生生会把其他话题，像你喜欢的 bags，或者是 gifts 这样的题目的回答说上去，就会很奇怪，如 I want to have beautiful robots. They are pretty, and my friends will also like them. 考官顿时就会疯了，美丽的机器人是什么，为什么你的朋友会喜欢机器人？

解决的办法是不要关注答案，要关注观点和表达，尽量用某些观点和解释去回答更多的题目，然后增加复习的范围。

演技派问题 4：停顿的地方不对

没有人说话是不停顿的，从头到尾像冲锋枪一样说话的人不是在聊天，而是在发病。

但是，背诵的人和交流的人的区别是，背诵的人是在单词上停顿，特别是在词伙中间停顿，而交流的人是在主要观点和内容出现之前停顿。

如考官问 Why are parks important to us? 你可以这么回答：

Parks are important because they are where people can get away from the hustle and bustle of urban life. They are fantastic place for you to relax.

那么背诵的人很有可能在 get away from，或者是 hustle and bustle 这些词的中间停顿，迟迟说不上来（或者是说不清楚），因为他们记得不够熟，所以他们在迟疑。

而交流的人，一般不会在固定的词伙那里停顿，因为他们既然想到了说这个词伙，肯定一下子就说出来了，他们更有可能是在 because, are where 这些表达的地方速度变慢，或者是停顿，因为他们可能是在思考下面的内容。

就好比中文交流也是如此，如果别人问我：你喜欢去公园吗？我说：去啊，那里会让我心情舒畅，可以帮助我解压。

你绝对不可能在“心情舒畅”中间停顿，也不可能在“解压”中间停顿。

解决的方法是不要背诵整个句子，而是选择背熟常用的表达，做到想到就说，一说就能说出来这些表达，而不是磕磕巴巴。

演技派问题 5：内容侧重点不对

很多同学喜欢背比较长的答案，因为比较好凑时间。主要的问题是在准备的题目和考场的题目不一致的时候，学生不知道恰当地调整，继续滔滔不绝地说，也会让考官知道你是在背答案。

很多题目问及细节，如 how, where, who, how often 等。

学生准备的题目是 Where do people in your country like to go swimming?

回答可能是这样的：Many people like to go to beach resorts for swimming, because the view is fantastic, and they love sunbathing.

但是考官在考场上可能问的并不是这个问题，而是问 Do you think swimming should be taught at school?

你也继续厚着脸皮说 Yes, students can go to beach resorts for swimming, because the view is fantastic, and they love sunbathing.

那考官不扣完你的分，也是天理不容。

解决的方法就是熟悉各种题目的类型，问法的不同导致回答的重心不同，在回答的时候考生懂得调整，使用问题里的关键词，来恰当回答。

2.3 口语 Part 2 考试备考攻略

2.3.1 Part 2 考试简介

口语 Part 2 的考试步骤如下：

- 考官会告诉你第一部分的考试已经结束，现在开始第二部分 (Part 2)。
- 然后给你一个 cue card (话题卡)、一支铅笔和一张白纸 (用于记录一些关键词)。
- 考官同时会提醒你，你有 1 分钟的时间准备，你可以在白纸上写思路 (尽量写词伙，不要写句子，时间不够)。
- 你会看到 cue card 上有一个题目，这个题目下面一般有 4 个小问题。

下面是一个例子：

Describe a paid job you ever did.

You should say:

what the job was

how you found this job

how long you did this job

and explain how you felt about this job.

- 一分钟后，考官会告诉你时间到了，你可以开始根据话题卡和自己写的提示回答 Part 2。你大概需要讲 2 分钟。
- 如果你的回答少于 1 分钟一般会扣分，但是如果不够 2 分钟，也没什么问题，不要害怕，多说自己的感受和原因；大于 2 分钟他会打断你但不会扣分。有时候，考官会提前打断你，并且问一两个附加问题（去检查一下你是否准备过这个话题，还是自己当场说的）。不要紧张，那是考官在故意质疑你，影响你的回答节奏，你要冷静应对。

- 讲的过程中，你未必要回答全话题卡上面所有的 4 个小问题，也未必一定要按顺序回答。一般来说，最后一个小问题比较重要。

Part 2 回答中要注意下面 10 件事情：

备考	① 备考的时候，可以优先考虑自己的真实经历；如果没有，可以编故事，选择自己比较熟悉的话题。 ② 不要背整个答案，考场上可能会因背漏、背错、背得很别扭而被考官识破；最好是想好一些故事，然后记住这些故事大概的思路，并背诵描述这些思路时可能用到的词伙。 ③ 备考中尽量注意避免出现低级错误（单复数、谓语动词错误、词性错误）。 ④ 减少使用网络上很多中国老师设计的套句和固定句型。 ⑤ 回答的第一句话一定要扣题。
考场	⑥ 一般来说 why，how do you feel 这两个问题比较重要。 ⑦ 注意看题目的时态，确保时态的准确性。 ⑧ 不要追求过分复杂的句子，内容连贯最重要。 ⑨ 小错误可以纠正一下，但是不要老是自我纠正，会影响流利度。 ⑩ 保持微笑，有自信，不要总是盯着自己的笔记。

2.3.2 Part 2 备考的步骤——双拼法

每个口语考试的季度（4 个月）大概会有 55 个左右的 Part 2 题目。

如果每个题目大家都事前想好故事，写好答案，备考会是一个比较长的过程。比较可行的方法是想 10～15 个故事，每个故事可以用于 3～5 个不同的题目，那么就比较轻松。

下面这是我们建议的备考步骤：

（1）拿到当季所有的 Part 2 题目（我们手把手的公共微信上有，搜索 gu_writing），阅读这些题目；

（2）随便找其中的一个题目，想一个故事；

（3）看看这个故事还可以套用在什么题目上（最好每个故事能够套用 3～5 个题目）；

（4）使用双拼法，看看所选择的题目有什么问题的回答是可以重复利用的；

（5）选择其中一个题目，写出词伙，自己大声说一下；

（6）说完后，看看有什么可以增加的内容，然后再说几次，直到熟练为止；

每天循环上面这个办法，准备 10～15 天，基本上当季的口语话题就准备好了。

我们现在可以用一些题目来体验一下这个方法。

步骤 1：阅读题库的题目

我看到一个题目是乡村的经历。

步骤 2：有可能借用的观点

- 年轻人支教；
- 富人提供奖学金，提高免费教育；
- 贫穷家庭的孩子可以免费获得教育；
- 他们以后可以找到工作，摆脱贫穷；
- 他们可以用知识建设家乡；
- 而不是犯罪；
- 减少社会不平衡。

步骤 3：串题

然后思考同一个故事有可能套用的题目：

- 国外工作（去外国支教）；
- 最喜欢的电影（一个农村老师的故事）；
- 一个团队项目（一个支教的团队）。

步骤 4：使用双拼法

所谓的**双拼法**，就是将 Part 2 的备考按照问题分成两部分。

- 一部分问题是我们可以标准化回答的（也就是标准化问题）；

也就是不管什么题目，我们都可以根据题目的小问题来事先想好拓展，这个称为 question-based expansion（以问题为基础的拓展）。一般来说，when, where, who, how often, how 属于这一类问题。

备考的同学可以参考附录 6，看看我总结的一些标准化问题回答的思路。

- 一部分内容我们很难标准化回答，但是可以通过类似的故事来准备（也就是故事化问题）。

这个是 idea-based or story-based expansion（以故事为基础的拓展）。一般来说，why, how do you feel, what did you do, what it is like 等属于这一类问题。

我们将上面 4 个题目的小题目罗列出来，看看什么小问题是互通的。

乡村的经历	一部最喜欢的电影
Describe a time you had good experience in the countryside. You would say: where you went what you did when you did it and explain why it was enjoyable.	Describe your favourite film. You should say: when you saw it where you saw it what the film was about and explain why it is your favourite film.
一位崇拜的领导	**一个团队项目**
Describe a leader who you admire. You should say: who this person is what this person did (has done) that you admire how you got to know this person and explain how this leader's qualities impressed you.	Describe a team project for study or entertainment. You should say: what the activity was when and where you did it who you were with and explain how you felt about being part of this group.

我们可以看到这 4 个题目中都有 where, when, who, how 4 个问题。

那么我们可以想想这些问题有没有什么固定的回答。

- 关于 **where**，我们可以说在一个贫穷的乡村，那里交通不好，人们生活很贫穷。
- 关于 **when**，我们可以说在暑假的时候，没有什么事情做，所以去教书。
- 关于 **who**，我们可以说一个人非常有爱心，总想帮助有需要的人，特别是帮那些生活有困难的人。
- 关于 **how**，我们可以说上网看新闻，看到一个视频，发现了这个。

然后，这些回答都要想好词伙。

步骤 5：开始练习

我们现在开始一个个练习上面的题目，都是用支教扶贫这个故事。

☆ Part 2 练习 1

描述一段乡村时光

Describe a time you had good experience in the countryside.

小问题	中文思路	词伙
Where you went 标准化的问题	在一个贫穷的乡村，那里交通不好，人们生活很贫穷	a poor village, poor access to transport, live in poverty
What you did 故事化的问题	去那里一个学校教一天的书，教当地的孩子一些英文句子	teach lessons, learn English
When you did it 标准化的问题	在暑假的时候，没有什么事情做，所以去教书	summer holiday
Why it was enjoyable 故事化的问题	我觉得很有意义，可以将我的知识帮助有需要的人。可能我的课能够启发学生，激发他们对英文的兴趣，以后甚至会因此而摆脱贫穷	needy people, fire enthusiasm, break the cycle of poverty

下面是回答的大致内容（大概 8～10 句话）。

Where you went

I'd like to talk about the experience working as a volunteer teacher in a poor village. The access to transport was poor in this place and all people lived in poverty.

What you did

I taught some lessons in the school of this village and taught children about how to learn English by teaching them some basic sentences and also vocabulary.

When you did it

It was during the summer holiday, when we didn't have many things to do, and I had a lot of free time at disposal. That's why I joined a volunteer programme and worked as a volunteer teacher with my classmates.

Why it was enjoyable

It's quite enjoyable because I could see how my work could help children. I had a sense of achievement because I could use my knowledge to help needy people. If my classes could fire children's enthusiasm for language learning, they may study hard to pick up this language. In the future, they are likely to break the cycle of poverty if they could master this language.

步骤 6：提升熟练度

可以掐表看看刚才自己有没有说到 2 分钟。

如果没有，可以想想哪里能增加一下内容，如关于 What you did 的问题，你完全可以说同时我们给小孩送去很多机构捐赠的书，小孩可以阅读这些材料。

We also gave these children many books for free. These books were donated by some charities and libraries. Children can use these books for self-study.

然后，多说两次，说到熟悉为止，记住，不要背诵，不要追求字字都能记忆。

我们现在重复步骤 4～6，将其他 3 个题目练习一次。

☆ Part 2 练习 2

描述一部最喜欢的电影

Describe your favourite film.

小问题	中文思路	词伙
When you saw it 标准化的问题	在暑假的时候，没有什么事情做，每天上网看电影	summer holiday, watch films online
Where you saw it 标准化的问题	上网看新闻，看到一个视频，发现了这个	watch online news
What the film was about 故事化的问题	叙述一个年轻人，去农村做老师，贫穷家庭的孩子可以免费获得教育	receive a formal education for free, from poor families
Why it is your favourite film 故事化的问题	学校没有设备，生活条件很差，孩子们认真学习，后来可以找到工作，摆脱贫穷	living conditions, study hard, find work, get rid of poverty

下面是回答的大致内容（大概 8～10 句话）。

When you saw it

My favourite film is about a teacher who volunteered to work in a village. I watched this film during the summer holiday. I had plenty of spare time, and I got nothing serious to do, so I spent a lot of time on the Internet every day.

Where you saw it

I watched the film online. I was watching online news, and there was a video which introduced this film, so I watched it.

What the film was about

The main character of the film is a young teacher who chooses to go to a small village and work there, although he received no pay. He is the only teacher there, but because of him, children from poor homes in this village are able to receive a formal education for free.

Why it is your favourite film

The film shot most scenes in a rural school, which doesn't have even basic equipment. Although living conditions are poor, all children study hard. They eventually find work and get rid of poverty.

可以掐表看看刚才自己有没有说到 2 分钟。

如果没有，可以想想哪里能增加一下内容，如关于 Why it is your favourite film 的问题，你完全可以说这部电影让我们看到教育的重要性，教育改变了一个人的人生，这部电影也改变了我对职业的看法。职业不是只为钱，也需要考虑对社会的贡献。

This film has taught me how important education is, and how education could change one's life. This film has also changed my perception of what defines a good job. Apart from the income, there are many other things which I should consider, for example, whether the job is meaningful or not.

然后，多说两次，说到熟悉为止，记住，不要背诵，不要追求字字都能记忆。

☆ Part 2 练习 3

描述一名领导

Describe a leader who you admire (for example, in sport, business or politics).

小问题	中文思路	词伙
Who this person is 标准化的问题	马云，非常有爱心，总想帮助有需要的人，特别是那些生活有困难的人	compassionate, help needy people, experience difficulties
What this person did (has done) that you admire 故事化的问题	建学校，购买设备，雇用老师提供奖学金，贫穷家庭的孩子可以获得正式教育	build schools, purchase equipment, recruit teachers, offer scholarships, from poor families, receive a formal education
How you got to know this person 标准化的问题	看视频，看微博	watch videos, check blogs

How this leader's qualities impressed you 故事化的问题	他非常有爱心，他知道很多地方生活条件很差，但是只要孩子们认真学习，就可以找到工作，摆脱贫穷 他相信他们可以用知识建设家乡 有了工作他们就不会犯罪 这样有助于减少社会不平衡	living condition, study hard, find work, get rid of poverty, commit crime, close the economic divide

下面是回答的大致内容（大概 8～10 句话）。

Who this person is

I'd like to talk about Ma Yun. He is a famous entrepreneur and also a philanthropist in China. He is very compassionate and willing to help needy people, especially those who experience difficulties in their lives.

What this person did (has done) that you admire

I admire him primarily because he has donated a lot of money to charities to build schools, purchase equipment and recruit teachers in rural areas.

He also offers scholarships to children from poor families to ensure that they can receive a formal education.

How you got to know this person

I got to know all these things he did when I watched videos and check blogs online. There were a lot of reports about what he did for education.

How this leader's qualities impressed you

As I said before, he is very compassionate. He knows that poor living conditions of children in rural areas, but as long as children study hard, they can find work and get rid of poverty eventually. He believes that these children can use their knowledge to make their hometowns prosperous in the future. They would not commit crimes if they have jobs. This can help close the economic divide.

可以掐表看看刚才自己有没有说到 2 分钟。

如果时间够了，多说两次，说到熟悉为止，记住，不要背诵，不要追求字字都能记忆。

☆ Part 2 练习 4

描述一个团队项目

Describe a team project for study or entertainment.

小问题	中文思路	词伙
What the activity was 故事化的问题	我们给一些低收入家庭的孩子提供免费教育，然后根据这些孩子的现状写一个报告	children from poor homes, disadvantaged children, free education, write a report
When and where you did it 标准化的问题	在暑假，去一些贫穷的地区，给学校的孩子教课，提供一对一的辅导	deprived areas, teach classes, on a one-on-one basis

Who you were with 标准化的问题	我的同学，他们都是很有同情心的人，希望帮助别人	those in need
How you felt about being part of this group 故事化的问题	感觉很好，因为我们深入了解贫穷家庭孩子遇到的挑战，知道教育对他们的重要性，我们也觉得有成就感，因为我们的工作可以让他们解决一些学习的问题	face challenges, children from less well-off backgrounds, a sense of achievement, solve problems, academic work

下面是回答的大致内容（大概 8～10 句话）。

What the activity was

It was my pleasure to join a team to conduct a survey about children from poor homes. In this project, we provided disadvantaged children with free education and wrote a report based on the situations of these children.

When and where you did it

It was during a summer holiday, and I went to some deprived areas of the city with my classmates. We taught classes to children for free, and provided tutorials on a one-on-one basis.

Who you were with

I did this project with my classmates. They all are very compassionate people, who are always willing to help those in need.

How you felt about being part of this group

I felt great because we were able to understand the challenges facing children from less well-off backgrounds. We did understand the importance of education to these children. We also had a sense of achievement, because I felt our work could help them solve some problems related to their academic work.

可以掐表看看刚才自己有没有说到 2 分钟。

如果没有，可以想想哪里能增加一下内容，例如说关于 Who you were with 的问题，你可以说我的同学在教学生的时候怎么细心，我们主要教什么东西等。

They are good at different subjects. Some of them taught children maths, how to deal with mathematical problems. Some of them taught children English, how to improve their vocabulary, etc.

然后，多说两次，说到熟悉为止，记住，不要背诵，不要追求字字都能记忆。

2.3.3 Part 2 双拼法使用的一些要点

我相信昨天大家练习过了双拼法，应该会觉得口语 Part 2 简单一点了。我们今天会讲一下双拼法使用过程中要注意的一些事情：

- 拓展合理：可以多拓展故事化的问题，而不是标准化的问题。
- 灵活扣题：使用同一故事的时候，要根据题目作出一定的调整。
- 偷梁换柱：标准化的问题可以不受题目限制。
- 词汇变化：为了避免自己的练习变得枯燥和单调，某些表达可以尝试进行替换。

这些建议比较理论化，我们通过实例来解释一下。我们还是根据昨天的6个步骤，一步步来练习。

步骤1：阅读题库的题目

我看到一个题目是想创建的小公司。

步骤2：有可能借用的观点

- 网络商务的发展，员工在家里工作，不用上下班；
- 有效地减少生意的成本，加大利润；
- 鼓励一些普通人创业；
- 比较自由；
- 能够平衡好工作和家庭之间的关系；
- 学会新的电脑技术，要用社交媒体推广；
- 如何和客户沟通，找到好的产品，提供好的服务是主要问题。

步骤3：串题

然后思考同一个故事有可能套用的题目：

- 想创建的小公司；
- 擅长的高薪工作；
- 喜欢去的网站；
- 生气的情形。

步骤4：使用双拼法

我们将上面4个题目的小题目罗列出来，看看什么小问题是互通的。

想创建的小公司	擅长的高薪工作
Describe a small business you would like to have. You should say: what it would be how you prepare for it where you would have this business and why you want to run this business.	Describe a well-paid job that you will be good at. You should say: what it is how you find this job what qualities it requires and explain why it is well-paid and why you think you will be good at this.
喜欢去的网站	**生气的情形**
Describe a website you like to visit. You should say: when you found it what it is about how often you visit it and why you like the website.	Describe a situation that made you a little angry. You should say: what made you angry where you were when it happened and why you were angry.

我们可以看到这 4 个题目中都有 where, when, how often, how 4 个问题。

那么我们可以想想这些问题有没有什么固定的回答。

- 关于 **where**，我们可以说在家里，通过网络、电话、传真机和别人联系。
- 关于 **when**，我们可以说在节日期间，想给家人买礼物的时候。
- 关于 **how**，我们可以听从朋友的建议，和朋友交流，增加知识。
- 关于 **how often**，我们可以不去思考这个问题，因为这个问题很少见，只出现了一次，可以不用理会。

然后，这些回答都要想好词伙。

步骤 5：开始练习

我们现在开始一个个练习上面的题目，都是用开网店这个故事。

☆ Part 2 练习 5

Describe a small business you would like to have.

小问题	中文思路	词伙
What it would be 故事化的问题	我想开网店，在网络上出售一些商品，获得利润	run an online shop, earn profits
How you prepare for it 标准化的问题	听从朋友的建议，和朋友交流，增加知识	follow advice, increase knowledge
Where you would have this business 标准化的问题	在家里，通过网络、电话、传真机和别人联系	at home, fax machines
Why you want to run this business 故事化的问题	比较自由，可以在家办公，成本比较低，可以增加商业经验	work from home, the running cost, business experience

下面是回答的大致内容（大概 8～10 句话）。

What it would be

The business I'd like to start is an online shop. I would sell products on the Internet to earn profits.

How you prepare for it

I would talk to friends who have experience in e-commerce, following their advice. Once I increase my knowledge about how to operate a business, I will start it.

Where you would have this business

I would work at home, using the Internet, mobile phones and fax machines to communicate with others.

Why you want to run this business

There are a number of benefits to running an online business. First of all, I can enjoy a high level of autonomy. I can work from home without having to go to work every day. The running cost is also low. I can increase my business experience.

现在我们说说双拼法的四大注意事项第一点：

拓展合理：可以多拓展故事化的问题，而不是标准化的问题。

上面这个回答字数不是很够，可能说不到两分钟。我们如果要拓展，尽量拓展故事化的问题，也就是 what 和 why 这两个问题。

原因在于，这 2 个问题的回答直接和题目相关，拓展起来会让你的回答更加充实；反之，如果你拓展的是 how 和 where，长篇大论地说，例如，你强调你家里很大，有多少房间什么的，那么考官会觉得你是在背诵。

关于 What it would be，你可以说你会将产品放在电商的网站上，消费者可以选购下订单，然后将产品寄给消费者。

I would put my products on some famous e-commerce websites, so customers can choose whatever they like easily and place an order. I'll deliver products to these customers.

关于 Why you want to run this business，你可以说现在网购是趋势，很多人都希望在家里购物，你希望把握商机。

I believe online shopping has gone mainstream, and many people now intend to shop online at home. I hope that I can seize this business opportunity.

将这两句话加入到刚才的回答，然后再说一次，可以掐表看看自己有没有说到 2 分钟。

然后，多说两次，说到熟悉为止，记住，不要背诵，不要追求字字都能记忆。

我们现在继续用网店这个故事，练习下面一题。

☆ Part 2 练习 6

Describe a well-paid job that you will be good at.

小问题	中文思路	词伙
What it is 故事化的问题	为网店工作	online business
How you find this job 标准化的问题	听从朋友的建议，和朋友交流，增加知识	follow advice, build up a network of contacts
What qualities it requires 故事化的问题	要有耐心，提供好的服务，和客户交流	show patience, good customer services
Why it is well-paid and why you think you will be good at this 故事化的问题	网店成本低，如果经营好，收入很高 网络商务是趋势，抓住的话可以赚很多钱	running cost, well-run shop, earn high profits online shopping, earn a fortune

下面是回答的大致内容（大概 8～10 句话）。

What it is

I think I can work for an online business. If it is highly profitable, I can earn a lot of money. As I study marketing at university, I believe I can find a decent job in this industry.

How you find this job

I would try to communicate with my friends who have a lot of experience in this field, and try to build up a network of contacts. I can follow my friends' advice as to how to find a good company.

What qualities it requires

I think if you want to be successful in running an online shop, you should be able to show patience when communicating with customers. You need to be able to provide good customer services if you want to make money.

Why it is well-paid and why you think you will be good at this

The main reason why I think this job would pay me well is that the running cost of an online shop is normally low. So if it is well-run, it can earn high profits. So I can benefit from it.

In addition, online shopping is fashionable. As long as you can grasp this opportunity, you can earn a fortune easily, possibly as the manager of an online success.

现在我们说说双拼法的四大注意事项第二点：

灵活扣题：使用同一故事的时候，要根据题目作出一定的调整。

我们很多同学在用一个故事套不同题目的时候，很容易被考官听出来是从其他题目的回答“偷”过来的，有时候考官会变得很不耐烦，甚至会惩罚性地给一个很低的分数。

那么如何解决这个问题？

在备考的时候，随着题目的变化，回答要尽量扣题。如这个题目有两个关键词，一个是 well-paid，一个是 good at。

也就是你要突出说这个工作的收入很高，也要突出说你擅长这个工作。

所以大家会发现，我在刚才的回答中加入了很多和题目相关的信息（画线部分），来不断突出我擅长这个工作，这个工作收入很高。包括我在回答的第一句话就说了 work for... 来突出我现在正在说的是一个工作。

大家平时自己练习的时候，也要形成这个习惯，就是在回答中，不时出现题目的关键词或者替换词，让考官知道你这个故事是连贯的。

如果一个同学傻乎乎地说自己开网店赚钱，那就会很怪异。因为开网店就不是一个 job，job 一般是你为别人打工。

好的，现在大家迅速按照上面的中文思维，说一次，掐表看看自己有没有说到 2 分钟。

然后，多说两次，说到熟悉为止，记住，不要背诵，不要追求字字都能记忆。

然后继续练习下面一题。

☆ Part 2 练习 7

Describe a website you like to visit.

小问题	中文思路	词伙
When you found it 标准化的问题	节日期间，想给家人买礼物的时候	festive season, buy gifts
What it is about 故事化的问题	一个网购的网站，很多产品，你可以和店主交流，下单，他们会发货给你	e-commerce website, shop owner, place an order, deliver products
How often you visit it 标准化的问题	我在家里就可以购买，通过网络和他们联系	in the comfort of my home
Why you like the website 故事化的问题	购物非常方便，价格非常便宜，经常打折，很容易比较产品，买到适合自己的东西	reasonable price, offer discounts, compare products, match needs

下面是回答的大致内容（大概 8～10 句话）。

When you found it

The website I'd like to talk about is a popular website in China for online shopping. I found it during the festive season last year, when I tried to buy gifts for my family.

What it is about

It's an e-commerce website which has possibly millions of products online. You can communicate with shop owners before you place an order. They will deliver products to you for free.

How often you visit it

I love browsing the website when I am at home. It's very nice to buy something in the comfort of my home and communicate with them on the Internet.

Why you like the website

The best part about this website is that it's convenient. Apart from this, the price is reasonable, and many shops offer discounts. So you can save money. It's also easy to compare products online, and you can find the products which match your needs easily.

现在我们说说双拼法的四大注意事项第三点：

偷梁换柱：标准化的问题可以不受题目限制。

很多同学可能会发现，上面的第三个问题，我并没有说 how often，而是说了 where。这里面有三个原因：

首先，雅思口语 Part 2 不要求你每个小问题都回答；

其次，雅思口语更加在意你故事的连贯性；

最后，很多标准化的问题（如 how, who, where, when, how often）其实边界不是很分明。

考官首先不会在意你是不是回答了 how often，他不会看题卡，来检查你是否回答了这个小问题。

其次，上述回答中，当我说完网站的特点，我就提到我可以在家里购物，然后和后面网站的优点连在一起说，非常连贯，对于听者来说，是一个连贯的故事。

最后，其实很多标准化的题目是可以互换的，如题目问你什么时候发现这个网站。

你说你朋友告诉我的，事实上更像是 who；

你也可以说我在家里发现的，事实上更像是 where；

你也可以说我通过朋友介绍知道的，事实上更像是 how；

简而言之，这些问题的回答完全可以相互借用，融会贯通。

好的，现在大家迅速按照上面的中文思维，说一次，掐表看看自己有没有说到 2 分钟。

然后，多说两次，说到熟悉为止，记住，不要背诵，不要追求字字都能记忆。

然后继续练习下面一题。

☆ Part 2 练习 8

Describe a situation that made you a little angry.

小问题	中文思路	词伙
What made you angry 故事化的问题	我买的产品迟迟不到，联系网店，老板一直没有说出解决方法，也没有退款	shop owner, offer a full refund
Where you were 标准化的问题	在家，我习惯在家购物，家里下单	in the comfort of my home, place an order
When it happened 标准化的问题	假日期间，想给家人买礼物	holiday season, buy presents
Why you were angry 故事化的问题	服务很不好，不尊重消费者的权益	consumers' rights

下面是回答的大致内容（大概 8～10 句话）。

What made you angry

I'm going to talk about the time when I bought something from an online shop, but they failed to deliver the product on time. When I contacted the shop owner, he didn't manage to solve the problem and he also refused to offer a full refund.

Where you were

I bought it online. I have a habit of buying things in the comfort of my home. When I see something interesting online, I'll place an order.

When it happened

It was during the holiday season, when I wanted to buy presents for family.

Why you were angry

The service was terrible, and the shop didn't respect consumers' rights.

说到这里，时间肯定不够，那么可以稍微拓展一下 Why。可以说一下网络购物的一些不好地方，第一个网店的广告很容易误导人，第二个就是产品可能质量比较差，服务不好。

然后加上这么几句话：

These are consequences of buying something online. First of all, the advertisements of online shops tend to be misleading. They tend to manipulate potential buyers. Secondly, the products they sell are possibly not of good quality. The standard of service is also poor.

这个时候再说一次，掐表看看自己有没有说到 2 分钟。

然后，多说两次，说到熟悉为止，记住，不要背诵，不要追求字字都能记忆。

现在说一下双拼法的四大注意事项第四点：

词汇变化：为了避免自己的练习变得枯燥和单调，某些表达可以尝试进行替换。

双拼法因为使用类似的故事，标准化的题目回答也比较类似，因此很多同学在练习过程中可能会觉得乏味。这个时候你可以尝试换一下表达：

如 festive season，可以是 holiday season；

buy gifts, 可以是 buy presents；

shop online, 可以是 buying something online。

这样的练习过程会有趣一点。

2.3.4 Part 2 要注意时态的准确

口语考试和作文考试的一个明显差异就是，口语的时态变化很厉害。考生要严格注意题目的时态，确保自己的时态准确。那么从什么地方可以看出时态的差异呢？

一般来说从题目的第一句话就可以看出来。

☆ 将来时态的提示单词有：will, would like to, plan to, is likely to, want to。

☆ 现在时态的提示单词一般是使用了一般现在时的动词，如 like, dislike, have, has 等。

☆ 过去时态的提示单词一般是使用了一般过去时的动词，如 met。

当然，也有一些时间副词或者短语可以体现时态的变化。

☆ 将来时态的提示单词有：in the future。

☆ 过去时态的提示单词有：recently, during your childhood。

注意：有些时候，某些题目的小问题可能涉及不同的时态，学生一定要灵活变化。

现在我找 4 个不同时态的题目，尝试使用前两天的复习步骤：

步骤 1：阅读题库的题目

我看到一个题目是很忙的时候。

步骤 2：有可能借用的观点

- 和我以后的就业有关；
- 压力很大；
- 体现了时间管理的重要性，需要分轻重缓急；
- 和同学一起交流，相互督促，分享；

- 复习以前的试卷；
- 需要有效的办法记忆；
- 收获很多；
- 获得了比较满意的成绩。

步骤 3：串题

然后思考同一个故事有可能套用的题目：

- 一个礼貌的人（帮助我备考的人）；
- 想再次阅读的书（关于备考的书）；
- 一个咖啡馆（去备考的地方）。

步骤 4：使用双拼法

我们将上面 4 个题目的小题目罗列出来，看看什么小问题是互通的。

繁忙的时刻	礼貌的人
Describe a time when you were very busy. You should say: when it was what you had to do during that time how you managed it and explain how you felt about being busy.	Describe a polite person you met. You should say: who this person was when and where you met this person how you met and explain why you think he or she was polite.
再次阅读的书	**喜欢的咖啡馆**
Describe a book that you would like to read again. You should say: what the book was about why you read it in the first place what you learned from the book and explain why you would like to read it again.	Describe a café or restaurant you like to visit. You should say: what it looks like where it is what you drink or eat and why you go there.

我们可以看到这 4 个题目，有 where, when, how, who 4 个问题。

那么我们可以想想这些问题有没有什么固定的回答。

- 关于 **where**，我们可以说在咖啡馆，比较安静，适合学习。
- 关于 **when**，我们可以说在考试期间，非常忙，还要在饭店打工。
- 关于 **who**，我们可以说一个学习成绩很好的人，掌握很多学习技能。
- 关于 **how you managed it**，可以转化成 who helped you manage it。
- 关于 **how you met**, 可以转化成 where you met this person。

步骤 5：开始练习

我们现在开始一个个练习上面的题目，都是用备考这个故事。

☆ Part 2 练习 9

Describe a time when you were very busy.

小问题	中文思路	词伙
When it was 标准化的问题	考试期间，非常忙，还要在饭店打工	nearly the exam time, a part-time job
What you had to do during that time 故事化的问题	考前，需要阅读很多书，复习笔记	before exams, read books, go through notes
How you managed it 标准化的问题	一个学习成绩很好的人，掌握很多学习技能	top student, study techniques
How you felt about being busy 故事化的问题	很有压力，时间不够，我使用了一些办法让我记住主要的概念和理论，最后分数不错	feel stressed, run out of time, key concepts, good grades

下面是回答的大致内容（大概 8～10 句话）。

When it was

I'd like to describe a time when I prepared for final exams in a semester. It's nearly the exam time, and I had a part-time job in a restaurant. It's not easy to manage my time.

What you had to do during that time

I had to read many books and go through many notes before exams.

How you managed it

I talked to one of my classmates. He was a top student who has a lot of study techniques. I managed to draw upon his ideas and experience.

How you felt about being busy

I felt stressed at the beginning, as I was running out of time. I wasn't sure whether I could read through all notes before the exam. I used some methods recommended by my friend to memorise some key concepts and theories. Eventually, I managed to get good grades. Overall, it's a rewarding experience.

我们可以看到这个题目是比较典型的使用过去时的题目，不仅题目中有 when you were very busy，而且 4 个小问题里也分别出现了过去时，when it was, had to do, managed it, how you felt。

所以我在回答中全部都用了一般过去时。

一般动词的过去时 managed	一般动词的现在时 manage/manages
系动词的过去时 was/were	系动词的现在时 is/are

情态动词的过去时	情态动词的现在时
could/might	can/may

掐表看看自己有没有说到 2 分钟。如果不够，增加点内容，重新再说一次。

然后，多说两次，说到熟悉为止，记住，不要背诵，不要追求字字都能记忆。

我们开始练习下面一个题目。

☆ Part 2 练习 10

Describe a polite person you met.

小问题	中文思路	词伙
Who this person was 标准化的问题	一个学习成绩很好的人，掌握很多学习技能	an excellent student, master study skills
When and where you met this person 标准化的问题	考试期间，非常忙，还要在饭店打工	the exam time, a tight timetable
How you met 标准化的问题	在咖啡馆，比较安静，适合学习	conducive to learning
Why you think he or she was polite 故事化的问题	他很有耐心地告诉了我一些学习技巧，怎么去看书更快，怎么去记忆一些内容，怎么去做模拟题	study skills, learn something by heart, practice tests

下面是回答的大致内容（大概 8～10 句话）。

Who this person was

I'd like to talk about a guy I met in a café. He is a very polite person. He's an excellent student who masters many study skills. I was lucky I could take advice from him about how to prepare for exams.

When and where you met this person

It was nearly the exam time. I had a tight schedule, not only spending a lot of time every day preparing for exams but also working in a restaurant on a part-time basis.

How you met

I went to a university café from time to time to do revision, because it's a quiet place. The environment was conducive to learning. It's not as noisy as other parts of the campus.

Why you think he or she was polite

He was having a coffee. When he found that I tried very hard to keep all notes well-organised, he volunteered to help me. He shared with me a lot of study skills with patience, including how to read books faster, how to learn something by heart more efficiently, and how to do practice tests.

I was touched by his politeness and patience. His ideas did help me achieve a high grade in exams.

这个题目也是用的过去时，题目里的 met 是 meet 的过去式，然后下面的小问题也是过去式，所以整篇回答都要以过去时为主。

例如，是 it was nearly exam time，而不是 it is nearly exam time；

I had a tight schedule，而不是 I have a tight schedule；

He was having a coffee，而不是 he is having a coffee。

掐表看看自己有没有说到 2 分钟。如果不够，增加点内容，重新再说一次。

然后，多说两次，说到熟悉为止，记住，不要背诵，不要追求字字都能记忆。

我们开始练习下面一个题目。

☆ Part 2 练习 11

Describe a book that you would like to read again.

小问题	中文思路	词伙
What the book was about 故事化的问题	关于一些学习的技巧，如怎么备考，怎么复习笔记	study techniques, read through notes
Why you read it in the first place 标准化的问题	（可以将这个题目看成是 when） 考试期间，非常忙，还要在饭店打工	final exams, a tight schedule
What you learned from the book 故事化的问题	要很好地管理时间，将比较重要的科目放在前面	manage time effectively, give priority to
Why you would like to read it again 故事化的问题	很多技巧可以用在工作中，如怎么做笔记，怎么去记忆一些主要信息，准备面试和 presentation 都用得到	take notes, memorise key concepts

下面是回答的大致内容（大概 8～10 句话）。

What the book was about

The book I'd like to talk about contains a lot of information about study techniques, including how to prepare for exams, and how to read through notes effectively.

Why you read it in the first place

I read the book when I prepared for final exams at college. I had a very tight schedule, not only studying but also working for a restaurant on a part-time basis.

What you learned from the book

The book told me how to manage time effectively. For example, the author suggests that we give priority to the most important subjects, instead of wasting time on the least important theories and chapters.

Why you would like to read it again

After I graduated, I have found that many of these techniques can be used in the workplace, such as how to take notes and how to memorise key concepts. I can use these skills for interviews and presentations. So I want to read it again, if I have time.

这个问题的题目是 would like to，应该用将来时态，所以最后我说了 I can, I want to 这样的表达。

例如，是 I want to read it again，而不是 I wanted to read it again。

但是，有 3 个小问题出现了过去时，包括 was about, you read (read 的过去时是其原形)，还有 what you learned。

所以在回答这些小问题的时候，我主要用的是过去时，包括 had, told。

I read the book when I prepared for final exams 里面的 read 这个单词，过去式和原形是一样的。

那么为什么有个地方用了一般现在时，suggests，因为我觉得书的内容不会变，现在也是如此，所以就用了一般现在时。

而后面之所以用 we give priority to，而不是 we should give priority to 是因为这是虚拟语气，可以不加 should。

掐表看看自己有没有说到 2 分钟。如果不够，增加点内容，重新再说一次。

然后，多说两次，说到熟悉为止，记住，不要背诵，不要追求字字都能记忆。

我们开始练习下面一个题目。

☆ Part 2 练习 12

Describe a café or restaurant you like to visit.

小问题	中文思路	词伙
What it looks like 故事化的问题	普通的 café，但是适合备考	revise for exams
Where it is 标准化的问题	比较安静，适合学习	conducive to learning
What you drink or eat 故事化的问题	不是很在意喝什么，主要是在那里可以专注学习，看书，或者看笔记	read through notes
Why you go there 故事化的问题	考试的时候压力很大，咖啡店放一下好听的钢琴曲，气氛轻松一点，记东西和做模考更加有效率	piano music, relaxed atmosphere, do practice tests

下面是回答的大致内容（大概 8～10 句话）。

What it looks like

The café I'd like to talk about is a university café. It looks ordinary from the outside, but it's a wonderful place for students to revise for exams.

Where it is

It's on campus. It's conducive to learning because all visitors are expected to keep their voices down when talking to each other.

What you drink or eat

To be honest, I don't care what I drink or eat right there, coffee or soft drink. What matters most is that I can concentrate on my books there and read through notes.

Why you go there

Preparing for exams can be very stressful. The café has very nice piano music, which can create a relaxed atmosphere. It can make the exam preparation less boring and more interesting. I can also memorise theories and do practice tests more efficiently.

这个题目主要用的是一般现在时，题目是 you like to visit，也就是你现在就经常去的 café。

下面的四个小问题也是一般现在时，体现在：

what it looks like，而不是 what it looked like；

where it is，而不是 where it was；

what you drink，而不是 what you drank；

why you go there，而不是 why you went there。

因此，我从头到尾基本上用的都是一般现在时。

现在掐表看看自己有没有说到 2 分钟。如果不够，增加点内容，重新再说一次。

然后，多说两次，说到熟悉为止，记住，不要背诵，不要追求字字都能记忆。

2.3.5 Part 2 如何避免故事雷同并保证说够时间？

很多考生在备考口语 Part 2 的时候，因为对自己的表达没自信，或者是对有些题目自己没有真实的经历（如和外国人交流的经历），因此很喜欢去使用网络上一些口语老师给的故事或答案。

这个方法最大的问题就是，如果你用的故事和很多同学相重，细节和思路也差不多，就会被考官发现，给你一个很低的分数。

有些考生会觉得非常委屈，可能看到的故事确实是想说的故事，确实是经历过了，难道不可以说吗？例如题目问的是想了解的一个名人，你想到了马云，可其他同学也说马云，那也没办法啊，因为中国的名人就那么几个。

我自己在一次口语考试中，也使用了马云，考官确实也一脸怀疑，并且加问了我两个问题，最后那次考试的分数是 7.5 分。虽然分数不高，但是也不是一个低分。

那么为什么考官不觉得我是在背故事呢？我使用的是三种办法：举个人例子、说感受、讲意义。

这三个办法刚好也能够帮助大家说够时间。

现在我找 4 个题目，还是重复过去三天的复习步骤，练习一下。与此同时，我们说一下上面三个不同的拓展方法的使用。

步骤 1：阅读题库的题目

我看到一个题目是国外工作。

步骤 2：有可能借用的观点

- 留学可以提升自己的语言能力（improve language skills）；
- 去好的大学读书，获得好的文凭；

- 打工可以增加自己的工作经历；
- 可以提升自己的独立生活能力；
- 缺点就是比较昂贵；
- 很多人会想家，适应不了当地的文化。

步骤 3：串题

然后思考同一个故事有可能套用的题目：

- 国外工作；
- 有趣的邻居；
- 等待；
- 看过的广告。

步骤 4：使用双拼法

我们将上面 4 个题目的小题目罗列出来，看看什么小问题是互通的。

国外工作	有趣的邻居
Describe a place in other countries where you would like to work. You should say: where you would like to go what kind of job you would like to have when you would like to go and explain why you want to work in that place.	Describe an interesting neighbour. You should say: who this person is how you know this person what this person likes to do and explain why you think this neighbour is interesting.
等待	**看过的广告**
Describe a time that you were waiting for something. You should say: when it happened where it happened what you were waiting for and how you felt about it.	Describe an advertisement you have seen recently. You should say: when and where you saw it what was advertised what the contents of the advertisements were and explain how you felt about it.

我们可以看到这 4 个题目，有 where, when, how, who 4 个问题。

那么我们可以想想这些问题有没有什么固定的回答。

- 关于 **where**，我们可以说在澳大利亚，一个说英文的国家，有很多世界知名的大学。
- 关于 **when**，我们可以说在大学毕业的时候，比较迷惘，不知道要不要读硕士，要不要开始工作。
- 关于 **who**，我们可以说这个人知识渊博，能够说流利的英文等。
- 关于 **how you know this person**，我们可以转化成 where，说这个人希望去澳大利亚留学，我们有很多话题。

步骤 5：开始练习

我们现在开始一个个练习上面的题目，都是用备考这个故事。

☆ Part 2 练习 13

小问题	中文思路	词伙
Where you would like to go 标准化的问题	在澳大利亚，一个说英文的国家，有很多世界知名的大学	prestigious universities
What kind of job you would like to have 故事化的问题	在语言学校工作，或者在饭店工作，主要是提升我的语言	improve language skills
When you would like to go 标准化的问题	在大学毕业的时候，比较迷惘，不知道要不要读硕士，要不要开始工作	graduate from the university, further education
Why you want to work in that place 故事化的问题	打工可以增加自己的工作经历，可以提升自己的独立生活能力	increase work experience, life skills, achieve a sense of independence

下面是回答的大致内容（大概 8～10 句话）。

Where you would like to go

I want to work in Australia. It's an English-speaking country. It has many prestigious universities. Some of my friends are studying in this country, and they all agree that it's a wonderful country to live and study.

What kind of job you would like to have

I'm not sure whether I'm able to find work there, but I'd rather work in a language school or a restaurant to improve my language skills.

When you would like to go

I'd like to go there when I gradate from university. I suppose I would be rather confused. I don't know whether I need to further my education, or whether I need to start working.

Why you want to work in that place

I believe that working in a foreign country can increase my work experience, for example, how to communicate with customers who speak English. That would be an amazing experience. In addition, I can improve my life skills and achieve a sense of independence. I have been relying on my parents to support my education, and I'd like to see whether I am able to survive in another country.

大家可以看到上面加彩的字，都是一些比较个人化的描述。

个人例子：

• Some of my friends are studying in this country, and they all agree that it's a wonderful country to live and study.（我的一些朋友在这个国家学习，他们觉得这是一个很好的地方。）

• how to communicate with customers who speak English（如何和说英文的顾客交流）

• I have been relying on my parents to support my education, and I'd like to see whether I am able to survive in another country.（我一直都靠父母去支持我的教育，我想知道自己是否能够在其他国家生存下来。）

感受：

- That would be an amazing experience.（这是一个很棒的体验。）

大家会发现，加入这些信息之后，整个故事就变得比较个人化，不那么生硬了。

现在大家可以按照上面的思路，说一下这个题目。

然后，多说两次，说到熟悉为止，记住，不要背诵，不要追求字字都能记忆。

☆ Part 2 练习 14

Describe an interesting neighbour.

小问题	中文思路	词伙
Who this person is 标准化的问题	这个人知识渊博，能够说流利的英文等	speak fluent English
How you know this person 标准化的问题	他想去澳大利亚，我对澳大利亚很感兴趣，所以一直有交流，我们有很多话题，说起澳大利亚一些好的大学	share interests, top universities
What this person likes to do 故事化的问题	他目前在一个跨国公司工作，经常去图书馆学习，提高自己的英文	multinational enterprise, have a good command of English
Why you think this neighbour is interesting 故事化的问题	他已经30多岁了，很多人都不会想着留学，因为费用很高，而且需要适应新的文化，但是他觉得这是人生重要的体验	afford tuition, adapt to the local culture, a life-changing experience

下面是回答的大致内容（大概8～10句话）。

Who this person is

The person is my neighbour. He is a very knowledgeable guy and speaks fluent English. I can learn a lot from him whenever I talk to him, especially when he shares some study techniques.

How you know this person

He wants to study in Australia, and I also have this plan, so we share many topics and interests. For example, he told me a lot about the top universities in Australia, and the courses provided by these universities.

What this person likes to do

He is currently working for a multinational enterprise. When he has spare time, he reads books in the library in order to have a good command of English. It's really nice to have a friend like him, who can serve as a good role model.

Why you think this neighbour is interesting

The main reason why I think he's an interesting guy is that he is in his thirties, and people of his age normally wouldn't consider the possibility of going abroad, not only because they cannot afford tuition but also they don't think they can adapt to the local culture of another country. More importantly, it's a life-changing experience. Studying abroad, according to him, can broaden our minds and expose me to different cultures.

大家可以看到上面加彩的字，使用的是举例、说个人感受和意义的方法去拓展，也使得一个故事产生变化，避免重复。

个人例子：

I can learn a lot from him whenever I talk to him, especially when he shares some study techniques.（我从他那里学到了很多，他会分享一些学习的技能。）

感受：

It's really nice to have a friend like him, who can serve as a good role model.（找到这样的朋友很好，他可以当我的榜样。）

意义：

Studying abroad, according to him, can broaden our minds and expose me to different cultures.（他说，海外学习可以开拓我们的视野，让我们接触不同的文化。）

现在大家可以按照上面的思路，练习一下这个题目。

然后，多说两次，说到熟悉为止，记住，不要背诵，不要追求字字都能记忆。

☆ Part 2 练习 15

Describe a time that you were waiting for something.

小问题	中文思路	词伙
When it happened 标准化的问题	在大学毕业的时候，比较迷惘，不知道要不要读硕士，要不要开始工作	continue studies
Where it happened 标准化的问题	在国内，我那时候想去澳洲留学，那里有一些很好的大学	world famous universities
What you were waiting for 故事化的问题	等待大学的 offer，我觉得可以提高语言，以后可能会更加容易找到好工作	have a good command of English, find a decent job
How you felt about it 故事化的问题	非常紧张，希望获得 offer 后，可以多一个选择，也担心自己适应不了外国的教育系统，会有文化差异的问题	a different education system, cultural shocks

下面是回答的大致内容（大概 8～10 句话）。

When it happened

I'm gonna talk about how I waited for the offer from an Australian university. I was about to graduate from university, but I was confused and restless. I was not sure whether it's a good idea to continue studies, or I had to look for a job.

Where it happened

I was in China. I was waiting for the offer from several universities in Australia. Australia has a number of world famous universities. If I go abroad, Australia is definitely the best choice. It would be fantastic to study there.

What you were waiting for

The offer from the university was important to me because I could improve my language skills. I also believed that a period of study overseas could help me find a decent job in the future. My friends working in investment firms told me that their companies would only recruit university graduates from universities in other countries.

How you felt about it

I was quite nervous. If I had the offer, I could have one more option. However, I was also worried that I couldn't adapt to a different education system in another country. I would have to handle cultural shocks. For example, I was not sure whether I could get used to eating local food. But after all, it would possibly push me to move out of the comfort zone and improve my skills.

大家可以看到上面加彩的字，使用的是举例、说个人感受和意义的方法去拓展，也使得一个故事产生变化，避免重复。

个人例子：

My friends working in investment firms told me that their companies would only recruit university graduates from universities in other countries.（我在投资公司工作的朋友和我说，他们公司只招聘来自其他国家的大学毕业生。）

For example, I was not sure whether I could get used to eating local food.（我不知道到时候我是否能够适应吃当地的食物。）

感受：

If I go abroad, Australia is definitely the best choice. It would be fantastic to study there.（如果我去外国，澳大利亚当然是最好的选择。在那里学习非常好。）

意义：

After all, it would possibly push me to move out of the comfort zone and improve my skills.（但是毕竟它让我离开安乐窝，促使我提高技能。）

现在大家可以按照上面的思路，练习一下这个题目。

然后，多说两次，说到熟悉为止，记住，不要背诵，不要追求字字都能记忆。

☆ Part 2 练习 16

Describe an advertisement you have seen recently.

小问题	中文思路	词伙
When and where you saw it 标准化的问题	在大学毕业的时候，比较迷惘，不知道要不要读硕士，要不要开始工作。我看到一个关于澳洲留学的广告，说澳洲有很多好的大学	reach a crossroads, take postgraduate courses, search for a job, renowned institutions

What was advertised 故事化的问题	这个广告推广的是留学申请服务，帮助学生申请去澳洲的大学	make an application
What the contents of the advertisements were 故事化的问题	这个广告说去澳洲读书可以有助于提升外语，也可以体验不同的文化，增加就业机会	master a foreign language, experience a different culture, improve job prospects
How you felt about it 故事化的问题	我觉得这个广告不错，给人启发，因为它告诉我们职途上的另外一个选择	career path

下面是回答的大致内容（大概 8～10 句话）。

When and where you saw it

The advertisement I'd like to talk about is about studying abroad. I watched the advertisement when I was about to complete a degree. My life reached a crossroads: I didn't know whether it's necessary to take postgraduate courses or search for a job. The advertisement highlighted the benefits of studying overseas, especially in Australia, where there are many renowned institutions.

What was advertised

The advertisement promoted the service of a company which helped students to apply for the admission to postgraduate courses in Australia. For example, if I wanted to study in the University of Sydney, the company could tell me how to get the offer.

What the contents of the advertisements were

The advertisement suggested that studying in Australia could help us master a foreign language. We can also have opportunities to experience a different culture. Qualifications gained overseas could improve our job prospects.

How you felt about it

The advertisement was quite inspiring and informative. It told me a different choice I could make in my career path. It has changed my perception of advertising. Many advertisements have focused on promoting their services by stressing their strengths, but this advertisement focuses on our needs and interests.

好，我们再次分析一下这些加彩的内容。

个人例子：

For example, if I wanted to study in the University of Sydney, the company could tell me how to get the offer.（例如，如果我想在悉尼大学学习，公司可以告诉我怎么获得 offer。）

意义：

Many advertisements have focused on promoting their services by stressing their strengths, but this advertisement focuses on our needs and interests.（很多广告都通过强调它们的优点来推广服务，而这个广告关注我们的需要和利益。）

现在大家可以按照上面的思路，练习一下这个题目。

然后，多说两次，说到熟悉为止，记住，不要背诵，不要追求字字都能记忆。

2.3.6 Part 2 传统雅思口语备考方法的弊端

传统的雅思口语备考方法一般是老师将口语题目分成五个类别：(1) 人物；(2) 地点；(3) 事件；(4) 物件；(5) 媒体。然后每个类别的题目想出 2～3 个素材，让学生去背好后，套在不同的题目上。

这种传统的方法有几个弊端。

弊端 1：背整个故事比较难，而且容易和其他学生重复。

传统的口语老师会设想好一个故事，想好了整个过程，如摘草莓，从坐车、买票、进去摘、吃草莓、和朋友分享心得、拍照、回家。

首先，一个学生不可能记得那么细致，除非背诵。一旦背诵，交流过程就会很不自然，考官容易听出来。

其次，如果真的背诵下来了，反而问题更严重。如果这个口语老师的其他学生也在同一个考场，考官就会非常清楚，这个故事是大家背好来考试的，那么给你一个 5 分甚至更低的分数都有可能。

弊端 2：一个故事套用到同一个类别的另外一个题目里很别扭。

传统的口语老师在对付人物类话题的时候会想好对一个人的描述，然后尝试放在所有关于人的题目上。

这个显然是不可取的，例如你描述一个名人，选的是姚明，说他很高，事业很成功，很有钱，喜欢做公益等。这种描述显然是不可能套用到其他的一些人物题目中去的，如你所熟悉的一个朋友，或者是对你影响很大的家人。

考官很容易听出来你是在用另外一个当季题目的回答来应付目前的题目，这样你的分数也会很低。

弊端 3：细节太多，不够合理和自然。

传统的口语老师非常强调时间要说得很够，所以他们非常注意细节。如描述一个建筑，他们会说门怎么样，窗怎么样，里面的柱子如何如何。又如描述一个动物，他们会说毛皮怎么样，眼睛多么大，生活习惯怎么样，一般生活在世界什么地点。

考官一听就知道你是准备好的，因为作为一个普通人，是不可能在一分钟之内想出那么多细节，像探索频道一样分享那么多知识的。

哪怕是描述一个人，传统的口语回答会说这个人的长相、身高、气质等，试问我们中文都不可能将自己最熟悉的人（哪怕是父母和好友）描述得很具体，那么我们怎么可能用英文描述得如此细致？考官是不可能相信的。

弊端 4：单词和表达过分高大上，不接地气。

传统的口语老师经常会在维基百科或者英文网站上找一些故事，然后稍微改动一下发给学生去背诵。这些故事里面的用词有时候太难，或者有很多的俚语，这些表达如果学生硬生生用到考试中，听起来会非常生硬和别扭。

特别是到了 Part 3 部分，学生的用词一旦和 Part 2 的级别相差很大，考官就会更加相信考生是背好了答案来考试的，也会大量扣分。

双拼法很好地解决了这些问题。

首先，双拼法并不是强调把整个故事都背下来，操作性强，避免重复。

在一些非故事问题的回答上，如 when，where，how，who 等，每个学生可以自己想一下说什么，所以不同的学生会有不同的回答，哪怕是用类似的故事。

可能大家都在说出国这个故事，但是有的人在回答 where 的时候，说去英国，因为那里有很多名胜古迹；有的人在回答 who 的时候，说一个人的工作，如建议我出国的人是一个成功的商人，他去各个国家做生意。这样大家就不会重复。

其次，双拼法让学生更加灵活地串故事。

如学生描述一个人，是比尔·盖茨，说这个人很喜欢阅读，会读很多的书，在书里获得知识和灵感，哪怕变得很富裕了还坚持读书。那么完全可以将读书这个事情用在不同类别的题目下。

如地点类题目，叫你描述一个咖啡店，你可以说你喜欢去的咖啡店，因为很方便读书。

如物品类题目，叫你描述送朋友的礼物，你可以说是一本书，这本书给了他很多阅读的乐趣。

如媒体类题目，叫你描述一个网站，你可以说喜欢去一个阅读的网站，有人在上面分享各种书的读后感。

如事件类题目，叫你描述一个和孩子相处的经历，你可以说教孩子看书。

等等……

大家会发现，双拼法不是强调人物的故事只能放在人物的话题上说，而是也可以放在其他类别的题目上说。

再次，双拼法不强调过多的细节。

双拼法将重心放在一个东西的意义或你的感受上，而不是放在对一个东西的过程描述上。

如读一本书，我们不强调学生要记住什么时候买、在哪里买、和谁一起买、买的时候发生了什么事情、花了多少钱等这种细节。因为我们觉得我们不可能记得住很多事情的细节。

反之，我们强调的是大家去说这本书的意义、你的感受等。这样听起来比较合乎常情。

然后，稍微加点细节的变化，如书的某部分内容，就已经足够。

最后，双拼法使表达更加容易掌握。

双拼法强调词伙的使用，而且是一个故事思路里出现的词伙，如果将这些词伙反复用在不同的题目下，会比较容易记得住。

词伙一般由简单的单词构成，也比较容易掌握。

2.4 如何克服口语考试的紧张感

很多考生口语考试紧张的原因有很多。

- 平时备考过程中听了很多关于雅思口语考试的负面报道，包括印度考官、5分老太、声音太低、语速太快等。到了考场的时候，也怕自己是受害人，进入考场前已经开始紧张。
- 等待的时间比较长，而考试的时间又比较短，考生总是觉得一不小心就会考不过，所以很紧张。
- 平时很少和外国人交流，考试的时候不知道对方是否能听懂、是否认可自己、是否能听出自己的错误等，这些想法也会导致紧张情绪。

- 备考的时候主要以背诵为主，背素材、背答案，到了考场怕自己背漏、背错，或者考到没背到的东西，所以也会高度敏感。
- 练习比较少，很怕自己卡壳、怕自己没话可说、怕自己说错单词和时态；遇到题目没想法、有想法没单词、有单词说不出、说出来不流畅或者说错等。

解决的方法主要 4 个：

方法 1：多练习。

很多考生备考口语的时候不喜欢开口，这是很大的问题。特别是在 Part 2，他们喜欢写答案然后背。

这个方法最大的弊病就是你写的东西往往是精雕细琢、改了又改的，一般不够自然、不够连贯，不是你平时想表达的一些东西。

解决的方法就是，大家在备考 Part 2 的时候，看到题目，自己思考 1 分钟就可以开始说，一边说一边写下一些用到的词伙，能说多少是多少，说到实在没话可说，就停下来，思考可以加什么内容，自己再说一次。这个过程其实就是一种交流和表达的练习过程。久而久之，你会熟练和上瘾，开口是很随意和简单的事情。

很多考生总想一次说够 2 分钟，一次说完一个完美的故事，却迟迟不愿意开口，这样就陷入了越不开口越难开口，越难开口越不开口的怪圈。最后考场一张嘴，结结巴巴，一不顺畅，更加紧张。很多单词写在纸上很简单，自己说却说不出来。

就如同学习保龄球一样，刚开始也觉得扔一个球特别不好意思，老怕出丑。因为害怕，所以不去尝试，结果真出手的时候，结果很糟糕。但是，如果你天天没事就扔，捡到就扔，你就会越来越熟练。

方法 2：熟悉考题。

每个月的口语题库一般来说都比较固定，大家可以看到题库里的题目就说，将自己的想法说出来，尽可能拓展，不要给自己限制（如我说 2 句话就够了，或者我说 3 句话就够了），能说就往下说。

也不要担心自己准备的题目考不到，或者自己的观点不够好，用词不够高大上。

对待任何的话题，都能够滔滔不绝，这本身就是交流能力的体现。

考试当日，可以在兜里揣着 1～2 页口语的题目和回答，进考场前自己看一下题目，闭着眼睛说一下回答，这样会让自己的嘴巴热身。

方法 3：开始说慢。

很多考生平时练习盲目追求语速，很多单词发音不清楚，到了考场上，考官一旦听不清楚，要你具体解释自己的回答，你就很容易紧张。

刚开始练习的时候，可以放慢速度，争取每个单词都发音清楚，特别是长单词，如 accomplish, babysitter, procrastination, paragraph 等。只有你嘴巴的肌肉熟悉了发长单词的音，你才会轻松发好每个单词的音，你才会更加自信。

方法 4：平时找老师或者朋友 1 对 1 练习。

自己一个人练习的弊端是没有对话的感觉。考场上，有时候考官会随机按照你的回答加问一些问题，这个时候你的随机回答能力很重要。

在和朋友练习的时候，可以叫对方多问你 why，逼迫你解释自己的回答，这样也可以提升你面对质疑时候的信心和交流能力。

第 3 章

词伙在雅思口语 Part 3 和写作中的应用

3.1 Part 3 考试介绍和备考攻略

雅思考试的口语 Part 3 紧跟在 Part 2 之后。很多老师都不太重视 Part 3，觉得没有什么规律，题目也变化多端。很多学生因此也忽视 Part 3。

按照我自己的经验，Part 3 其实在口语考试里非常重要。我自己在口语考试里，Part 1 都没什么好说的，因为大家说的东西都差不多，Part 2 我的故事比较 boring，毕竟上年纪了，但是到了 Part 3，因为我教了很多年写作，很多 Part 3 的题目就是写作题目，我反而能够滔滔不绝地回答。

考官如何判断一个人的口语交流水平？

其实就是看这个人是否能交流，能表达自己的想法，有内容可以说。

很多同学 Part 1 和 Part 2 精心准备，到了 Part 3 却磕磕碰碰，经常卡壳，这样分数不可能高。反之，我们很多同学上了网课后，口语上了 7 分，就是因为我们非常强调要每天练习作文的内容和口语 Part 3。包括口译作文的段落，练习口语考试的 Part 3，哪怕是考试没有遇到原题，一样可以获得好分数。

为什么？

原因 *1*：很多题目的观点和例子是可以互用的。

原因 *2*：你在练习中会增加自己交流的信心，表达会更加熟练和流利，而这就是考官看重的东西。你的表现会比那些在 Part 3 上不知所措的学生要好得多。

口语 Part 3 要注意下面一些要点：

注意 *1*：关注时态，不要犯错。

注意 *2*：尽可能拓展，多说原因、影响、例子等。

注意 *3*：少用冗长的套句，不要重复一些内容。

注意 *4*：不要担心你的立场问题，只管继续说。

如题目是问 Do you agree that...，你开始说 Yes, I agree...，说到中间，没东西说了，这个时候，你可以说 On the other hand, I think...，说相反的立场，也是可以的。雅思口语考试不要求你从头到尾紧扣题目。

注意 *5*：不要用太长的个人例子表述。

当你用自己的经历举例的时候，尽量长话短说。否则考官会说这是你个人的例子，我想知道更加普遍的情况。

注意 *6*：不要用大词或者自己不熟悉的词。

考官往往会问这个词是什么意思，或者为什么你觉得是这样的。他们想知道你是否真正了解这个单词的意思。

注意 *7*：遇到听不懂的题目，可以叫考官重复问题。

比较直接的方式是 “Pardon me” “I beg you pardon” “Could you please rephrase the question?” 等，也可以比较间接地问，如 “Did you mean...”，将自己对题目的理解说一下，考官会进行解释，帮助你准确了解题目。

注意 *8*：回答的第一句话一定要扣题，出现题目关键词。

我们很多考生都喜欢先说很多背景，然后再回答题目，这种思路不符合英文母语者的习惯。他们喜欢先回答题目，再开始说背景和解释。

注意 *9*：遇到不懂的题目，可以说自己不是很懂，但是尽量回答所有问题。

你可以说 “I am not sure” “It’s a difficult question” “It’s difficult to say. I’m not an expert on this topic” 等，但是这种表达如果在一次考试中出现了 2～3 次，你的分数基本上会很难看。考官会觉得你的交流能力有问题。

注意 *10*：注意句子的衔接和逻辑，不要让人觉得你前言不搭后语。

3.2 口语 Part 3 和写作的共通点

雅思口语 Part 3 的考试和写作考试有很多类似之处，可以联合一起复习。

下面的表大概解释了口语 Part 3 和写作的共同点和不同点。

	共同点	不同点
拓展	在口语 Part 3，一定要注意拓展。考官会期待考生在口语 Part 3 给出比较充分的回答，从而判断考生的语言水平。	在拓展方面，作文要求会更高。在写作的主体段，一般尽量要避免语言和内容的重复。在口语中，有点重复有时候并无大碍。毕竟写作是白纸黑字，任何重复都很容易看出来。但是在口语考试中，如果考生解释不清楚一个观点，口语考官会不断问 why，基础不好的考生就崩溃了。
连接	作文和口语 Part 3 的回答都要注意连接，回答要有逻辑关系。可以通过这些方法来增加连贯性：① 连接词；② 关键词重复或者近义词的使用；③ 代词的使用。	口语中，出现常规的连接词，如 firstly, secondly, last but not least, finally，没有任何问题。在写作中，使用这些连接词则会有模板嫌疑。
举例	口语和作文都建议用例子来拓展，不仅可以让内容丰富，然后也可以让你的回答脱颖而出，不至于太过俗套（因为大家的观点可能差不多，区别体现在例子上）。	口语的例子可以更加个人化。口语 Part 3 有些时候会问一些关于你自己国家的事情，这种问题中经常会出现 in your country，或者是关于 your family, your experience，in your case，这个时候用你自己的具体情况回答也可以。而作文使用个人的例子缺乏概括性和普遍性。

用词	不要重复使用一个单词或者表达，要懂得使用替换词或者替换的表达,这样才可以展示你的词汇量。	有些替换词在口语里可以接受，但是作文里不建议，如用 kids 替换 children。又如用 tons of/loads of 替换 many/a large number of。
大词和陌生的词伙	雅思考官是 native speakers，对于用词的恰当性和地道性有很高的要求。大家拿不准的表达千万不要用。	在口语中，用大词和复杂的词更加危险。一来如果考生发音有问题，考官未必能听懂。二来如果考生使用单词不当，或和语境不符，考官会打断考试，问一些关于这个单词的问题，考生马上就乱了。
语法	口语和写作对于语法都有专门的评分标准。语法越准确，分数越高。	在口语中，有时候有些语法错误是可以接受的。因为即便我们说中文，也不是每句话都没有语法错误。在考场上，考生可以在发现错误的时候自我纠正一下，或者即便有错误也继续说，不破坏流畅性。而在写作中，语法非常重要，因为写前写后都有时间思考和检查，考官对语法错误的容忍度很低。
句子结构	句子结构的变化在口语和写作中都是考查的对象。	在口语中，不要因为追求复杂句而损失了流畅性。更不要因为追求复杂的语法而说一些别扭的句子，导致考官不理解你的回答。简而言之，口语中 fluency 更重要。
时态	时态准确也是语法的一个要素，在口语和写作中都重要。	口语的时态变化要比 Task 2 写作复杂得多。主要原因是口语 Part 3 问的问题非常多变和广泛，会问你关于过去的记忆和未来的预想，还会让你对比不同东西。

正是因为口语 Part 3 和作文的这些类似之处，我在这本词伙书中建议大家用“嘴巴写作文”的方式学习词伙和常见观点。在回答口语 Part 3 的时候使用作文的拓展方式，这样可以让回答变得更加有内容（不至于考场上支支吾吾填不满时间）。复习作文不用笔写，而是用嘴巴说，这样可以加快复习速度，使考生能复习更多题目、拓宽复习的范围。

当然，我也要提醒一下，本书 80 道口语 Part 3 练习题目基本上都含有两个观点，每个观点都有比较详细的拓展。很多考生会担心两个观点：① 考场上说不出那么多；② 考场上没说完，考官就打断。

我的建议是不用担心这些，平时多练习，能说多少说多少，在考场上，给考官一种口若悬河、“左右逢源”的感觉，也好过吞吞吐吐在那里凑字数。

3.3 百搭观点的介绍

很多考生在雅思作文和口语考试中遇到的一个麻烦就是看到题目想不出观点。原因有二：① 雅思题库很大，话题很广泛，很多题目并不是我们日常讨论的话题，我们很少去思考这些话题的观点；② 很多同学平时较少阅读，缺乏背景知识。

想不到合适的观点对于写作和口语考试的影响都很大：

首先，没观点会让很多考生在作文中会没东西可写，只能写套句凑字数，而在口语考试中，结果更悲惨，考官会以为你听不懂题目，不断追问你。

其次，没有合适的观点就很难拓展和论述，必然会影响到句子的连接、内容的连贯和词汇的表达（中文都不知道说什么，英文的单词就更加不用说了）。

因此，要解决口语 Part 3 和大作文，我们首先要处理观点的问题。

那么如何帮助考生在短时间内熟悉雅思大部分的考题，然后增加背景知识呢？

我想出了“百搭观点”这个方法。

所谓的“百搭观点”，就是一个可以用在多个相关作文和口语题目上的观点，这些题目论述的思路类似。考生通过熟悉百搭观点，可以掌握不同题目的相关性，在考场上比较迅速地想出观点。

我们看一下下面这个教育类题目的百搭观点，说的是教育的重要性。

教育的提供和老师的教育有助于：

A 小孩增加知识，以后方便找工作，减少失业率。

B 年轻人懂得道德和社会规范。

C 小孩学会如何和人交流。

D 加深对不同科目的认识，方便以后大学做研究和产品创新。

E 不同的学校和校外活动塑造年轻人的性格和品质。

F 培养人们的技能并提升他们的能力，方便他们不断学习，实现自己的梦想。

G 掌握知识和技术可以提高工作效率和产出。

那么这个观点可以用在下面这些作文题目中。

题目 1

Some working parents believe childcare centres can provide best care for children, while others think other family members like grandparents can do this job. Discuss both views and give your own opinion. （考试日期：20150314）

这个 2015 年的作文题目是关于幼教中心的重要性的。

那么我们可以使用上面百搭观点 F 的观点。

作文主体部分的一个观点可以是：

去幼教中心，可以提升小孩的能力（如技术能力、读写能力、动手能力），方便他们不断学习，以后实现自己的梦想。

题目 2

Young people who commit crimes should be treated in the same ways as adults by authorities. To what extent do you agree or disagree? （考试日期：20150425）

这个 2015 年的作文题目是关于青少年罪犯的惩罚措施的。

那么我们可以使用上面百搭观点 A 的观点。

作文主体部分的一个观点可以是：

年轻人不应该被判刑坐牢，这样他们可以继续完成学业，增加知识，方便以后找工作，不用因为失业而继续犯罪。

题目 3

More and more people want to study at university, so competition for university places is increasing. Why more and more people want to study at university? Is it a positive or negative development?（考试日期：20150606）

这个 2015 年的作文题目是关于为什么大家要读大学的。

我们可以使用上面百搭观点 G 的观点。

作文主体部分的一个观点可以是：

读大学可以使人们掌握更多的知识和技术，使工作更有效率、产出更高，更加容易获得雇主的青睐。

从这三个例子可以看出，一旦你熟悉一些百搭观点，然后不断在不同的题目中使用，就会在很短时间之内成为一个“雅思通”，在考场上遇到新题、偏题，也能够融会贯通，得心应手。这比准备一道道真题要容易得多，毕竟雅思作文过去十年的题目就有差不多 500 道，而口语的 Part 3 题目也非常多。

百搭观点在使用中要注意三个问题：

- 要注意题目的变化。

百搭观点里的每个观点不是在每个题目里都可以使用的，随着题目的变化，针对的人和事物也在改变，需要选择恰当的观点。

如，第三个题目是关于“人们为什么要读大学”，那么我们显然不能使用“B 教育可以让人学会道德和社会规范”这个观点。虽然大学有这么一个功能，但是大家不是为了学会道德才进大学。

- 观点要有所延伸或者调整。

题目变化的时候，我们使用一个百搭观点，最好再补充一些题目的关键词，去增加观点和题目的联系。

如第二题，关于如何惩罚年轻的罪犯，当我们说到“年轻人可以找工作”，后面要加上“从而避免再次犯罪”这种关键词来扣题（因为题目说的是青年罪犯的问题）。

- 要使用例子。

也有的考生会担心如果大家都在考场上用一个观点，考官会不会扣分。首先，雅思考试不会因为大家的观点差不多就扣分。其次，即便写了同一个观点，每个人的语言水平不同决定了用词、语法、拓展和论述的不同。最后，如果担心自己写的东西和别人差不多，可以通过举例去区分。

如第一个题目可以解释一下小孩能学会什么具体的技能，第二个题目可以举例说年轻人能找到什么具体的工作（如修车）。

3.4 写作和口语常考十大类话题

现在我们开始讲百搭观点。为了方便大家记忆和理解，我将雅思作文和口语按照话题分成 10 大类，我们可以看看每个话题大概的出题方向是什么，分别有什么百搭观点。

当然，考生想出观点是第一步，第二步就是决定了观点之后要用地道的语言表达出来。这里涉及词伙的应用。因此，在每个百搭观点之后，我都会给一个口语 Part 3 的题目，给出相关的词伙，大家可以大声地说一下，这样，观点和词伙都得到了练习。

在《顾家北手把手教你雅思写作》一书中，我主要是解决学生关于审题、扣题、逻辑、拓展、语法及句子结构和段落结构的问题，而本书解决的是学生观点和用词的问题。

3.4.1 常考写作和口语话题 1：政府类

政府类是雅思作文和口语一个很大的话题。政府拥有立法权和支配社会资源的能力，所以政府对各个领域影响很大。常考的次话题有下面一些：

政府次话题 1：立法和惩治犯罪

政府次话题 2：政府对社会弱势群体（包括妇女、老人）的帮助

政府次话题 3：政府对教育和科技的投资和支持

政府次话题 4：政府对文化活动和设施（包括博物馆、艺术馆、古建筑）的投资

政府次话题 5：政府对民生（包括医疗、住房、交通设施）的影响

政府次话题 1：立法和惩治犯罪

政府立法在雅思考试中包含的范围非常广泛，包括：税法、环境法、交通法规、针对广告的法律、针对食品和快餐的法律、针对工作时间的法律。

关于惩治犯罪，雅思常考的话题是如何能够减少犯罪。

百搭观点 1

A 加大惩罚力度，如罚款
B 服刑
C 社区服务和做义工
D 加强法律教育
E 扶贫
F 提供职业培训，减少失业
G 增加警察，甚至是配枪警察
H 设置视频监控系统
I 政府教大家如何保护自己

有助于减少犯罪。

Crime 相关词伙

act as a deterrent

1. a deterrent effect 威慑作用
2. escape punishment 逃避惩罚
3. think twice 再三考虑
4. prevent crime 阻止犯罪
5. curb crime 遏制犯罪
6. combat crime 打击犯罪
7. commit a crime 犯罪
8. break laws 违反法律
9. violate laws 触犯法律
10. catch criminals 抓捕罪犯
11. an escaping criminal 在逃罪犯
12. armed police 武装警察
13. carry weapons 携带武器
14. pay a fine 支付罚款
15. serve a prison term 服刑
16. work as a volunteer 作为志愿者
17. reduce poverty 减少贫穷
18. vocational/job training 职业培训
19. surveillance cameras 视频监控

口语 Part 3 练习题目

Question: What are the benefits to having police officers in the community?

大家先看着中文思路自己回答一次，然后使用词伙再回答一次。

结构	思路	词伙
观点 1	震慑犯罪	a good deterrent
原因	罪犯觉得自己很难逃脱惩罚，所以会三思而后行	escape punishment, think twice
结果 1	预防犯罪	prevent crime
结果 2	社区更加安全	make the community a safer place to live
观点 2	抓罪犯	catch criminals
举例	配枪警察可以射击罪犯	armed police, shoot an escaping criminal
结果	保护民众	protect the public

大家看一下下面的回答，自己再练习，说到熟练为止。

观点 1：I think the benefit is that the presence of police officers is **a good deterrent**.

原因：Potential offenders think they cannot **escape punishment**, so they will **think twice** if they want to commit a crime.

结果 1：It can **prevent crime**.

结果 2：If the number of officers on patrol increases, it can **make the community a safer place to live**.

观点 2：Another benefit is that the police can **catch criminals**.

举例：For example, **armed police** can **shoot an escaping criminal** who is likely to do something harmful to **innocent citizens**.

结果：This can help **protect the public**.

雅思作文相关真题

> ***Many people are afraid to leave home because of crimes. Some believe that more action should be taken to prevent crimes, but others feel little can be done. Discuss both views and give your opinion.***（考试日期：20150903）

政府次话题 2：政府对社会弱势群体（包括妇女、老人）的帮助

妇女和老人的题目在口语中特别是在 Part 3 中考查的频率很高。在作文考试中，老年人的话题考的比女性的题目更加频繁。

妇女话题一般涉及女性在家庭、学业和工作中所遇到的问题和歧视。

百搭观点 2

A 女性接受教育的机会增加

B 家庭经济压力增加导致男性的收入不够养家

C 企业注意女性的特质，如细心

D 女性对职业成就越发有追求

E 科技发展让很多职业都减少了体力和身体要求

从而促进了女性进入职场，提升了女性的地位，减少了男女歧视，并且促进了性别平等。

Gender Discrimination 的相关词伙

1. gender discrimination 性别歧视
2. discrimination on the grounds of sex 性别歧视
3. gender bias 性别偏见
4. gender equality 性别平等
5. the equal access to education 教育公平
6. gender differences 性别差异
7. gender gap narrows 缩小性别差距
8. managerial skills 管理技能
9. business leaders 商业领袖
10. members of the board 董事会成员
11. shatter the glass ceiling（女性）打破职位提升的障碍
12. enter the workforce 进入职场
13. close the gender gap 减少男女歧视
14. raise a family/start a family 养家糊口

口语 Part 3 练习题目

Question: Many women are earning more money now; does it mean that they can become leaders?

大家先看着中文思路自己回答一次，然后使用词伙再回答一次。

结构	思路	词伙
观点 1	女性可以成为好领导是因为有平等享受教育的权利	have equal access to education
解释	可以在大学学到管理知识	learn managerial skills
结果 1	她们可以像男性那样有效管理公司	manage the company as effectively as their male counterparts do
结果 2	性别的差距在不断减小	gender gap
观点 2	现在不存在性别歧视 大公司不重男轻女，女性也可以进入董事会	gender discrimination, gender bias
举例	员工甚至都习惯听命于女性上司	take an order from
结果	在相同的职位上，女性可以挣和男性一样多的钱	earn as much money

大家看一下下面的回答，自己再练习，说到熟练为止。

观点 1：I think one reason why women can become **business leaders** today is that they today have **equal access to education**.

解释：They can **learn managerial skills** at university.

结果 1：It means that they can also **manage the company as effectively as their male counterparts do**.

结果 2：The **gender gap** is narrowing in terms of workplace performance.

观点 2：Another reason is that we don't have any **gender discrimination**. Many big companies today don't have **gender bias** when choosing **members of the board**.

举例：Employees are comfortable with **taking an order from** female supervisors.

结果：Women can **earn as much money** as men do in the same positions.

雅思作文相关真题

Nowadays, both men and women work full-time. Therefore, they have to share household tasks equally. To what extent do you agree or disagree? (考试日期：20140510)

百搭观点 3

女性被认为是

A 以家庭为重

B 生育影响事业

C 身体不能从事高强度工作

D 女性天生比较有同情心，没什么野心

E 比较多愁善感和情绪化

都会影响其事业的发展和工作的选择。

Women in the Workplace 相关词伙

1. male-dominated industries 男性占主导地位的行业
2. clerical work 白领工作
3. juggle different roles 扮演不同的角色
4. balance work and family commitments 平衡工作和家庭责任的关系
5. domestic responsibilities 家庭责任
6. domestic work 家务活
7. child-rearing duties 抚养孩子的责任
8. raise children 抚养孩子
9. high-paying industries 高薪行业
10. advance one's career 发展某人的事业
11. a fulfilling career 令人满意的事业
12. career success 事业成功
13. maternity leave 产假
14. physically demanding jobs/manual work 体力活
15. career choices 职业选择

口语 Part 3 练习题目

Question: Do you think there's any difference between males and females when it comes to choosing a future career?

大家先看看中文思路自己回答一次，然后使用词伙再回答一次。

结构	思路	词伙
直接回答	是的，我相信他们会考虑不同的因素	take different factors into consideration
解释	男人更愿意在一个高薪行业工作，这帮助他们挣大钱	in a high-paying industry
结果	这就是为什么银行和 IT 通常是男性居多的行业	male-dominated industries
对比	相比之下，女人通常喜欢挑战性较小的工作，例如白领工作，这工作通常不需要她们加班，所以她们能更容易地平衡工作和家庭责任之间的关系	clerical work, work overtime, balance work and family commitments
举例	例如，大多数女人想要做教师，因为有寒假和暑假	have winter or summer holidays
其他观点	另一个不同是职业发展的机会	advance one's career
解释	男人是有志向的，他们想有一个令人满意的事业	have a fulfilling career
对比	女人是缺乏事业心的。她们更注重她们的家庭责任	domestic responsibilities

大家看一下下面的回答，自己再练习，说到熟练为止。

直接回答：Yes, I believe they **take different factors into consideration**.

解释：For men, they are more willing to work **in a high-paying industry** which helps them to **earn a large amount of money**.

结果：This is why banking and IT are normally **male-dominated industries**.

对比：By contrast, women usually prefer less challenging jobs, such as **clerical work**, which normally do not require them to **work overtime**, so they can **balance work and family commitments** more easily.

举例：For example, most women intend to work as teachers and they **have winter or summer holidays**.

其他观点：Another difference is the opportunity to **advance one's career**.

解释：Men are ambitious and they want to **have a fulfilling career**.

对比：Women **are less driven by career success**. They **pay closer attention to** their **domestic responsibilities**.

雅思作文相关真题

In many countries women are not able to join the army to share the same opportunities as men to serve the country. However, some people think women can be a member of the army, navy and air-force. To what extent do you agree or disagree? (考试日期：20160519)

老年人的题目主要是考查老龄化社会里老人遇到的各种问题和挑战，如何解决这些问题。也考查老人和年轻人的主要差别。

百搭观点 4

老年人被认为是

A 保守

B 不愿意接受新的科技

C 和世界缺乏接触

D 身体不好

E 没有收入，比较节省

所以被认为会

A 阻碍创新

B 阻碍社会发展

C 和年轻人有矛盾

D 不适合继续工作

E 对家庭和社会产生经济负担

Older People 相关词伙

1. older people 老人
2. the elderly 老者
3. senior citizens 年长者
4. the older generation 老一辈
5. out of touch with the world 跟不上时代
6. resistant to change 抵触改变
7. old-fashioned ideas 过时的观念
8. fit into the modern world 适应现代社会
9. adopt advanced technology 采用高科技
10. sensible advice 明智的意见
11. life experience 生活经历
12. take risks 冒险
13. make a rash decision 做轻率的决定
14. risk averse 风险规避
15. out of touch with the world 与世界脱节
16. a source of income 收入来源
17. hold back social progress 阻碍社会进步
18. a financial burden on 财政负担

口语 Part 3 练习题目

Question: Do you think you will take advice from older people?

大家先看着中文思路自己回答一次，然后使用词伙再回答一次。

结构	思路	词伙
直接回答	是的，我认为我们能从老人的生活经验中收获很多	the life experience, elderly people

解释	他们能给年轻人合理的建议并帮助年轻人理解自己的行为和选择的潜在后果	sensible advice potential consequences
举例	根据我的经历，当我从大学毕业的时候，我的父亲要求我在决定做什么工作之前和我的老师们交谈，还要和大学的求职顾问交谈，同时在网上搜寻信息	job adviser made choices
总结	我认为他们不愿意去冒险，所以他们将收集信息去避免做出轻率的决定	take risks, collect information, make a rash decision
相反的观点	另一方面，有时，老人也许跟不上时代	out of touch with the world
解释	他们是对改变有抵触的，也不愿意去适应高科技	resistant to change, adopt advanced technology
结果	他们过时的理念可能不适应现代社会	old-fashioned ideas, fit into the modern world

大家看一下下面的回答，自己再练习，说到熟练为止。

直接回答：Well, I suppose that we can benefit a lot from **the life experience** of **elderly people**.

解释：They can give young people **sensible advice** and help young people understand the **potential consequences** of their behavior and choice.

举例：In my experience, when I was about to graduate from the university, my father asked me to talk to my teachers, the **job adviser** of the university and also **search for information** on the Internet, before I **made choices** about jobs.

总结：I think they are less willing to **take risks**, so they will **collect information** to avoid **making a rash decision**.

相反的观点：On the other hand, sometimes, older people may be **out of touch with the world**.

解释：They are **resistant to change** and not willing to **adopt advanced technology**.

结果：Their **old-fashioned ideas** may not **fit into the modern world**.

雅思作文相关真题

> ***The leaders or directors of organisations are often older people. But some people say that young people can also be a leader. Do you agree or disagree?*** （考试日期：20150110）

政府次话题 3：政府对教育和科技的投资和支持

这一类话题常考的题目主要有：政府要不要提供免费的大学教育，是不是应该资助贫困的学生，是不是应该帮助乡村的孩子读书，如何减少贫富差距等。

百搭观点 5

政府对教育的支持主要体现在

A 开设更多公立学校
B 提供社区的职业培训
C 给大学生提供奖学金、学生贷款，甚至减免学费
D 提高老师待遇
E 在社区设置图书馆，方便大家免费看书
F 提高宽带服务，让大家更容易从网络上获得知识

Educational Equality 相关词伙

1. from less well-off backgrounds 来自贫穷的家庭
2. disadvantaged students 贫穷的学生
3. children from poor homes 来自贫穷家庭的孩子
4. children from deprived backgrounds 贫穷的孩子
5. from less well-off families 来自普通家庭
6. exempted from tuition fees 免除学费
7. drop out of school 辍学
8. educational equality 教育的公平
9. the equal access to education 教育公平
10. study at university 在大学学习
11. free-interest loans 无息贷款
12. financial support 财政支持
13. the cost of learning 学习的成本
14. break the cycle of poverty 摆脱贫穷
15. reduce poverty 减少贫穷
16. vocational/job training 职业培训
17. bridge the gap between rich and poor 减少贫富差距
18. close the economic divide 减少贫富差距
19. the education system 教育系统
20. the school system 学校系统
21. higher education 高等教育
22. receive a good education 接受好的教育
23. a well-educated workforce 受过良好教育的劳动力队伍
24. public schools 公立学校
25. set scholarships 设立奖学金
26. student loans 学生贷款
27. free education 免费教育
28. free access to knowledge 免费获取知识
29. broadband internet services 宽带服务

口语 Part 3 练习题目

Question: Do you think the government should subsidise all university students?

大家先看着中文思路自己回答一次，然后使用词伙再回答一次。

结构	思路	词伙
观点 1	政府应该把钱投入到中小学教育中	put money in
原因	有许多孩子来自不富裕的家庭，负担不起学费	children from less well-off backgrounds, afford tuition fees
结果	他们不得不因为贫穷辍学，而且将来无法找到工作	drop out of school, find employment
对比	大学生可以通过工作和节约生活费来自己支付学费	study at university

观点 2	更多的资源应该用来帮助来自贫困家庭但却在大学入学考试中表现出色的学生	allocate resources to, disadvantaged students, university entrance exams
解释	经济支持可以有各种形式，如奖学金或助学贷款	financial support, interest-free loans
结果	这可以帮助这些年轻人完成学位并且打破世代贫穷的恶性循环	pursue a degree, break the cycle of poverty
对比	如果要免除所有学生的学费，政府是资助不了的	exempted from tuition fees

大家看一下下面的回答，自己再练习，说到熟练为止。

观点 1：No. Firstly, the government should **put money in** primary and secondary education.

原因：There are many **children from less well-off backgrounds** who cannot **afford tuition fees**.

结果：They have to **drop out of school** because of poverty and cannot **find employment** later.

对比：University students can work and save money to pay the cost of **studying at university**.

观点 2：Secondly, **the resources** should **be allocated to** help **disadvantaged students** who have performed well in **university entrance exams**.

解释：**Financial support** can come in various forms, scholarships or **interest-free loans**.

结果：This can help these young people **pursue a degree** and **break the cycle of poverty**.

对比：The government couldn't support them, if all students were **exempted from tuition fees**.

雅思作文相关真题

Some people think that government should establish free libraries in each town. Others believe that it is a waste of money since people can access the Internet to obtain information. Discuss both sides and give your own opinion. (考试日期：20120112)

政府次话题 4：政府对文化活动和设施（包括博物馆、艺术馆、古建筑）的投资

雅思作文和口语经常会有一些题目是问政府是否应该在文化活动和文化项目上花钱，如博物馆要不要继续开，要不要在艺术、电影和音乐行业上花钱等。

百搭观点 6

政府的资金有限，钱应该多花在和普通民众生活直接相关的服务上

A 教育　　B 医疗

C 交通　　D 养老金

E 住房等

而不是花在一些本身有一定盈利能力的项目上

A 音乐　　B 电影

C 艺术　　D 某些科学项目（如医药）

E 博物馆　　F 古建筑和文化景点

也不是在回报期比较长的项目（如 A 太空科技 B 医药）上。

Film 相关词伙

1. the film industry 电影行业
2. top-grossing films 最卖座的电影
3. go to the cinema 去电影院
4. big-budget films 大预算电影
5. special effects 特技效果
6. star famous actors 由巨星主演
7. the box office 票房
8. talented filmmakers 有天赋的电影人（制片人）
9. produce high-quality films 制作高质量的电影
10. domestically produced films 国产电影
11. locally produced films 当地制作的电影

口语 Part 3 练习题目

Question: Do you think it is necessary for the government to invest in the film industry?

大家先看着中文思路自己回答一次，然后使用词伙再回答一次。

结构	思路	词伙
反对的观点	电影行业赚钱	the film industry
原因	很多卖座电影，人们注意休闲活动，喜欢看电影	top-grossing films, leisure activities, go to the cinema
举例	大制作电影有特效、著名影星，票房高	big-budget films, special effects, star famous actors and actresses, box office
结果	政府应该在其他地方花钱	
相反的观点	应该资助有才华的制作人	talented filmmakers
原因	帮助他们拍高质量电影	high-quality films
举例	记录民俗、传统生活方式的本国电影	domestically produced films, traditional ways of life
对比	没有资助，国产电影很难成功	locally produced films

大家看一下下面的回答，自己再练习，说到熟练为止。

反对的观点：No, I do not think governments should invest in **the film industry**.

原因：**The film industry** is a highly profitable business, and many **top-grossing films** are produced every year. Many people pay closer attention to **leisure activities** nowadays and they love to **go to the cinema** to **kill time**.

举例：For instance, some people like **big-budget films** which have **special effects** and **star famous actors and actresses**. These films attract many movie-goers and perform well in **the box office**.

结果：Instead of spending money on filmmaking, governments can invest in public services which cannot attract the investment of **the private sector**.

相反的观点：However, governments can provide funds for some **talented filmmakers** sometimes.

原因：These filmmakers need the investment to produce **high-quality films** which can compete with **foreign movies**.

举例：For instance, some **domestically produced films** feature customs as well as **traditional ways of life**.

对比：Without government funds, these **locally produced films** can hardly succeed.

雅思作文相关真题

Some people think that creative artists should be supported financially by the government of their country, while others believe that they should find financial support from other sources instead. Discuss both views and give your opinion. （考试日期：20151031）

当然，我们也会发现，艺术和文化活动如果没有政府的资助，也很难发展。我们生活如果没有了艺术和各种文化活动，也会乏味很多。

百搭观点 7

A 政府投资博物馆和艺术馆

B 资助艺术家

C 艺术展和博物馆免费入场

D 举办音乐会和参加音乐活动

E 看电影

F 上社区的艺术课

G 去图书馆看书

可以丰富我们的文化生活，有助于文化产业的发展，有助于文化的多样性。

Museums 相关词伙

1. art museums 艺术博物馆
2. war museums 战争博物馆
3. exhibit artefacts 展览文物
4. organise an exhibition 举办一个展览
5. a connection to the past 连接历史
6. cultural heritage 文化遗产
7. enrich cultural lives 丰富文化生活
8. admission fees 门票
9. open to the public 对公众开放
10. free admission 免费入场
11. free entry 免费进入

口语 Part 3 练习题目

Question: Should museums be open to the public for free?

大家先看着中文思路自己回答一次，然后使用词伙再回答一次。

结构	思路	词伙
直接回答	是的，我认为我们能免费进入	free admission
观点 1	有时对那些想要和家人度过一个美好周末的人来说博物馆是个合适的选择	spend a nice weekend, a possible option
举例	父母希望帮助他们的孩子深入理解过去发生的事情并培养孩子的认同感	develop a sense of identity

解释	博物馆展出很多手工艺品和历史文物，这些能联系过去	exhibit artefacts, connections to the past
观点 2	一些博物馆给孩子一个拓展艺术、科技、文化和历史知识的机会	expand knowledge
解释	参观这些博物馆能丰富他们的文化生活	enrich cultural lives
对比	设置门票可能会剥夺孩子的机会	admission fees

大家看一下下面的回答，自己再练习，说到熟练为止。

直接回答：Yes, I think we can offer **free admission**.

观点 1：Museums are sometimes **a possible option** for those who want to **spend a nice weekend with family**.

举例：Parents intend to help their children **deepen their understanding of** what happened in the past and **develop a sense of identity**.

解释：Museums **exhibit a lot of artefacts**, **historical items**, which are **connections to the past**.

观点 2：Some museums can also give children a good opportunity to **expand knowledge** about art, technology, cultures and history.

解释：Visiting these museums can **enrich their cultural lives**.

对比：**Admission fees** may **deprive children of** this opportunity.

雅思作文相关真题

Public museums and art galleries are not needed because people could see historical objects and works by using computers. To what extent do you agree or disagree? (考试日期：20101204)

政府次话题 5：政府对民生（包括医疗、住房、交通设施）的影响

政府在民生项目上的投资是雅思考试的常考话题，所谓民生就是和我们衣食住行直接相关的一些基础设施和公共服务。

百搭观点 8

政府可以通过

A 资助公立医院

B 投资医药研究，发明新药

C 进行健康和防疫等方面的宣传

D 免费给居民打疫苗，防止传染病

E 加强城市卫生管理（包括厕所、垃圾处理、用水等）

F 增加房屋供应，避免高密度居住条件下产生的传染病蔓延

G 通过对烟酒、快餐食品加税等方式来引导人们注意生活健康

提升大众健康，延长寿命等。

Medical Services 相关词伙

1. easier access to medical services 更加容易接触医疗服务
2. public hospitals 公办医院
3. medical equipment 医疗设备
4. clinical experience 临床经验
5. receive medical treatments 接受医疗
6. contract an illness 患病
7. high medical expenses 高医疗费用
8. a long waiting list 排长队
9. medical research 医疗调查
10. improve our health 促进我们的健康
11. in the pharmacy industry 在医药行业
12. invent new drugs 发明新药物
13. cure diseases 治愈疾病
14. previously incurable diseases 以前不可治疗的疾病
15. waste management 垃圾管理
16. spread of diseases 传播疾病
17. infectious/contagious diseases 传染病
18. healthy living 生活健康
19. improve life expectancy 延长寿命
20. boost public health 提升大众健康

口语 Part 3 练习题目

Question: Do you think people in your country have become healthier than twenty years ago?

大家先看着中文思路自己回答一次，然后使用词伙再回答一次。

结构	思路	词伙
观点 1	人们更加健康，因为医疗系统不断发展	medical system
原因	人们看病容易，政府花很多钱在公立医院上	easy access to medical services，public hospitals
举例	购买医疗设备、聘请经验丰富的医生	medical equipment, clinical experience
结果	人们更容易获得治疗，尽管医疗费用高，需要排队	receive medical treatments, medical expenses, a long waiting list
观点 2	医药研究不断发展	medical research
原因	医药行业大公司开发新药	the pharmacy industry, invent new drugs
结果	一些不治之症可以被治愈了	incurable diseases

大家看一下下面的回答，自己再练习，说到熟练为止。

观点 1：Yes, I think people have become healthier in these decades in my country due to the development of the **medical system**.

原因：People have **easier access to medical services** today, because governments have increased the funds for **public hospitals**.

举例：For instance, hospitals have adequate money to purchase **medical equipment** and doctors who have a lot of **clinical experience** are paid well.

结果：As a result, patients will find it easy to **receive medical treatments** when they **contract an illness**, although problems such as high **medical expenses** and **a long waiting list** have not yet been solved.

观点 2：The advances in **medical research** have also helped improve our health.

原因：Big companies **in the pharmacy industry** have **invented new drugs** to **cure diseases**.

结果：Therefore, some patients who suffer from previously **incurable diseases** can recover now.

雅思作文相关真题

Some people think that good health is a basic human need, so the medical service should not be run by profit-making companies. Do you think the disadvantages of the private health care outweigh the advantages? (考试日期：20061104)

3.4.2 常考写作和口语话题 2：科技类

科技类话题在雅思考试中主要考查以下内容：

科技次话题 1：电脑、网络和手机的影响

科技次话题 2：农业科技的影响

科技次话题 3：机械化和机器人的影响

科技次话题 4：太空科技的影响

科技次话题 5：空航的影响（这个次话题会在全球化的话题中讨论）

科技次话题 6：医疗科技的影响（这个次话题可以参照政府类话题讨论）

我们先用实例讲解一下科技类话题比较概括的一个观点。

百搭观点 9

科技的发展对我们有很多积极的影响，包括

A 环保科技改善环境，减少污染

B 医疗科技减少疾病，延长寿命

C 农业科技增加产量，减少饥荒

D 电脑、机械、机器人、空航等提高效率

E 太空科技给我们提供了研究方向，促进各方面的技术发展

Technology 相关词伙

1. technological advances 科技的进步
2. state-funded scientific research 政府资助的科学研究
3. scientific institutions 科学机构
4. medical advances 医学进步
5. technological innovations 技术的创新
6. technological change 技术的改变
7. advanced technology 先进科技
8. new technology 新技术
9. state-of-the-art technology 最新技术
10. cutting-edge technology 高新技术
11. technological breakthroughs 技术突破
12. the hi-tech industry 高新技术产业
13. improve the environment 保护环境
14. reduce diseases 减少疾病
15. fight hunger 减少饥荒
16. space technology 太空技术

口语 Part 3 练习题目

Question: How has technology influenced our lives?

大家先看着中文思路自己回答一次，然后使用词伙再回答一次。

结构	思路	词伙
观点	科技进步对我们的生活水平有很大影响	technological advances
举例 1	国家投资的药物科研已经成功地帮助我们找到了一些以前的致命疾病的治疗方法并且延长了人们的寿命	state-funded research, new drugs, cure for diseases, improve life expectancy
举例 2	医疗发展减少了我们由于健康问题经历的痛苦	medical advances, experience suffering, health problems
举例 3	农业上的科技革新已经增加了土地产量	increase the yield
举例 4	机械和工业机器人的使用能让工厂更快以更低成本生产产品	industrial robots, at a lower cost
结果	这就是对我们生活产生巨大影响的科技突破	technological breakthroughs, make a huge difference

大家看一下下面的回答，自己再练习，说到熟练为止。

观点：**Technological advances** have had a huge influence on our living standards.

举例 1：The **state-funded scientific research** on **new drugs**, for example, has successfully helped us find **a cure for some previously fatal diseases** and **improved life expectancy**

举例 2：**Medical advances** have minimized the **suffering** we **experience** as a result of **health problems**

举例 3 + 举例 4：**Technological innovations** in agriculture have **increased the yield** of farmland and the use of machines and **industrial robots** has enabled factories to produce products faster and **at a lower cost**.

结果：It is these **technological breakthroughs** that have **made a huge difference** to our lives.

雅思作文相关真题

Technological progress in the past century has its negative effect, despite its remarkable contribution. To what extent do you agree or disagree? (考试日期：20100227)

科技次话题 1：电脑、网络和手机的影响

这些工具是我们现代生活中不可或缺的，也是雅思写作和口语常考话题。方便和省时是它们的主要优点，而它们对我们社会关系和社会技能的影响是主要的隐患。

百搭观点 10

电脑、网络和手机主要的好处是可以让信息的传递更加方便，允许人们

A 在家里办公
B 通过手机和电脑看书和新闻
C 用手机来拍照和上传照片
D 在家里可以通过视频上课
E 通过社交网络发布新闻
F 在网络和手机上浏览网店可以更好地比价和选择产品
G 浏览网站即可，不用去博物馆和艺术馆
H 和家人朋友同事视频聊天

Internet 相关词伙

1. web-based technology 网络科技
2. work from home 在家里工作
3. teleworking, telecommuting, work at home 远程办公
4. shop online 上网购物
5. attend online courses 上网课
6. travel to work 去公司
7. travel a long distance to work 上班路程远
8. save time 省时间
9. face-to-face communication 面对面的交流
10. attend meetings 开会
11. avoid rush-hour traffic 避开交通高峰时段
12. in a formal setting 正式的场合
13. watch videos online 在网上看视频
14. social networking websites/social media 社交媒体网站
15. video chat programme 视频聊天软件

口语 Part 3 练习题目

Question: Do you think technology can save our time?

大家先看着中文思路自己回答一次，然后使用词伙再回答一次。

结构	思路	词伙
立场	可以	
原因 1	有了电脑和手机，人们可以不用去公司上班，他们可以在家里工作	travel to work
结果	省时间，他们不需要每天早起去避开交通拥挤的时段	save time, rush-hour traffic
对比	面对面的交流会耗费时间，包括开会	face-to-face communication, attend meetings
原因 2	人们可以在家里上课，参加在线教育	study from home, attend online courses
结果	不用在正式的环境下上课	in a formal setting

大家看一下下面的回答，自己再练习，说到熟练为止。

立场：Yes, I think technology can **save a lot of time**,

原因 1：because we don't have to **travel to work** every day.

结果：We can **save** our **time** for other meaningful things, we don't have to **get up early** to **avoid rush-**

hour traffic.

对比：By contrast, relying on **face-to-face communication** may be time-consuming for the simple reason that you have to go to the office **to attend meetings** or report everything to the supervisor.

原因 2：People can **study from home**, and **attend online courses**.

结果：They don't have to take courses **in a formal setting**.

雅思作文相关真题

> ***Around the world, more adults can work from home and more children can study from home as computer technologies become cheaper and more accessible. Do you think it is a positive or negative development?*** (考试日期：20110319)

电脑话题和网络话题基本上是不可分割的，毕竟电脑都可以上网。

Computers 相关词伙

1. computer games 电脑游戏
2. educational games 教育类游戏
3. computer skills 电脑技能
4. computer literacy 计算机素养
5. connect to the Internet 联网
6. download software 下载软件
7. use online communication tools 使用在线交流工具
8. store information 存储信息
9. process documents 处理文件
10. edit photos 编辑照片
11. produce videos 制作视频

口语 Part 3 练习题目

Question: What are the advantages of computer games?

大家先看着中文思路自己回答一次，然后使用词伙再回答一次。

结构	思路	词伙
观点 1	有利于熟悉电脑	computer literacy
原因	你需要懂得怎样上网，如何下载软件，怎么和其他的 players 交流	connect to the Internet, download software, use online communication tools
结果	电脑技术的进步对工作也有帮助	computer skills
观点 2	有些人觉得对大脑好	brain development
举例	教育游戏，譬如说下棋，quiz	educational games, play chess
结果	增强大脑活动	boost brain activity

大家看一下下面的回答，自己再练习，说到熟练为止。

观点 1: I think one benefit of **playing games on the computer** is that players can **improve computer literacy**.

原因：They understand how to **connect to the Internet**, **download software** and **use online communication tools** to talk with different gamers.

结果：If they **improve computer skills**, they can perform well in the workplace.

观点2：Some people also think it is beneficial to children's **brain development**.

举例+结果：**Educational games** such as **playing chess**, doing quizzes etc. can **boost brain activity**.

雅思作文相关真题

Many parents today spend little time with their children, and they use television and computer games to make their children quiet. What are the reasons for this situation? Do you think it is good or bad? (考试日期：20131121)

口语还经常考的一个话题是关于使用 digital cameras 和 smartphones 拍照的。这个话题事实上也是在讨论电脑和手机的影响。

Photos 相关词伙

1. take phones 拍照
2. take pictures 拍照
3. take a selfie 拍自拍照
4. a photo album 相册
5. portable device 可移动设备
6. capture special moments 捕捉特别的瞬间
7. relive experiences 重温一些（美好的瞬间或者日子）
8. upload photos 上传相片
9. social networking websites 社交网站
10. digital camera 数码相机
11. edit images 编辑相片
12. brighten colours 让颜色更加鲜艳
13. make slow motion movies 制作慢动作电影

口语 Part 3 练习题目

Question: Do you prefer to use a camera or a phone to take photos?

大家先看着中文思路自己回答一次，然后使用词伙再回答一次。

结构	思路	词伙
直接回答	我更喜欢用我的智能手机拍照片	take photos
原因1	它是个可携带的设备	a portable device
解释	这意味着我随时随地都可以带着它，用它来拍照	take pictures
举例	当我和我同事吃饭的时候，我可以拍下一些特殊的时刻，而使用照相机就不是很方便	capture special moments
原因2	我还可以把这些照片储存在我的电脑里，并上传照片到社交网站上	store pictures, upload photos, social networking websites
结果	我可以在未来的某个时刻重温这些照片里的经历	relive these experiences

对比	照相机没有这个功能，你不得不小心地看管你的相册	photo albums
原因 3	用智能手机可以更加容易地编辑图片	edit images
举例	我可以提亮颜色，移除颜色，甚至制作慢镜头电影	brighten colours, remove colours, make slow motion movies

大家看一下下面的回答，自己再练习，说到熟练为止。

直接回答：I prefer to **take photos** by using my smartphone.

原因 1：It is **a portable device**.

解释：This means I can take it with me wherever I go and **take pictures** whenever I like.

举例：For example, I can **capture some special moments**, when I have a great dinner with my colleagues. Using a camera is not convenient.

原因 2：I can also **store these pictures** in my computer and **upload photos** to **social networking websites**.

结果：I can possibly **relive these experiences**, with these pictures at some point in the future.

对比：In contrast, the camera doesn't have this function. You have to take care of **a photo album** carefully.

原因 3：Finally, it is always easier to **edit images** by using the smartphone.

举例：I can **brighten colours**, **remove colours** and even **make slow motion movies**.

我们在使用网络和手机交流的过程中比较大的问题是：它们可能会影响我们的社会关系、交流技能、写作技能等。

百搭观点 11

A 过分使用社交网站

B 手机和电话交流

C 依赖电邮工作，不去见客户和同事

D 喜欢独居

E 生活在大城市或者国外，离家人和朋友很远

F 喜欢看电视和打游戏，不喜欢社交

G 工作狂，长时间工作

会减少面对面交流和社会活动以及家庭活动，导致交流水平下降，使人和人之间缺乏情感联系。

Communication 相关词伙

1. face to face communication 面对面交流
2. communication skills 交流能力
3. human interaction 人际交往
4. interpret messages 解释信息；翻译信息
5. facial expression 面部表情
6. body language 肢体语言
7. avoid misunderstandings 避免误解
8. a sign of respect 以示尊敬
9. listen to others 倾听别人
10. a good listener 一个好的听众
11. a good communicator 良好的沟通能力；出色的沟通者
12. form strong relationships 形成牢固的关系
13. live alone 独居
14. live far away from family 住得离家很远
15. social activity 社交活动
16. family life 家庭活动

口语 Part 3 练习题目

Question: What are the advantages of communicating face-to-face with people?

大家先看着中文思路自己回答一次，然后使用词伙再回答一次。

结构	思路	词伙
观点 1	我认为面对面交流使你能够更容易理解他人	face to face communication
原因	因为你可以通过他们的面部表情和身体语言解读他们想传达的信息	interpret messages, facial expression, body language
结果	你可以清楚地明白他们关心的是什么、他们真正想说的是什么。这可以避免误会	have a clear idea, avoid misunderstandings
观点 2	如果你愿意亲自交流，你是在表示对他人的尊重	a sign of respect
原因	这体现了你愿意去倾听他人	listen to others
结果	这可以帮助形成牢固的人际关系	form strong personal relationships

大家看一下下面的回答，自己再练习，说到熟练为止。

观点 1：I think **face to face communication** enables you to understand other people more easily.

原因：It is because you can **interpret their messages** by their **facial expression** and **body language**.

结果：You can **have a clear idea** what they are concerned about and what they really want to say. This can **avoid misunderstandings**.

观点 2：It is also clear that if you are willing to talk to each other in person, you are actually showing respect to others. It is **a sign of respect**.

原因：It reveals that you are willing to **listen to others**.

结果：This can help **form strong personal relationships**.

我们看看怎么把百搭观点用到家庭生活的话题里。

Family 相关词伙

1. family life 家庭生活
2. spend quality time 度过宝贵时光
3. achieve a work-life balance 实现工作和生活的平衡
4. family commitments 家庭责任
5. family dinners 家庭聚餐
6. family ties 家庭关系
7. family activities 家庭活动
8. a loving family 一个有爱的家庭
9. feel lonely 感到孤独
10. a sense of loneliness 孤独感
11. a sense of isolation 孤立感
12. emotional support 情感上的支持

口语 Part 3 练习题目

Question: Do you think long working hours can have an effect on family lives of employees?

大家先看着中文思路自己回答一次，然后使用词伙再回答一次。

结构	思路	词伙
观点	长时间工作对职场人的家庭生活有消极的影响	family life
原因	他们不能花宝贵的时间和家人在一起。很难达到工作与家庭的平衡	spend quality time
举例	例如，他们不能参加家庭聚餐。当他们的孩子想玩游戏或做作业的时候，他们不能陪孩子	family dinners
结果 1	这会威胁到家庭关系	family ties
结果 2	他们会感到孤独和无助，因为当他们在生活中面临挑战的时候，他们得不到家人的情感支持	gain emotional support, face challenges in lives

大家看一下下面的回答，自己再练习，说到熟练为止。

观点：Yes, **working long hours** may have a negative effect on working people's **family life**.

原因：They cannot **spend quality time** with family. It is difficult to **achieve a work-life balance**.

举例：For example, they cannot attend **family dinners**. They cannot stay with their children when their children want to play sport and do homework.

结果 1：This can pose a threat to **family ties**.

结果 2：They feel **lonely and helpless** because they cannot **gain emotional support** from their family when they **face challenges in lives**.

雅思作文相关真题

In some countries, many people have chosen to live by themselves in recent years. What has caused this to happen? Does it have a positive or negative effect on the development of society?（考试日期：20140927）

科技次话题 2：农业科技的影响

农业科技除了种植庄稼和水果蔬菜之外，还涉及工业农场（factory farming），就是在很小的空间里养殖猪、牛、羊、家禽等。这些科技都旨在增加产量以解决全球食物短缺的问题。

百搭观点 12

A 使用农药和化肥　　B 密度种植
C 基因科技　　D 使用防腐剂
E 机械化种植

都可以让农作物生长得更快，农田产量更多，减少食品短缺的问题。

Food Technology 相关词伙

1. increase yields 增加产量
2. food production 食品生产
3. grow crops 种庄稼
4. cultivate crops 种庄稼
5. a good harvest 收成很好
6. chemical fertilisers 化肥
7. apply pesticides 使用杀虫药
8. pest disease 病虫害
9. food prices 食品价格
10. GM food 转基因食品
11. genetic engineering 基因工程
12. high-yield crops 高产量的庄稼
13. resistant to pests 抗虫害
14. intensive farming 高密度农场
15. use preservatives 使用防腐剂
16. mechanised farming 机械化种植
17. grow faster 生长得更快
18. food shortage 食物短缺

口语 Part 3 练习题目

Question: What effects has modern technology had on the way food is produced?

大家先看着中文思路自己回答一次，然后使用词伙再回答一次。

结构	思路	词伙
观点 1	现代科技增加食物产量	food production
原因 1	化肥让农作物生长更快	chemical fertilisers
原因 2	杀虫剂防止病虫害	prevent the pest disease
结果	提高土地产量，蔬菜食物价格更低	the yield of farmland, food prices
观点 2	科技影响食物种类	the variety of food
举例	转基因食物流行，基因工程创造高产作物	GM food, genetic engineering, high-yield crops
结果	作物有抗虫性，科技的变化保证了好收成	resistant to pests

大家看一下下面的回答，自己再练习，说到熟练为止。

观点 1：I think one major impact is that **modern technology** can **increase food production**.

原因 1：Some **chemical fertilisers** can be used to make **crops grow faster**.

原因 2：Pesticides have also been applied to **prevent the pest disease**.

结果：This can **increase the yield of farmland**, and **food prices** are cheaper than ever.

观点 2：Technology has also affected **the variety of food**.

举例：**GM food** has become popular and **genetic engineering** has created some **high-yield crops**.

结果：These crops are **resistant to pests**. This technological change can guarantee **a good harvest**.

雅思作文相关真题

> ***Some people support the developments in agriculture such as factory farming and creations of new types of fruit and vegetables, while others oppose this view. Discuss both views and give your opinion.*** (考试日期：20080712)

科技次话题 3：机械化和机器人的影响

机械化和机器人作为技术变革的产物，主要的目的是取代人力、增加效率、增加利润，从而促进经济发展。但是在雅思考试里经常要讨论它的一些缺陷。

百搭观点 13

A 电脑化　　B 机械化

C 机器人　　D 自动化

让很多工作，特别是体力工作，变得更加有效率、更加有质量保证，还能减低成本，对经济有一定促进作用。

Mechanisation 相关词伙

1. improve productivity 提高生产力
2. improve efficiency 提高效率
3. do repetitive tasks 执行重复任务
4. replace human labour 取代人类劳动力
5. reduce the workforce 减少劳动力
6. mechanise tasks 机械化任务
7. mechanised assembly lines 机械化装配线
8. mechanised farming 机械化耕作
9. automate the process 过程自动化
10. done by hand 手工完成
11. computerise the service 服务电脑化
12. industrial robots 工业机器人
13. reduce the labour cost 减少劳动力成本
14. grow the economy 促进经济

口语 Part 3 练习题目

Question: How do you think modern technology has changed the way we work?

大家先看着中文思路自己回答一次，然后使用词伙再回答一次。

结构	思路	词伙
支持的观点	一些技术已经减少了体力劳动	manual work
解释	自动化和机器的使用显著提高了效率和生产力，它们将我们从重复劳动中解放出来	improve efficiency，repetitive tasks
结果	机器取代人力劳动	replace human labour

举例	机械化耕作使许多任务变得机械化，如播种和收获作物，耕作变得比以往任何时候都容易	mechanised farming，sow seeds，harvest crops

大家看一下下面的回答，自己再练习，说到熟练为止。

支持的观点：Yes, there have been many changes brought by the use of machines. Some technologies have reduced the amount of **manual work** we need to finish every day.

解释：Automation and the use of machinery have significantly **improved efficiency** and **productivity**, and they have freed us from some **repetitive tasks**.

结果：This is why machines have **replaced human labour**.

举例：For example, **mechanised farming** has mechanised many tasks such as **sowing seeds** and **harvesting crops**, so farming has become easier than ever.

雅思作文相关真题

Food can be produced much more cheaply today because of improved fertilisers and better machinery. However, some of the methods used to do this may be dangerous to human health and may have negative effects on local communities. To what extent do you agree or disagree? （考试日期：20120519）

科技的进步很多时候也有一些不好的影响，包括会对就业产生一定的冲击。此外，行业的变化会让很多人失业，人们需要重新找工作。

百搭观点 14

A 机械化　　B 电脑化

C 机器人的增加　　D 经济危机，企业收入下降

E 外国进口货品的增加　　F 老龄化趋势导致推迟退休

都会减少工作机会，影响人们的收入。

Job Creation 相关词伙

1. lose jobs 失去工作
2. out of work 失业
3. the jobless rate 失业率
4. reduce unemployment 减少失业问题
5. create jobs 创造就业机会
6. provide job opportunities 提供就业机会
7. make a living 谋生 / 维持生计
8. earn salaries 赚取薪水
9. earn money 赚钱
10. feed family 养家
11. live comfortably 生活得好 / 过上好日子
12. economic recession/an economic crisis 经济危机
13. population ageing 老龄化
14. foreign brands 外国产品

口语 Part 3 练习题目

Question: What effect does new technology have on employment?

大家先看着中文思路自己回答一次，然后使用词伙再回答一次。

结构	思路	词伙
观点 1	我认为科技通常是造成人们失业的原因	lose jobs
原因	机器和工业机器人已经在很多领域（比如制造业和农业中）取代了人类劳动力	
结果 1	很多工作已经裁员了，所以很多人无法谋生	make a living
结果 2	他们不能够赚钱养家	earn salaries, feed family
观点 2	同时，新科技创造了一些新的工作岗位	create jobs
举例 1	如果电脑没有被发明出来，也就不会有电脑程序员了	computer programmers
举例 2	相似的是，农业部门可以提供很多工作机会，因为更多的人去打包和运送食品到其他国家	the farming sector
结果	他们可以挣到钱，从而去舒适地生活	live comfortably

大家看一下下面的回答，自己再练习，说到熟练为止。

观点 1：I think technology is often responsible for people **losing their jobs**.

原因：Machines and **industrial robots** have replaced people in areas like manufacturing and agriculture.

结果 1：**Jobs have been cut**, and many people are not able to **make a living**.

结果 2：They cannot **earn salaries** to **feed their family**.

观点 2：At the same time, **jobs** might **be created** thanks to **new technology**;

举例 1：there would be no **computer programmers** if the computer hadn't been invented.

举例 2：Similarly, **the farming sector** can provide many **job opportunities** since more people can be hired to package and **ship food products** to other countries.

结果：They can **earn money** to **live comfortably**.

雅思作文相关真题

> ***Nowadays many people work longer time and got more stressful jobs than ever before. What causes this? How can employers make the worker's lives easier?***（考试日期：20080726）

科技次话题 4：太空科技的影响

雅思作文关于太空科技的题目历史上有考过，但是不是很频繁。口语考试主要是在 Part 3 零星出现过几次。

百搭观点 15

私人企业很多时候不会投资

A 太空科技　　B 新能源

C 道路和其他公共设施　　D 传统艺术

E 老建筑的维护　　G 老人院，学校

H 自然保护区

因为这些项目要么回报率很低，要么很久都没有回报。

Space Technology 相关词伙

1. space missions 太空任务
2. space exploration 太空探索
3. space science 太空科学
4. advance knowledge 先进的知识
5. habitable planets 适合居住的星球
6. population explosion 人口增长
7. provide shelter for 为……提供避难所
8. sustain our civilisation 保护我们的文明
9. used commercially 商业化地使用
10. protective clothes 保护衣
11. in the hostile environment 在恶劣的环境里
12. on the ground 在地面上
13. travel in outer space 太空旅行
14. an immediate payoff 马上有回报

口语 Part 3 练习题目

Question: Do you think it is necessary to spend money on space missions?

大家先看着中文思路自己回答一次，然后使用词伙再回答一次。

结构	思路	词伙
观点 1	有必要。太空探索可以让我们更加熟悉宇宙，找到可以居住的星球	advance our knowledge, habitable planet
背景	现在地球人口不断增长，环境问题严重	population explosion
结果	我们需要找到可以为人类提供庇护的星球，维持我们的文明	provide shelter for, sustain our civilisation
观点 2	太空探索也可以推进我们的科技发展	technological innovations
原因	政府需要不断投资航天科学的项目，支持宇航员的太空旅行，很多科技可以用于商业用途	travel in space, be used commercially
举例	给宇航员穿的保护衣服可以用于保护在恶劣环境工作的人	protective clothes, the hostile environment

大家看一下下面的回答，自己再练习，说到熟练为止。

观点 1：Yes, investment in **space missions** is very important. Space exploration **advances our knowledge** about the whole universe and possibly helps us find **habitable planets** in the future.

背景：We have been struggling with different problems, such as **population explosion** and **environmental issues**, on Earth.

结果：We are desperate to find another planet that **provides shelter for** human beings, so we can **sustain our civilisation**.

观点 2：**Space research** can also lead to **technological innovations**.

原因：Governments need to invest in projects related to **space science** in order to support astronauts **travelling in outer space**. Many new technologies can also **be used commercially**.

举例：For instance, astronauts' **protective clothes** can be used to protect the people who work **in the hostile environment** on the ground.

雅思作文相关真题

Space travel has been possible for some time. Some people think space tourism would develop in the future. Do you think space tourism is a positive or negative development? (考试日期：20130706)

3.4.3 常考写作和口语话题 3：城市化

城市化的话题有下面一些次话题：

城市化次话题 1：汽车和交通的问题

城市化次话题 2：绿化和城市拓展的问题

城市化次话题 3：房屋供应的问题

百搭观点 16

很多人去城市居住，因为

A 工作机会多

B 设施比较完备

C 教育好

D 思想比较先进

但是问题是

A 人口增加导致物价飞涨

B 房屋紧缺

C 交通堵塞

D 空气污染严重

E 基础设施和服务（如医疗）供不应求

F 城市的公园和绿地减少

G 很多人找不到工作，犯罪率提高

H 人口流动，人们没有社区的感觉

Urbanisation 相关词伙

1. relocate to cities 搬去城市
2. employment opportunities 就业机会
3. keep pace with the demand 满足需求
4. reduce the quality of life 影响生活质量
5. afford home ownership 买得起房子
6. a growing population 不断增长的人口
7. population expansion 人口扩张
8. put pressure on 增加压力
9. public transport service 公共交通服务
10. transport costs 交通费用
11. low income people 低收入群体
12. housing shortage 房屋紧缺
13. population is mobile 人口流动大
14. valuable services/essential services 和民生有关的服务

口语 Part 3 练习题目

Question: What are some of the serious problems associated with living in big cities?

大家先看着中文思路自己回答一次，然后使用词伙再回答一次。

结构	思路	词伙
观点 1	主要问题是大城市日益拥挤	increasingly crowded
原因	很多人搬去大城市寻求就业机会	relocate to, in search of, employment opportunities
结果 1	城市没有足够的设施去匹配需求	keep pace with
结果 2	这会降低很多城市居民的生活质量，因为很多人买不起房	city dwellers, afford home ownership
观点 2	不断增长的人口也给城市的基础建设带来压力	a growing population, put pressure on
举例	公共交通服务会被过度使用	be overused
结果	交通费会涨，低收入人群最容易受影响	transport costs, low income people, among the most affected

大家看一下下面的回答，自己再练习，说到熟练为止。

观点 1：The main problem is that **cities** are **increasingly crowded**.

原因：Many people have **relocated to** large cities **in search of employment opportunities**.

结果 1：Cities do not have facilities to **keep pace with** the demand.

结果 2：This can **reduce the quality of life** of many **city dwellers** because many people are not able to **afford home ownership**.

观点 2：**A growing population** also **puts pressure on** the city's infrastructure.

举例：The public transport service, for example, will **be overused**.

结果：**Transport costs** will also increase, and **low income people** will be **among the most affected**.

城市化次话题 1：汽车和交通的问题

城市人多，交通是个大问题，如何减少交通堵塞是雅思作文和口语考试的高频话题。

百搭观点 17

A 拓宽马路并增加道路的数量

B 增加汽油税，鼓励大家不开车

C 增加路考难度，提高驾照发放标准

D 发展公共交通工具

E 鼓励大家移居市郊，同时公司也搬到市郊

F 设立步行街

G 鼓励大家走路或骑车上班

H 拼车

I 让人们在家里上班

都有助于减少交通堵塞，减少汽车量，减少尾气污染，也会提高效率，增加产出。

Traffic Congestion 相关词伙

1. reduce traffic congestion 减少交通阻塞
2. cope with traffic jams 处理交通阻塞
3. rush-hour traffic 高峰期的交通
4. cycle to work 骑自行车去上班
5. within walking distance 步行就可以到
6. driving test 驾照考试
7. driving license 驾驶执照
8. curb private car use 限制私人汽车的使用
9. car ownership 拥有汽车
10. fuel tax 汽油税
11. congestion tax 交通阻塞税
12. broaden roads 扩宽道路
13. build new roads 修路
14. raise standards 提升标准
15. use public transport 使用公共交通
16. pedenstrianise streets 步行街
17. car pooling 拼车
18. reduce car emissions 减少汽车尾气

口语 Part 3 练习题目

Question: What can the government do to deal with traffic jams?

大家先看着中文思路自己回答一次，然后使用词伙再回答一次。

结构	思路	词伙
方法 1	鼓励大家骑车或者走路上班	cycle to work
原因	路上汽车减少	
结果	减少拥堵	reduce traffic congestion
特定化	特别是在工作地步行就可以到的情况下	within walking distance
方法 2	征税	impose a tax
原因	费用上升	expenses increase
结果	用车减少	curb private car use

大家看一下下面的回答，自己再练习，说到熟练为止。

方法 1：I think the government can encourage citizens to **cycle to work** or walk.

原因：There will be less traffic on the road.

结果：It can **reduce traffic congestion**.

特定化：This is particularly effective when offices and shops are **within walking distance**.

方法 2：Another method is to **impose a tax on car ownership** or **make driving tests tougher**.

原因：This will cause an **increase in expenses** and make it difficult for people to obtain **driving licenses**.

结果：This can help **curb private car use**.

雅思作文相关真题

In some cities, governments have tried to reduce traffic congestion. For instance, they have imposed a congestion tax during rush hour. Do you think this development is positive or negative?(考试日期：20160130)

城市化次话题2：绿化和城市拓展的问题

城市人口增长，人类活动增加，会导致绿地的减少，雅思会考查这个趋势的影响。

百搭观点18

城市人口增加导致

A 修路和拓展道路

B 修高楼

从而减少绿地、花园、树木等，导致

A 污染变得严重

B 人们看不到绿色植物心情不好

C 缺乏运动和室外活动的地方

D 人们没有乘凉的地方

E 缺乏一些能举办文化活动（如音乐节或赏花会）的场所

F 一些野生动物和鸟类不再栖息于城市

Trees 相关词伙

1. plant trees 种树
2. cut down trees 砍树
3. tree-lined avenues 林荫大道
4. lined with trees（街道）两边种满了树
5. a view of nature 自然景观
6. feel close to nature 亲近自然
7. provide the shade 提供阴凉
8. provide shelter 提供休憩处
9. absorb dust 吸尘
10. ever-green trees 常青树
11. plant life 植物
12. flower garden 花园

口语 Part 3 练习题目

Question: Do you think it is a good idea to spend more funds on planting more trees in the city?

大家先看着中文思路自己回答一次，然后使用词伙再回答一次。

结构	思路	词伙
观点	应该加大投入，因为树多好处多	
解释1	看到自然的景色，人们更开心、放松	a view of nature
举例	当他们走在林荫大道时会觉得很放松	tree-lined avenues, feel relaxed
解释2	树为人们遮阳，吸引他们在树下聚会	provide shade, bring together
举例	人们可以聊天或做一些户外活动，如放风筝	have a chat, do outdoor activities
解释3	可以净化城市的空气	
背景	空气污染越来越严重	air pollution
解释4	树木可以吸收灰尘和烟雾	absorb dirt and smoke
结果	提高空气质量	improve air quality

大家看一下下面的回答，自己再练习，说到熟练为止。

观点：I believe that more money should be put/invested into the green spaces in the cities, which can benefit all people who live in cities.

解释 1：First of all people tend to feel happy if they have **a view of nature in** cities.

举例：For instance, they are likely to **feel relaxed** when walking in **tree-lined avenues**.

解释 2：Trees can also **provide shade** and **bring people together** especially in summers. They gather around trees and enjoy the shade provided by trees.

举例：They can **have a chat** together and **do some outdoor activities** such as flying a kite.

解释 3：The third benefit is that trees can also help keep our cities clean.

背景 + 解释 4：As you know, **air pollution** in many cities has become a highly serious problem and trees can **absorb dirt and smoke**.

结果：It can **improve air quality**.

雅思作文相关真题

Some people think that it is more important to plant more trees in open areas in towns and cities than provides more housing. To what extent do you agree or disagree? (考试日期：20150312)

城市化次话题 3：房屋供应的问题

城市拥挤、房价高涨，这些情况在全世界都差不多。房屋决定了人们的生活质量，给人们安全感，甚至会影响健康（过分拥挤的房子会让流行病蔓延，而潮湿的房子会导致风湿病）。因此，雅思作文和口语有大量关于房子的问题，包括：

- 租房还是买房
- 住大房子好还是公寓好
- 住城市好还是农村好
- 是否应该拆旧房建新房

百搭观点 19

A 政府提供房屋补助

B 政府提供福利房

C 拆旧房建新房

D 鼓励人们移居小城镇或者郊区

E 建高楼

F 减少公园和公共场所多建房子

解决城市的住房问题。

Housing 相关词伙

1. housing shortage 住房短缺
2. urban planning 城市规划
3. densely populated cities 人口很多的城市
4. redevelop run-down urban areas 重新开发破旧城区
5. make room for 为……腾出空间
6. residential buildings 住宅楼
7. the housing market 住房市场
8. provincial towns 乡镇
9. state housing 国家房，即有政府补贴的“公租房”，福利房
10. pay a mortgage 按揭付款
11. housing developers 房产开发商
12. high-rise buildings 高层建筑
13. accommodate people 容纳人
14. low-density neighbourhoods 低建筑密度的社区
15. land-scarce cities 土地稀缺城市
16. meet the growing demand for housing 满足对住房日益增长的需求
17. demolish old buildings 拆除老房子

口语 Part 3 练习题目

Question: What do you think can the government do to tackle the housing shortage?

大家先看着中文思路自己回答一次，然后使用词伙再回答一次。

结构	思路	词伙
观点 1	政府应该首先密切关注城市规划	urban planning
举例	在人口密集的城市，政府可以重新开发破旧的老城市区域	redevelop run-down urban areas
结果	从而为住宅楼的建设腾出空间	make room for, residential buildings
观点 2	政府同样可以鼓励居民搬到郊区或村庄	move to suburbs or rural areas
结果	这个政策可以缓解城市住房市场的压力	alleviate the pressure, the housing market
解释	这些可以通过将一些产业和工作岗位迁移到乡镇来实现	provincial towns
观点 3	提供“公租房”同样非常有必要	state housing
解释	即为不能负担房租或按揭付款的弱势群体提供的免费住房	disadvantaged people
举例	政府可以补贴开发商建造高层建筑	housing developers
结果	这些高层住房可以建在低建筑物密度社区，容纳尽可能多的人	low-density neighbourhoods
特定化	这些政策在土地稀缺的城市非常有效，这些城市不能满足对住房日益增长的需求	in land-scarce cities, meet the growing demand for

大家看一下下面的回答，自己再练习，说到熟练为止。

观点 1：Governments should first pay closer attention to **urban planning**.

举例 + 结果：In densely populated cities, governments can also **redevelop run-down urban areas** to **make room for** the construction of **residential buildings**.

观点 2：The government can also encourage inhabitants to **move to suburbs or rural areas**,

结果：and this policy can **alleviate the pressure** on **the housing market** in cities.

解释：This can be achieved by moving industry and jobs to the countryside or **provincial towns**.

观点 3 + 解释：It is also necessary to provide **state housing**, namely, free housing available for **disadvantaged people** who are unable to afford rent or pay a mortgage.

举例 + 结果：The government can subsidise **housing developers** to build high-rise buildings which can accommodate many people in **low-density neighbourhoods**.

特定化：These policies are effective **in land-scarce cities**, which cannot **meet the growing demand for** housing.

雅思作文相关真题

The restoration of old buildings in major cities in the world costs enormous government expenditure. This money should be used in new housing and road development. To what extent do you agree or disagree? (考试日期：20130727)

3.4.4 常考写作和口语话题 4：社会文化和价值观

社会文化和价值观的话题在雅思作文和口语中考查得非常广泛，主要有下面这些次话题：

社会文化和价值观次话题 1：快乐如何定义；压力的来源

社会文化和价值观次话题 2：应该自私和贪婪，还是应该注意社会责任和社会规范

社会文化和价值观次话题 3：应该注重事业和工作，还是注重家庭生活，劳逸结合

社会文化和价值观次话题 4：存钱，还是消费

社会文化和价值观次话题 1：快乐如何定义；压力的来源

所谓价值观和社会文化，就是人们做什么事情能让他们快乐。

百搭观点 20

人们

A 赚大量的钱变得富裕

B 事业上功成名就

C 捐钱让社会其他人更加开心

D 陪伴家人，或者享受家人的陪伴

E 自己生活得很自由和独立

F 享受朋友、邻居和同事的陪伴

G 大手大脚花钱购物

H 存钱为退休时过稳定的生活做准备

I 注意减少压力，保持健康

都会感到快乐。

Happiness 相关词伙

1. achieve happiness 获得幸福（结果）
2. experience happiness 感受幸福（过程）
3. find enjoyment 找到乐趣
4. find joy 找到乐趣
5. cover basic needs 满足基本需求
6. improve living standards 改善生活水平
7. a higher standard of living 更高的生活水平
8. live comfortably 过上舒适的生活
9. feel stressed out 感到紧张
10. non-financial factors 非经济因素
11. family life 家庭生活
12. social life 社会生活
13. feel lonely 感到孤独
14. earn a decent income 有体面的收入
15. earn money 挣钱
16. achieve career success 实现职场成功
17. enjoy a happy retirement 享受快乐的退休时光
18. donate money 捐钱

口语 Part 3 练习题目

Question: Do you think money is important to your life? Why or why not?

大家先看着中文思路自己回答一次，然后使用词伙再回答一次。

结构	思路	词伙
支持的观点	金钱能满足基本需要	basic needs
原因	金钱决定了我们的生活水准	living standards
结果	有了钱，我们才可以过舒适的生活	live comfortably
对比	没钱就会有压力	stressed out
反对的观点	一些非物质的东西也很重要	non-financial factors
原因	家庭和社会生活决定了我们是否幸福	achieve happiness
解释	和朋友在一起也会找到乐趣	find enjoyment
对比	有钱却没有家人的陪伴，反而会觉得孤独	the company of family

大家看一下下面的回答，自己再练习，说到熟练为止。

支持的观点：Yes, I think money is important, because it **satisfies our basic needs**, like food, clothes, and housing.

原因：Money has a direct impact on our **living standards**.

结果：With money, we can **live comfortably**, and then experience happiness.

对比：Without it, you would possibly **feel stressed out**.

反对的观点：On the other hand, some **non-financial factors** are also important.

原因：For example, your family life can determine whether you can **achieve happiness**.

解释：You can **find enjoyment** in the time you spend with your friends.

对比：If you are very wealthy, but you do not have **the company of family**, you are likely to feel lonely.

雅思作文相关真题

As economy develops, people get richer. Studies show that people in developing countries feel happier than before, while people in developed countries feel less happy. Why do you think is it? What lessons can we learn from it? (考试日期：20111126)

社会文化和价值观次话题 2：应该自私和贪婪，还是应该关注社会责任和社会规范

雅思作文和口语经常考查一些关于是否应该帮助他人，年轻人是否应该做义工，有钱人是不是应该捐钱，企业要不要关注社会责任的题目。核心就是人到底是应该关注个人利益，还是关注社会和社区的利益。

百搭观点 21

A 学校重视学习好的学生

B 竞技体育鼓励年轻人战胜别人

C 媒体推崇那些暴富的人，强调金钱的重要性

D 学校和父母没有注意对孩子进行道德和无私的教育

E 社会不注意无私和道德的公益宣传

F 工作竞争激烈

导致年轻人现在更加关注自己的成就和利益，而不去关心和体谅别人。

Selfish People 相关词伙

1. give a helping hand 伸出援手
2. with a heart of gold 有颗金子般美好的心
3. show compassion 同情
4. responsive to emotional needs 响应情感需求
5. behave selfishly 做事自私
6. driven by self-interest 受自身利益驱使
7. motivated by greed 出于贪婪
8. cheat in exams 在考试中作弊
9. gain an unfair advantage over 获取不公平的优势
10. make easy money 不劳而获
11. teach moral values 灌输道德观
12. traditional values 传统的价值

口语 Part 3 练习题目

Question: Do you think it is necessary to teach children to be unselfish?

大家先看着中文思路自己回答一次，然后使用词伙再回答一次。

结构	思路	词伙
立场	这是很重要的	
观点 1	它让孩子变得更会社交	sociable persons
解释 1	如果孩子不自私，他们就更愿意带着他们金子一样的心去帮助别人	give a helping hand, with a heart of gold

解释 2	他们更有可能同情其他人，更能够回应其他人的情感需求	responsive to emotional needs
结果	在这种情况下，他们更容易交朋友	
观点 2	防止犯罪	prevent some crimes
解释	自私的小孩会用暴力去对抗不同意他们观点的人	tend to be aggressive
举例 1	如果他很自私的话，他可能在考试时作弊	driven by self-interest, cheat in exams
举例 2	如果他贪婪，他可能通过犯罪，比如偷盗，来赚快钱	motivated by greed, commit crimes, make easy money
对比	这些问题都可以预防的，如果他们懂得不自私并且关心他人的利益	conscious of other people's interest

大家看一下下面的回答，自己再练习，说到熟练为止。

立场：Yes, it is important.

观点 1：First of all, it can make children **sociable persons**.

解释 1：If children are unselfish, they are more willing to **give a helping hand** to others **with a heart of gold**.

解释 2：They are more likely to **show compassion for** others, and more **responsive to** others' **emotional needs**.

结果：In this case, they are more likely to make friends.

观点 2：Second, it can also **prevent some crimes**.

解释：A child who behaves selfishly **tends to be aggressive** when others don't agree with him.

举例 1：If he is **driven by self-interest**, he might **cheat in exams** in order to **gain an unfair advantage over** others.

举例 2：If he is **motivated by greed**, he may also **commit crimes** such as theft in order to **make easy money**.

对比：These problems are all preventable if they learn to be unselfish and **conscious of other people's interest**.

雅思作文相关真题

Some people think that education should help students to be useful to the whole society, other people think that education should provide students with opportunities to achieve personal ambitions. Discuss both views and give your opinion. (考试日期：20140412)

与此同时，我们还会考查这么一个话题：人是要我行我素，还是要注意自己的行为，使其符合社会的行为规范和标准。

百搭观点 22

A 在公共地方遵守秩序
B 使用礼貌语言
C 在公共场合不抽烟
D 在公共场合遵守手机使用的社会规则
E 开会和赴约要准时
F 遵守穿衣的标准
G 诚实
H 平时尽量不要制造噪音
I 要遵守餐桌礼仪
J 送礼物

属于社会规范和标准，体现了人们在意别人、体贴别人。

Clothes 相关词伙

1. follow a dress code 遵守着装要求
2. wear uniforms 穿制服
3. dress formally 穿着正式
4. casual dress 休闲服装
5. present a professional image 展现专业形象
6. make a good impression 留下好印象
7. social rules 社会规则
8. social norms 社会规范
9. social etiquette 社交礼仪
10. public places/spaces 公共场所

口语 Part 3 练习题目

Question: What kinds of clothes should people wear at work?

大家先看着中文思路自己回答一次，然后使用词伙再回答一次。

结构	思路	词伙
观点 1	穿制服	wear uniforms
原因	遵守严格的穿衣标准，体现员工受过良好训练	a strict dress code
举例	员工知道怎么有礼貌地和客人交流	in a friendly manner
观点 2	穿着正式也很重要	dress formally
原因	当人们穿得很正式，他们会更加重视自己的专业形象	present a professional image
举例	例如，参加会议的时候，他们会很准时；和别人交流的时候，谈吐非常得体	attend meetings on time, in a formal way
对比	如果穿得很随意，就代表他们不是非常重视这些社会规则，别人也未必很舒服	social rules

大家看一下下面的回答，自己再练习，说到熟练为止。

观点 1：Well, normally people **wear uniforms** in the workplace.

原因：This normally shows that the company has **a strict dress code** and employees are well-trained.

举例：For example, **uniformed staff** may learn how to communicate with clients **in a friendly manner**.

观点 2：Also, it is necessary to **dress formally in formal settings**.

原因：When people **dress up**, it'll **present a professional image**.

举例：People who **wear formal dresses** would be more conscious of their images; they **attend meetings on time** and communicate with others **in a formal way**.

对比：In contrast, people who **dress casually** may not pay attention to **social rules and business etiquette**, and other people may feel uncomfortable.

社会文化和价值观次话题3：注重事业和工作，还是注重家庭生活和劳逸结合

这也是雅思作文和口语频繁考查的话题。为什么现在大家那么忙？为什么现在大家很少和家人在一起？为什么现在大家喜欢自己住？为什么大家晚婚？为什么家庭越来越小？等等。

主要原因就是现代人非常看重工作，工作时间变长，压力增大，而花在家庭上的时间越来越少。

百搭观点23

A 物价飞涨

B 城市生活费用很高

C 大家现在喜欢买奢侈品，变得很物质

D 失业率高

E 经济波动大

F 人们对个人成就的追求提升了

G 电话和网络让人们在下班时间也可以工作

H 缺乏时间管理能力，而且还经常犯拖延症

都导致人们越来越忙，工作时间变长，忘记了家庭生活。

Stress相关词伙

1. economic pressure 经济压力
2. financial difficulties 财政困难
3. combine work and family commitments 协调好工作和家庭之间的关系
4. work commitments 工作投入
5. a tight schedule 时间很紧
6. find time 找到时间
7. put a severe strain on 对……施加更大的压力
8. reduce stress 减少压力
9. cope with stress 应付压力
10. a source of stress 压力的来源
11. feel stressed 感到压力
12. feel relaxed 感到轻松
13. cost of living 生活费用
14. material goods 物质的东西
15. avoid procrastination 避免拖延
16. time management skills 时间管理

口语Part 3练习题目

Question: Why do many people today fail to achieve a work-life balance?

大家先看着中文思路自己回答一次，然后使用词伙再回答一次。

结构	思路	词伙
观点1	生活成本比任何时候都高，这让人们活在极大的经济压力之下	economic pressure

结果	他们必须努力赚钱去满足基本生活所需	basic needs
举例	那些没有付清房贷的人有经济困难	financial difficulties
观点 2	经济衰退也是人们不能平衡家庭和工作的另一大原因	combine work and family commitments
结果	他们必须延长工作时间来取悦老板但长期加班让他们没空陪伴家人	impress employers, overworking
结果的拓展	这给工作的人带来了巨大的压力	put a severe strain on

大家看一下下面的回答，自己再练习，说到熟练为止。

观点 1：I suppose the first reason is that the cost of living has been higher than ever, which has put many people under **economic pressure**.

结果：They have to work harder to earn more money to cover **basic needs**.

举例：For example, many people **have experienced financial difficulties** when they fail to repay home loans.

观点 2：The economic downturn is another reason why many people cannot **combine work and family commitments**.

结果：They have to work long hours to **impress employers**, but **overworking** has made it difficult for them to find time for family.

结果的拓展：This can **put a severe strain on** working people.

雅思作文相关真题

Today, there is less communication between family members than in the past. What has caused this? Do you think it is a positive or negative development? （考试日期：20081108）

除了通过和家人团聚之外，人们还可以通过社会活动（和朋友一起出去玩）还有文化活动来达到休闲的目的，从而解压。

百搭观点 24

社会活动

A 参加聚会　　B 和朋友一起去旅游

C 聚餐　　D 逛街

和文化活动

A 看电影　　B 听音乐

C 参加乐队　　D 看画展

E 去博物馆　　F 参观古建筑

有助于释放一些不好的情绪，可以暂时不去思考工作，有利于消除疲惫，重燃活力。

Social Life 相关词伙

1. cultural activities 文化活动
2. do social activities 参加社会活动
3. social life 社会生活
4. mix with others 和他人来往
5. socialise with neighbours 和邻居来往
6. cut stress 减少压力
7. release stress 释放压力
8. tasks at hand 手边的工作
9. forget about work 忘记工作
10. reduce anxiety 缓解紧张情绪
11. join the choir 参加合唱团
12. a pleasurable experience 非常有趣的经历
13. visit art galleries 参观艺术馆
14. join a band 参加乐队

口语 Part 3 练习题目

Question: Do you think it is important for us to study singing?

大家先看着中文思路自己回答一次，然后使用词伙再回答一次。

结构	思路	词伙
观点 1	唱歌是一种解压的方式	cut stress
解释	人们可以暂时忘记手头的工作	tasks at hand
结果	这样会减少紧张	reduce anxiety
观点 2	唱歌也是一种社会活动	social activity
解释	可以和其他有共同爱好的人一起学习唱歌	common interests
举例	可以参加合唱团	join the choir, practise singing
结果	和别人交流是一种好的经历，对健康也有好处	pleasurable experience

大家看一下下面的回答，自己再练习，说到熟练为止。

观点 1：I agree that we can benefit from singing, because it is an effective way to **cut stress**.

解释：People may forget about **tasks at hand** when they learn singing.

结果：This can help **reduce anxiety** and make them happier.

观点 2：It is also true that singing is also **a social activity**.

解释：People can learn how to sing with others who have **common interests**.

举例：For example, many school students **join the choir** to **practise singing**.

结果：Communicating with their peers can be **a pleasurable experience**. This can have a beneficial effect on their health as well.

雅思作文相关真题

Some people think that personal happiness is directly related to economic success. Others argue that happiness depends on different factors. Discuss both views and give your own opinion. (考试日期：20121011)

社会文化和价值观次话题 4：存钱，还是消费

雅思作文和口语会考一些消费类的话题：为什么大家经常负债？电子商务的优缺点是什么？为什么很多人现在有经济压力？广告是不是在鼓励人们去买自己不需要的东西？给小孩买礼物的坏处是什么？

百搭观点 25

A 广告
B 信用卡付账
C 电子商务
D 经济发展导致收入增加
E 产品不断更新
F 某些商品的价格不断下降
G 追求时尚的名人不断在媒体上出现
H 人们追求物质享受

导致了消费文化的盛行：人们喜欢攀比，喜欢大手大脚花钱，喜欢买很多东西。

Shopping 相关词伙

1. a strong appetite 需求很高
2. a growing demand 需求很高
3. consumer goods 消费品
4. electrical equipment 电子设备
5. household appliances 家庭用具
6. shop online 网络购物
7. online stores 网络商店
8. online retailers 网络零售商
9. in the comfort of their homes 在舒适的家里
10. on high streets 在购物街
11. shopping malls 购物中心
12. shopping streets 购物街
13. buy...on impulse 冲动买……
14. steep discounts 大降价
15. consumer society 消费社会
16. consumer culture 消费文化
17. pay by credit card 用信用卡付账

口语 Part 3 练习题目

Question: Do young people today spend a lot of time shopping?

大家先看着中文思路自己回答一次，然后使用词伙再回答一次。

结构	思路	词伙
直接回答	是的，年轻人比他们的父母更爱花钱	
观点 1	人们的收入增加	earn more money
解释	可以购买各种消费品	consumer goods
举例	购买电器	electrical equipment
结果	生活更加方便	
观点 2	电子商务不断发展	e-commerce
解释	人们可以在家购物	in the comfort of their homes
结果	他们不再去实体店消费	on high streets

大家看一下下面的回答，自己再练习，说到熟练为止。

直接回答：Yes, I think many young people today are more willing to spend money buying things than their parents do.

观点 1：First of all, they are able to **earn more money** today, and this is a result of economic growth.

解释：They have a **strong appetite for** different **consumer goods**.

举例：For example, many young couples prefer to purchase **electrical equipment**,

结果：which can bring convenience to their lives.

观点 2：The fast **growing e-commerce** has also encouraged consumers to **shop online**.

解释：They can enjoy shopping **in the comfort of their homes**,

结果：instead of buying things **on high streets**.

在人们消费文化里，名人也扮演着很重要的角色。因为名人曝光率很高，名人是很多人的偶像，名人效应引导人们购买商品。

Celebrities 相关词伙

1. self-made celebrities 依靠自己努力而出名的人
2. start from scratch 白手起家
3. lead a life of luxury 过奢侈的生活
4. live a frugal life 过节约的生活
5. designer clothes 名牌的衣服
6. drive prestigious cars 开豪车
7. extravagant parties 奢华的派对
8. set a bad example 树立坏的榜样
9. pursue material goods 追求物质的东西
10. admire celebrities 羡慕名人
11. pop singers 摇滚歌手
12. famous entertainers 有名的娱乐圈人士
13. movie stars 电影明星
14. achieve fame 成名
15. positive role models 正面的榜样
16. devoted fans 忠实粉丝

口语 Part 3 练习题目

Question: Many young people today spend a lot of time reading news and magazines about celebrities. Do you think it is a positive trend?

大家先看着中文思路自己回答一次，然后使用词伙再回答一次。

结构	思路	词伙
观点 1	很多时候，影响是不好的	most of the time, a negative effect
原因	很多明星过着奢侈的生活	lead a life of luxury
举例	买名牌的衣服，驾驶名牌车，开奢侈的派对	designer clothes, prestigious cars, extravagant parties
结果	这些行为都会给年轻人树立不好的榜样，使年轻人也去追求物质的东西	set a bad example, pursue material goods
观点 2	有时候，年轻人从崇拜的名人那里学到很多	admire celebrities

原因	一些运动员、演员、企业家都是白手起家的名人	self-made celebrities
举例	他们非常勤奋，而且成名后也非常节俭	achieve fame, live a frugal life
结果	给年轻人树立了好的榜样	positive role models

大家看一下下面的回答，自己再练习，说到熟练为止。

观点 1：**Most of the time**, **the coverage of celebrities** in the media can have **a negative effect** on the younger generation.

原因：Many celebrities **lead a life of luxury**.

举例：For example, many movie stars buy **designer clothes** whenever they show up in the media, drive **prestigious cars** and have **extravagant parties**.

结果：They will **set a bad example** for the young adults, encouraging their fans to **pursue material goods**.

观点 2：On the other hand, young people can also learn a lot from **the celebrities they admire**.

原因：Some well-known and influential people like sportsmen, actors and businesspeople are **self-made celebrities** who **start from scratch**.

举例：They are very diligent, and some of them may **live a frugal life** even after they **achieve fame**.

结果：As a result, they are **positive role models for** their devoted fans.

雅思作文相关真题

Advertisements encourage consumers to buy in quantity rather than promote quality. To what extent do you agree or disagree? (考试日期：20120707)

3.4.5 常考写作和口语话题 5：生活方式

生活方式主要包括两个次话题：运动和饮食。

生活方式次话题 1：运动

百搭观点 26

A 加强锻炼
B 走路上班
C 注意劳逸结合，减少工作时间
D 少吃快餐
E 不抽烟喝酒
F 好的作息习惯，不要熬夜看电视打游戏和工作
G 少发脾气
H 经常体检，生病得到及时救治
I 注意一些健康活动，如读书、旅游、解压
J 不要总是待在城市或者污染严重的地方
K 住通风好的、宽敞的房子

都有助于健康。

Sport 相关词伙

1. play sport 做运动
2. gentle physical exercise 温和的身体锻炼
3. moderate intensity activities 强度适中的运动
4. mild exercise 温和的锻炼（不刺激的运动）
5. go for a jog 去慢跑
6. take a brisk walk 去快跑
7. go for a swim 去游泳
8. burn calories 燃烧卡路里
9. increase blood circulation 促进血液循环
10. build strength 增强体力
11. keep a good body shape 保持好的身材
12. improve health 促进身体健康
13. lead an inactive life 不运动的生活
14. suffer injuries 受伤
15. extreme sports 极端运动
16. professional trainers 专业的教练

口语 Part 3 练习题目

Question: Do you think playing sport can benefit everybody?

大家先看着中文思路自己回答一次，然后使用词伙再回答一次。

结构	思路	词伙
支持的观点	在多数情况下，体育锻炼对我们有好处	play sport
举例	即便是温和的运动，比如慢跑、散步或游泳也能燃烧卡路里，增强我们的体力并帮助我们保持好的身材	gentle physical exercise, go for a jog, take a brisk walk, burn calories, build strength, keep a body shape
特定化	对于平时不怎么运动的人来说	lead an inactive life
解释	一些强度适中运动比如跑步、网球能提高血液循环并有益健康	moderate intensity activities increase blood circulation
相反的观点	对于运动员来说，最大的问题就是人们可能会由于过度训练而受伤	suffer injuries
举例	为了玩极限运动，比如攀岩，人们要接受高强度的训练	receive intensive training, play extreme sports
措施	除非他们受到专业教练的指导，否则是很容易受伤的	professional trainers
结果	缓和的运动只适合老年人	mild exercise

大家看一下下面的回答，自己再练习，说到熟练为止。

支持的观点：Yes, in most cases, **playing sport** is beneficial to us in many aspects.

举例：For example, even some **gentle physical exercise** such as **going for a jog**, **taking a brisk walk** and swimming can **burn calories**, **build our strength** and help us **keep a good body shape**.

特定化 + 解释：For those people who **lead an inactive life**, some **moderate intensity activities** such as running and playing tennis can **increase blood circulation** and improve their health.

相反的观点：However, the main problem of playing sport is that some people may **suffer injuries** because of overtraining.

举例：They **receive intensive training** for **playing some extreme sports** such as rock climbing.

措施：Unless they participate in these sports with the guidance of **professional trainers**, they may be hurt.

结果：**Mild exercise** is recommended for older people only.

雅思作文相关真题

Doctors said in many countries there are not enough physical exercises. What has caused that problem? What should be done for that? (考试日期：20080522)

很多同学在写作文的时候，经常很随便地说“这个对健康有益”，但是为什么我们需要健康呢？健康的好处是什么？这些问题的答案却很少有同学说得上来。这样就缺乏拓展，观点不够有说服力。

百搭观点 27

健康的好处多多，包括

A 可以工作赚钱

B 享受生活，做各种各样的事情

C 实现事业的梦想

D 减少病假，劳动产出会更高，给企业和国家带来经济价值

E 减轻医疗系统的压力，政府可以投资到其他的民生项目上

Health 相关词伙

1. stay healthy 保持健康
2. a sedentary lifestyle 一个久坐的生活方式
3. endanger health 危害健康
4. harmful to health 对健康有危害
5. concentrate on work 专注于工作
6. suffer from heart diseases 患上心脏病
7. improve physical health 促进身体健康
8. sick leave 病假
9. prone to health problem 容易有健康问题
10. see doctors 看医生
11. achieve ambitions 实现自己的梦想
12. attain goals 实现自己的目标
13. economic value 经济价值

口语 Part 3 练习题目

Question: Why do people need to play sports?

大家先看着中文思路自己回答一次，然后使用词伙再回答一次。

结构	思路	词伙
观点	通过做体育运动可以保持健康	stay healthy

解释	久坐的生活模式会危害我们的健康，因为这样会缺乏锻炼	a sedentary lifestyle, endanger health
举例	一些人工作的时候无法专注，还有一些人可能会患上心脏病，因为他们超重了	concentrate on work, heart diseases
拓展 1	运动可以促进身体健康，使工作更有效率，减少病假次数	improve physical health, reduce sick leave
拓展 2	减轻医疗系统的压力，因为我们不用经常去看医生	medical system, see doctors

大家看一下下面的回答，自己再练习，说到熟练为止。

观点：We can **stay healthy** by **doing sports**.

解释：**A sedentary lifestyle** can **endanger our health** because of the lack of **physical activity**.

举例：Some people cannot **concentrate on their work**, and some other people may **suffer from heart diseases** because they are overweight.

拓展 1：Playing sports can **improve our physical health** and **reduce sick leave**. We are more productive and less **prone to health problems**.

拓展 2: This can also ease the pressure on **the medical system** because we are less likely to **see doctors**.

雅思作文相关真题

Some people think it is more important for government to spend more money on promoting a healthy lifestyle in order to prevent illnesses than the treatment for people who are already ill. To what extent do you agree or disagree? (考试日期：20090321)

生活方式次话题 2：饮食

饮食话题也是常考话题，特别是在口语中。主要是因为我们工作忙，还有快餐广告多，另外就是大量的国际快餐连锁店，导致我们现在很依赖快餐和垃圾食品。

百搭观点 28

A 在家做饭　　B 少吃快餐

C 多吃素菜，少吃肉类　　D 少吃零食

E 少吃进口食品，多吃本地新鲜食品

会减少体重，减少得一些健康疾病，包括肥胖和心脏病等的概率。

Food 相关词伙

1. cook a meal 做饭	2. cooking skills 做饭技能
3. life skill 生活技能	4. prepare meals 准备饭菜
5. fruits and vegetables 水果和蔬菜	6. a healthy diet 健康的饮食
7. a balanced diet 均衡的饮食	8. eat fatty food 吃脂肪过多的食物
9. fast food 快餐	10. fish and chips 鱼和薯条
11. fizzy drinks 碳酸饮料	12. high in salt and sugar 高盐高糖的
13. fresh ingredients 新鲜的食材	14. combat obesity 对抗肥胖问题

口语 Part 3 练习题目

Question: Do children need to learn cooking? Why?

大家先看着中文思路自己回答一次，然后使用词伙再回答一次。

结构	思路	词伙
观点	父母和老师应该教孩子如何做饭，因为这是一项重要的生活技能	cook a meal, life skills
解释	他们可以学习如何用新鲜食材做饭	fresh food, prepare meals
结果	他们可以拥有健康的饮食，也会吃更多的水果和蔬菜	have a healthy diet, fruits and vegetables
对比	否则，他们会吃高脂食物，这对他们的健康有害	fatty food
结果	快餐如炸鸡、鱼和薯条、汽水含有盐和糖，会导致健康问题包括心脏病、肥胖症	fizzy drinks, health problems, heart diseases

大家看一下下面的回答，自己再练习，说到熟练为止。

观点：Yes, I agree that parents or teachers should teach children how to **cook a meal**, because it is **an important life skill**.

解释：They will learn how to use **fresh food** to **prepare meals**.

结果：They can thus **have a healthy diet**. They will possibly **eat more fruits and vegetables**.

对比＋结果：Otherwise, they may eat **fatty food**, which is **harmful to their health**. **Fast food** such as **fried chicken, fish and chips, fizzy drinks** contain salt and sugar which can **cause health problems** including **heart diseases** and obesity.

雅思作文相关真题

Those foods that have scientifically proven to be bad to health should not be allowed to be sold at stores. Do you agree or disagree? (考试日期：20141213)

3.4.6 常考写作和口语话题 6：工作类

雅思的工作类话题在写作和口语都有涉及。考过的题目也比较多样，包括：

- 网络工作的优缺点
- 工作时间和放假的长短
- 人应该换工作还是坚持做一份工作很多年
- 人应该创业还是打工

这些题目的大部分观点都可以从马斯洛的需求原理角度（读人力资源或者管理学的学生对这个理论应该不陌生）来思考。

百搭观点 29

A 工作的收入　　B 工作的稳定性

C 工作的升职和发展机会　　D 和同事上司的关系

E 工作的环境　　F 工作时间和放假时间的长短

G 工作的自由度　　H 实现自己才华的机会

能够决定工作满意度。

Job Satisfaction 相关词伙

1. well-motivated employees 很积极的员工
2. a good motivator 一个好的激励因素
3. improve motivation 提高积极性
4. a sense of progress 进步感
5. live a comfortable life 过舒服的生活
6. raise a family 养家糊口
7. pay rise 加薪
8. a sense of belonging 归属感
9. a good working environment 一个好的工作环境
10. obtain job satisfaction 获得工作满意度
11. inspire loyalty 让员工更加忠诚
12. achieve ambition 实现个人的野心
13. the atmosphere in the workplace 工作环境
14. working conditions 工作条件
15. flexible patterns of work 灵活的工作模式
16. working relationship 工作关系
17. a steady career 稳定的职业

口语 Part 3 练习题目

Question: How does a company motivate its staff to work?

大家先看着中文思路自己回答一次，然后使用词伙再回答一次。

结构	思路	词伙
观点 1	或许，钱是一个好的动力	a good motivator
解释 1	人们为了增加他们的收入会更努力地工作，这样就可以过上更加舒适的生活	increase their earnings, live a comfortable life

解释 2	这也就是为什么加薪时很多员工非常兴奋，特别是那些在大城市买房或是需要赡养家庭的人	get pay rises, home buyers
观点 2	除此之外，公司同样要为员工提供职业培训	job training
原因	因为员工们想要提高自己的工作能力并且在事业上取得进步	advance their career
结果	这就是员工获得进步的感觉并且实现他们人生中的雄心壮志的方式	a sense of progress, achieve ambitions

大家看一下下面的回答，自己再练习，说到熟练为止。

观点 1：Perhaps money is **a good motivator**.

解释 1：People tend to work harder to **increase their earnings** so as to **live a comfortable life**.

解释 2：This is why many employees are really thrilled when they **get pay rises**, especially for **home buyers** in large cities and for those who have to **raise a family**.

观点 2 + 原因：In addition to this, a company can also provide staff with **job training** because they want to improve job skills and **advance their career**.

结果：This is how they can gain **a sense of progress** and **achieve some ambitions** in their lives.

选择工作的时候是不是应该首先考虑收入，或者是收入是不是唯一考虑因素，也是常考话题。

Living Standards 相关词伙

1. steady jobs 稳定的工作
2. steady income 稳定的收入
3. a well-paid job 收入很高的工作
4. cover living expenses 支付生活费
5. live comfortably 过很舒适的生活
6. afford tuition fees 支付学费
7. pay bills 支付生活杂费
8. pay off the mortgage 还清房贷
9. lead a happy life 过快乐的生活
10. financial difficulties 经济困难

口语 Part 3 练习题目

Question: Do Chinese people change jobs very often? Why?

大家先看着中文思路自己回答一次，然后使用词伙再回答一次。

结构	思路	词伙
立场	这取决于年龄	depend on
观点	老年人或中年人更喜欢稳定的工作	senior people, middle-aged people, steady jobs
原因	因为他们想赚取稳定的收入	steady income
结果 1	可以支付生活费用，并过得舒适	cover living expenses, live comfortably

举例	他们可以负担得起学费、账单房贷	afford tuition fees, pay off the mortgage
结果 2	因此他们可以过上幸福的生活	lead a happy life
对比	如果他们没有高收入的工作，他们可能时常处于经济困难中	a well-paid job, from time to time, financial difficulties

大家看一下下面的回答，自己再练习，说到熟练为止。

立场：It **depends on** the age.

观点：**Senior people** or **middle-aged people** normally prefer **steady jobs**,

原因：because they want to **earn steady income**.

结果 1：This can **cover living expenses** and they can **live comfortably**.

举例：For example, they can **afford their children's tuition fees**, **pay bills** and **pay off the mortgage**.

结果 2：They can thus **lead a happy life** if their family have a good quality of life.

对比：If they did not have **a well-paid job**, they might experience **financial difficulties** from time to time.

然后我们再将工作满意度的百搭观点放在网络工作的话题上。

Teleworking 相关词伙

1. work from home 在家远程办公
2. work at home 在家工作（工作地点是自己的家）
3. paperless office 使用现代办公设备（如传真机和电脑）的办公室，也可以说 "无纸办公室"
4. travel to and from work 上下班
5. show discipline 自律
6. stay self-motivated 保持积极性
7. show initiative 表现主动性
8. enter the workforce 参加工作
9. combine work and raising a family 兼顾工作和家庭
10. flexible work hours 灵活的工作时间
11. work commitments 工作的责任
12. sacrifice family life 牺牲家庭生活

口语 Part 3 练习题目

Question: What kinds of people work from home?

大家先看着中文思路自己回答一次，然后使用词伙再回答一次。

结构	思路	词伙
观点 1	希望自主和自律的人可以在家办公	want autonomy, show discipline
解释	他们可以专注于工作并且及时完成工作	focus on their work
结果	他们希望独自工作，而不是被其他人监督或者打扰	working alone
观点 2	残疾人也可以在家办公	work from home

解释	他们不能像正常人一样上下班	travel to and from work
结果	在家工作能为他们带来进入职场的可能性	create new possibilities, enter the workforce
观点 3	想要兼顾工作和家庭的人也喜欢在家工作	combine work and raising a family
解释	这些人需要弹性的工作时间，而且他们也要做很多家务	flexible working hours
结果	他们不用为了工作牺牲家庭生活	work commitments

大家看一下下面的回答，自己再练习，说到熟练为止。

观点 1：I think normally people who **want autonomy** and **show discipline** can **work from home**.

解释：They can **focus on their work** and finish every job on time.

结果：They enjoy **working alone** without being supervised or interrupted by others.

观点 2：**People with disabilities** may also **work from home**.

解释：These people are not able to **travel to and from work** every day as ordinary people.

结果：Telecommuting can **create new possibilities** for them to **enter the workforce**.

观点 3：Those who want to **combine work and raising a family** may also prefer to work at home.

解释：These people want **flexible working hours**, and they have to do a lot of housework.

结果：They don't have to sacrifice their family life because of **work commitments**.

雅思作文相关真题

Some people tend to take temporary jobs (working for a few months), for they have the time to do other things they are interested in. Do the advantages outweigh the disadvantages? (考试日期：20091203)

3.4.7 常考写作和口语话题 7：环境类

环境类主要涉及下面一些次话题：

环境次话题 1：能源的消耗，新能源的开发

环境次话题 2：水资源的使用和水污染

环境次话题 3：垃圾的产生

环境次话题 4：动物保护

环境次话题 1：能源的消耗，新能源的开发

在我们的生活中，用电、取暖、使用交通工具都会导致能源的消耗。雅思写作和口语经常讨论化石能源(石油、天然气、煤)产生的影响，还有和其他能源的对比(包括太阳能、风能、潮汐能、水电、地热、核能等)。

百搭观点 30

A 工厂使用节能科技

B 家庭使用节能设备

C 建筑使用节能材料

D 开发新能源，包括太阳能和风能，去发电

E 开发电动汽车和混合能源车

有助于减少化石资源的使用，更加环保。

Energy Consumption 相关词伙

1. alternative energy sources 可替代能源
2. clean energy 清洁能源
3. renewable resources 可再生资源
4. energy conservation 能源保护
5. energy consumption 能源消耗
6. generate electricity 发电
7. natural light 自然光
8. sustainable materials 可持续材料
9. electric cars 电动汽车
10. hybrid cars 混合能源汽车
11. car giants 汽车业巨头
12. traditional fossil fuels 传统化石燃料
13. environmentally friendly materials 环保材料
14. energy-saving technology 节能科技
15. energy efficiency 节能

口语 Part 3 练习题目

Question: Do you agree that technology has caused many environmental problems?

大家先看着中文思路自己回答一次，然后使用词伙再回答一次。

结构	思路	词伙
观点 1	是的，这是部分正确的，但我想说科技也对很多环境问题给出了解决方法	environmental problems
举例	例如，当今许多新的建筑使用的是环保的和持续的材料，建筑师试图充分利用自然光，采用太阳能面板发电的方式为屋主提供电力	sustainable materials
观点 2	我们也能看到许多汽车巨头研发电动汽车和混合动力车	car giants
解释	这些车靠电能或者可再生资源驱动	alternative energy sources
结果	因此我们能减少对传统化石燃料的依赖	traditional fossil fuels

大家看一下下面的回答，自己再练习，说到熟练为止。

观点 1: Yes, it is partly right, but I'd like to say technology has also been a solution to many **environmental problems**.

举例：For example, many new buildings today use **environmentally friendly** and **sustainable materials**, and architects also try to make the most of **natural light**, use **solar panels** to **generate electricity** for homeowners.

观点 2：We also see many **car giants** develop **electric cars** and **hybrid cars**.

解释：These cars are **powered by electricity** and **alternative energy sources**,

结果：so we can reduce reliance on **traditional fossil fuels**.

雅思作文相关真题

Nuclear energy is a better energy source for countries to meet the ever-increasing energy demand. To what extent do you agree or disagree? (考试日期：20130907)

环境次话题 2：水资源的使用和水污染

水资源的话题在写作中考得不多，口语经常考，包括靠近水的地方、和水相关的运动等话题，考官在 Part 3 往往会问考生关于水资源缺乏和水污染的相关话题。

百搭观点 31

A 使用农药

B 工业排污

C 家庭污水

D 海洋垃圾

E 森林破坏导致水土流失

F 人口增长

G 不注意节约用水

都会导致水资源减少，或者水污染增加。

Water 相关词伙

1. fresh water 淡水
2. tap water 自来水
3. a threat to public health 一个对公众健康的威胁
4. water pollution 水污染
5. contaminate water 污染水
6. underground water 地下水
7. heavily polluted 污染严重
8. boil water 开水
9. a clean water supply 一个干净水源
10. poor sanitation 恶劣的卫生状况
11. bottled water 瓶装水
12. water consumption 耗水量
13. soil erosion 水土流失
14. efficiency in water use 有效用水
15. untreated sewage 未经处理的废水

口语 Part 3 练习题目

Question: How to get fresh water in your country?

大家先看着中文思路自己回答一次，然后使用词伙再回答一次。

结构	思路	词伙
观点 1	来自水龙头，需要煮沸	turn on the taps, boil water
原因	主要原因是工业化，工业废料导致了水污染；农业的化肥也在很大程度上污染了水	water pollution, chemical fertilisers, contaminated water
结果	水龙头的水未必干净	tap water
观点 2	买灌装水	bottled water
原因	城市的卫生条件不好	poor sanitation
结果	很难保证水源的纯净	maintain a clean water supply

大家看一下下面的回答，自己再练习，说到熟练为止。

观点 1：Whenever you want fresh water in China, what you need to do is to **turn on the taps**, but you need to **boil water** before you drink it.

原因：The main reason is that many cities have been industrialised, **industrial waste** has **caused water pollution**. In addition, **chemical fertilisers** have also **contaminated water** to a large extent.

结果：This is why **tap water** is not sterile.

观点 2：Many people also buy **bottled water** for convenience.

原因：**Poor sanitation** in urban areas means that people normally are not confident in the water available in public places.

结果：It is not easy to **maintain a clean water supply** in these cities.

雅思作文相关真题

The natural resources such as oil, forests and fresh water are being consumed at an alarming rate. What problems does it cause? How can we solve these problems? (考试日期：20150801)

环境次话题 3：垃圾的产生

垃圾问题是雅思常考话题，和社会文化话题下的消费话题、广告话题、机械化生产的话题有直接联系。

百搭观点 32

A 广告和消费文化鼓励大家消费

B 城市没有垃圾回收设备

C 政府没有提高大家的垃圾回收的意识

D 工厂没有垃圾处理的技术和设备

E 很多产品都是由不可降解的物质做成的

导致垃圾大量增加，从而

A 影响土壤和水源

B 垃圾的毒素影响我们的食物

C 动植物死亡

Waste 相关词伙

1. consumer goods 消费者商品
2. household goods 家庭用品
3. consumer products 消费者产品
4. end up in landfill sites 填埋在垃圾场
5. contaminate the environment 污染环境
6. household waste 家庭垃圾
7. industrial waste 工业浪费
8. household rubbish 家庭垃圾
9. drop litter 扔垃圾
10. dump waste 扔垃圾
11. incinerate waste 焚烧垃圾
12. dispose of waste 处理垃圾
13. enter the food chain 进入食物链
14. hazardous waste 有害的垃圾

口语 Part 3 练习题目

Question: Do you think economic development can improve our living standards?

大家先看着中文思路自己回答一次，然后使用词伙再回答一次。

结构	思路	词伙
支持的观点	收入更高	earn a higher salary
结果 1	购买很多产品	consumer goods
举例	家庭用品	household goods
结果 2	享受这些消费品带来的便利	consumer products
相反的观点	过度消费	overconsumption of goods
结果 3	垃圾增加，扔到垃圾堆，影响环境	household waste, landfill sites, contaminate the environment
拓展结果	垃圾有很多有毒的物质，进入我们的食品体系，伤害野生动植物	toxic substances, enter our food chain, harm wildlife

大家看一下下面的回答，自己再练习，说到熟练为止。

支持的观点：Yes, economic development means that you can **earn a higher salary**,

结果 1：so you are able to afford many **consumer goods**,

举例：such as **household goods** like refrigerators.

结果 2：You will enjoy the convenience brought by these **consumer products**.

相反的观点：On the other hand, the **economic boom** normally leads to **overconsumption of goods**.

结果 3：In this case, **household waste** increases. It will end up in **landfill sites** and **contaminate the environment**.

拓展结果：Most rubbish contains **toxic substances** which can **enter our food chain** and also **harm wildlife** living near landfills.

雅思作文相关真题

> ***Nowadays people live in the society where consumer goods are relatively cheaper to buy. Do you think its advantages outweigh its disadvantages?*** (考试日期：20090404)

环境次话题4：动物保护

动物保护主要是考查动物对人类的重要性，动物和人类的关系，包括吃肉、打猎、用动物来制作衣服、制药、医疗实验、养宠物、建动物园等一系列事情。

百搭观点33

人口增长，导致人类活动增加

A 过分耕种
B 过分放牧
C 砍伐树林
D 使用化肥
E 房地产开发
F 建厂发电
G 开矿和开采石油

会破坏环境，尤其是动植物栖息地，导致动物灭绝，影响生物多样性。

Wildlife Preservation 相关词伙

1. human activities 人类活动
2. poor farming practices 不好的耕种模式
3. destroy the forest 破坏森林
4. mine coal 开采煤田
5. oil drilling 开采石油
6. animal die out 动物灭绝
7. biodiversity loss 生物多样性下降
8. intensive farming 密集耕种
9. the loss of biodiversity 生物多样性的缺失
10. improve biodiversity 改善生物多样性
11. endangered species 濒危物种
12. rare animals 稀有物种
13. cause damage to the environment 对环境造成危害
14. toxic chemicals 有毒的化学品
15. habitat destruction 栖息地破坏
16. face a high risk of extinction 面临很高的灭绝风险
17. on the verge of extinction 濒临灭绝

口语 Part 3 练习题目

Question: In what ways does human activity result in the extinction of some animal species?

大家先看着中文思路自己回答一次，然后使用词伙再回答一次。

结构	思路	词伙
直接回答	许多人类活动会对环境造成破坏	human activities, cause damage to the environment
举例1	集约农业使用化学品去增加土地的产量，但是这些有毒的化学品会污染土壤	intensive farming, productivity of farmland toxic chemicals

结果	这些化学品能危害野生动植物，一些物种将因此而灭绝	harm wildlife, die out
举例 2	采伐森林，过度伐木和开荒会破坏栖息地	habitat destruction
结果	许多动物可能不得不迁移到容易找到食物的地方	move to
总结	这就是很多物种已经濒临灭绝的原因	on the verge of extinction

大家看一下下面的回答，自己再练习，说到熟练为止。

直接回答：Many **human activities** can **cause damage to the environment**.

举例 1：For instance, **intensive farming** has used chemicals to **increase the productivity of farmland**, but these **toxic chemicals** can **contaminate soil**.

结果：These chemicals can **harm wildlife**. Some species will thus **die out**.

举例 2：Deforestation, overlogging and **land clearance** can cause **habitat destruction**.

结果：Many animals may have to **move to** some areas where they can find food easily.

总结：This is the reason why many species have been **on the verge of extinction**.

百搭观点 34

A 偷猎　　B 将动物用于表演

C 将动物关在动物园里　　D 用动物做实验

E 吃动物的肉　　F 养宠物

都会对动物造成伤害，不够人道。

Zoo 相关词伙

1. animal in captivity 被关住的动物
2. locked in cages 被关在笼子里
3. lose freedom 失去自由
4. freedom is restricted 自由受到限制
5. natural behaviour 天生的行为
6. hunting instincts 狩猎的天性
7. fierce animals 猛兽
8. reintroduce species 将动物放回（野外）
9. in the wild 在野外
10. human-caused disturbances 人类（对动物造成）的干扰
11. manmade environment 人工环境
12. artificial environment 人工环境
13. illegal hunting 非法狩猎
14. exhibit animals 展出动物
15. animal testing 动物实验
16. kill animals for meat 杀动物来吃肉
17. raise pets 养宠物

口语 Part 3 练习题目

Question: What are the differences between keeping animals in zoos and putting them in the natural environment?

大家先看着中文思路自己回答一次，然后使用词伙再回答一次。

结构	思路	词伙
观点 1	把动物关在动物园不利于动物的幸福	animals' well-being
原因	会被关在笼子里	locked in cages
结果	动物失去自由和天性	lose freedom, change natural behabiour
举例	如果被限制了自由，猛兽会失去捕猎天性，如狮子、老虎	hunting instincts
结果	无法回归到本物种的自然栖息地	reintroduce these animals to natural habitats
对比	在野外，这个问题不太可能发生	in the wild
观点 2	把动物留在自然栖息地，很难保护它们不受人为的干扰	human-caused disturbances
结果	很难保护生物多样性	preserve biodiversity

大家看一下下面的回答，自己再练习，说到熟练为止。

观点 1：I think keeping animals in zoos may not be beneficial to **animals' well-being**.

原因：They will be **locked in cages**.

结果：This means that animals will **lose freedom** and **change their natural behaviour**.

举例：For example, tigers, lions and other fierce animals may lose their **hunting instincts**, if their freedom is restricted.

结果：As a consequence, it is difficult to **reintroduce these species to** their **natural habitats** again.

对比：If animals are **in the wild**, this problem is unlikely to happen.

观点 2：Another difference is that if we leave animals in their natural habitats, it is not easy to protect them from **human-caused disturbances**.

结果：It will be difficult to **preserve biodiversity**.

雅思作文相关真题

Some people think zoos are cruel and all the zoos should be closed. However, some people think zoos can help protect the rare animals. Discuss both these views and give your opinion. (考试日期：20100318)

Animal Testing 相关词伙

1. animal tests 动物实验
2. animal experiments 动物实验
3. conduct experiments 做实验
4. animal welfare groups 动物权益团体
5. develop a new drugs 研发一种新药
6. show promising results 有好结果
7. side effect 副作用
8. exposed to abuse 受到虐待
9. medical tests 药物实验
10. alternative methods of research 可代替的研究方法
11. medical products 医用品
12. skincare products 护肤品

口语 Part 3 练习题目

Question: Do you think we should stop animal testing?

大家先看着中文思路自己回答一次，然后使用词伙再回答一次。

结构	思路	词伙
观点 1	我认为禁止动物实验不必要	animal experiments
原因	实验可以帮助开发新药，测试产品的安全性，例如护肤品	develop new drugs, test the safety of products, skincare products
结果	我们应该在实验室动物身上实行实验，来看新药品是否有效，是否有任何副作用	show promising results, side effect
观点 2	另一方面，我觉得政府应该仔细审查动物实验	put animal experimentation under scrutiny
原因	很多动物在实验室遭到虐待	be exposed to abuse
结果	除非没有其他能够替代的研究方法，在医学实验中使用动物应该被禁止	alternative methods

大家看一下下面的回答，自己再练习，说到熟练为止。

观点 1+ 原因：No, I don't think it is necessary to ban **animal experiments**, because these tests can help us **develop new drugs** and **test the safety of products** such as **skincare products**.

结果：We should **conduct experiments on** lab animals to see whether new drugs **show promising results** and whether there is any **side effect**.

观点 2：On the other hand, I would argue that authorities should **put animal experimentation under scrutiny**.

原因：Many animals **are exposed to abuse** in the lab.

结果：Using animals in **medical tests** is not allowed unless there are no **alternative methods of research**.

3.4.8 常考写作和口语话题 8：媒体类

媒体类主要是考查三个次话题：

媒体次话题 1：新闻媒体的发展和影响

媒体次话题 2：不同信息来源的对比（包括电视、网络、广播、书本）

媒体次话题 3：广告的影响

媒体次话题 1：新闻媒体的发展和影响

雅思有很多题目是关于新闻媒体对我们生活的影响的，包括我们为什么要依赖新闻和新闻的信息是不是都准确等。

百搭观点 35

新闻媒体不报道真实信息的主要原因是

A 要夸大坏信息来增加收视率

B 迫于政治或者经济压力去隐瞒和修改信息

C 无法去实地报道新闻，只能捏造

D 新闻工作者不够客观

E 为了迎合观众制造假新闻

News 相关词伙

1. news reports 新闻报道
2. news outlets 新闻机构
3. news organisations 新闻组织
4. news media 新闻媒体
5. professional reports 专业报道
6. gather first-hand information 收集第一手资料
7. broadcast news 播放新闻
8. a reliable source of information 一条有可靠来源的信息
9. increase ratings 提高收视率
10. expand the readership 拓展读者群体
11. sensationalise crimes 夸大犯罪事实
12. cover up political scandals 掩盖政治性的丑闻
13. mislead the public 误导公众
14. fake news 虚假新闻
15. political pressure 政治压力
16. in an opinionated way 带有主观看法
17. on the spot 现场
18. conceal the truth 隐瞒真相

口语 Part 3 练习题目

Question: Is news trustworthy?

大家先看着中文思路自己回答一次，然后使用词伙再回答一次。

结构	思路	词伙
支持的观点	如果是一些比较大型的新闻机构，新闻可信	news outlets
原因	这些机构有专业新闻工作者现场收集信息	professional reporters, gather first-hand information
结果	信息可信	a reliable source of information
相反的观点	很多时候新闻未必可信	in most cases
举例 1	新闻媒体可能会夸大犯罪事实，这样会提高收视率，吸引读者	sensationalise crime, increase ratings, expand the readership

举例 2	新闻有时候也会出于政治压力，掩盖一些政治丑闻	political pressures, cover up political scandals
结果	这样会误导观众	mislead the public

大家看一下下面的回答，自己再练习，说到熟练为止。

支持的观点 + 原因：**News reports** can be reliable if they are prepared by some well-established **news outlets**, since these organisations have **professional reporters** who **gather first-hand information on the spot** for the public.

结果：As a result, the **news broadcast** by these organisations is **a reliable source of information**.

相反的观点：On the other hand, many people, including me, believe that **news media** may not be trustworthy **in most cases**.

举例 1：For example, in order to **increase ratings** as well as **expand the readership**, some **news organisations** might **sensationalise some crimes**, and many people think crime is widespread.

举例 2：Also, many journalists may choose to **cover up political scandals** due to **political pressure**.

结果：They report news in a way that **misleads the public**.

雅思作文相关真题

Nowadays, we rely on news for our knowledge, but we are uncertain about the truth of these news. Should we believe journalists? What qualities should a good journalist or correspondent have?

（考试日期：20110604）

媒体次话题 2：不同信息来源的对比（包括电视、网络、广播、书本）

近年来考的比较多的话题是人们到底是通过上网使用社交媒体，还是通过报纸或电视新闻看新闻。还有就是人们到底是喜欢看纸质书，还是在电脑或手机上看书。

百搭观点 36

通过

A 网络　　B 手机

C 听广播

获得信息，主要是

A 快捷　　B 方便

而传统媒体

A 电视　　B 杂志和报纸

C 书本

的优点是

A 有深度的分析　　B 有更多的图像信息

Online News 相关词伙

1. read news online 在网上看新闻
2. read news stories 看新闻
3. check online news 阅读网上新闻
4. have free time 空闲时间
5. keep up to date with what is happening 了解最近发生的事情
6. watch videos online 看网络视频
7. have faster access to news in real time 更快了解到实时新闻
8. the live coverage of 实况转播
9. the delivery of visual information 视频信息的呈现
10. TV news 电视新闻
11. news programmes 新闻节目

口语 Part 3 练习题目

Question: Do people like to read news on the Internet?

大家先看着中文思路自己回答一次，然后使用词伙再回答一次。

结构	思路	词伙
观点 1	是的，因为网上的新闻阅读起来非常方便	read news online
解释	大家现在都使用智能手机和电脑，利用空闲时间可以顺便查看新闻	free time
举例	很多人在上下班期间都会在地铁上用手机上网看新闻，了解最近发生的事情	travel by underground, keep up to date with
对比	在家看电视新闻不够方便	watch news on TV
观点 2	网络新闻现在还可以看视频	watch videos
结果	人们可以看到实时新闻	in real time
举例	可以看到实时转播的体育赛事，国际会议等	live coverage of
对比	这曾经是电视新闻的一个优点，但现在在线新闻也有这个功能了	visual information

大家看一下下面的回答，自己再练习，说到熟练为止。

观点 1：Yes, I do think so, mainly because it is more convenient to **read news online**.

解释：Most people use smart phones and laptops today, so it's easy for them to **read news stories** whenever they have **free time**.

举例：For example, many commuters can **keep up to date with** what is happening throughout the world by checking **online news**, when **traveling by underground**.

对比：In contrast, it's inconvenient for them to **watch news on TV** at home.

观点 2 + 结果：Online news has become popular also because people can **watch videos** online, so they have **faster access to news in real time**.

举 例：The **live coverage of** the some **sports events** like Olympics and international conferences is available online now.

对比：The delivery of **visual information** used to be a feature of **TV news** but now online news has this function as well.

雅思作文相关真题

> ***Anyone can post information on the Internet. Some people say most of what we read on the Internet is inaccurate. To what extent do you agree or disagree?*** (考试日期：20111022)

媒体次话题 3：广告的影响

广告是雅思口语和写作常考话题，主要是讨论广告对我们的影响，包括对儿童的影响。广告是如何鼓励我们大量消费的也是一个常考题目。很多同学在广告话题上会有的一个常见的错误观点就是"广告有色情和暴力内容"，这个观点和事实不相符，事实上广告一般是有没有色情和暴力内容的。

百搭观点 37

广告

A 告诉我们消费很快乐，不断鼓励我们花钱

B 通过明星代言来让我们购买奢侈品和不需要的东西

C 推广一些不好的生活方式，如吃快餐、喝酒、玩游戏等

D 夸大产品的功效，鼓励大家购买

导致大家乱花钱，影响生活质量，甚至使某些人债台高筑。

Consumer Society 相关词伙

1. consumer societies 消费型社会
2. buy more than they need 买的东西多过自己需要的
3. spend more than they earn 入不敷出
4. excess shopping 过度购物
5. the latest gadgets 最新的电子设备
6. get into debt 负债
7. pay off debts 还清债务
8. financial problems 经济问题
9. low income families 低收入家庭
10. economic pressure 经济压力

口语 Part 3 练习题目

Question: What do you think is the impact of advertising on children?

大家先看着中文思路自己回答一次，然后使用词伙再回答一次。

结构	思路	词伙
观点	一般都是负面的影响	negative impact
原因	广告将购物和快乐联系到一起	associate...with...

举例	小孩觉得如果买了玩具和小电子设备就可以和其他小孩有更多话题	the latest gadgets
结果 1	他们意识到物质的重要性，长大后很可能会成为购物狂乱买东西，甚至会负债	material possessions, shopaholics, buy more than they need, get into debt
结果 2	他们也会缠着父母买东西，这会给低收入家庭造成压力	nag parents to, economic pressure

大家看一下下面的回答，自己再练习，说到熟练为止。

观点：I think in general, **the impact of advertisements** on children **is negative**.

原因：Many advertisements have been trying to **associate shopping with happiness**.

举例：For example, children will be persuaded to believe that if they buy a toy or **the latest gadgets**, they'll have something to talk about with other kids.

结果 1：Children will be increasingly conscious of **material possessions**. In the future, when they grow older, they're likely to become **shopaholics**. They may **buy more than they need**, and sometimes, they even **get into debt**.

结果 2：They also **nag their parents** to buy more. This can put low income families under **economic pressure**.

雅思作文相关真题

> ***Advertising encourages consumers to buy in quantity rather than promoting quality. To what extent do you agree or disagree?*** (考试日期：20120707)

3.4.9 常考写作和口语话题 9：全球化

全球化的话题主要是考查三个方面：

全球化次话题 1：人的迁移（包括游客、移民、商人、工作者、学生）

全球化次话题 2：商品和钱的流通（包括国际品牌、食物、国际援助、国际投资）

全球化次话题 3：文化交流（包括国际电影、音乐、电视节目、语言交流）

全球化次话题 1：人的迁移

人的迁移包括：游客和投资者的移动有利于贫穷国家增加收入，移民、留学生和打工者的到来可以减少劳动力紧缺的问题，也会给地区带来先进技术。

百搭观点 38

A 保护城市的老建筑　　B 维持一些传统文化和习惯

C 发展文化产业（包括艺术、音乐等）　　D 保护自然风景

可以吸引游客，这些游客的消费会为社区带来收入，工作机会增加。

Tourism 相关词伙

1. create revenues 产生收入
2. attract tourists 吸引游客
3. tourist attractions 旅游胜地
4. tourist destinations 旅游目的地
5. the tourist sector 旅游业
6. go sightseeing 去观光
7. a driver of economic growth 一个经济增长的驱动力
8. an important part of the economy 经济的重要组成部分
9. a source of income 收入来源
10. create jobs 创造就业机会
11. create employment/generate employment 创造就业机会
12. charge admission fees 收取门票
13. creative industry 创意产业

口语 Part 3 练习题目

Question: Do you think it is a waste of money for the government to maintain historic buildings?

大家先看着中文思路自己回答一次，然后使用词伙再回答一次。

结构	思路	词伙
立场	很有必要花钱保护历史建筑	historic buildings
原因 1	可以吸引游客、创造收入	attract tourists, create revenues
原因 2	这些建筑可以成为有着独特建筑风格的著名文化景点	with unique architectural styles, cultural attractions
举例	中国一些城市的宝塔在西方国家游客中非常受欢迎	pagodas
结果 1	当地社区可以收取门票费用	charge admission fees
结果 2	企业在某些行业，如酒店还可以赚取更多的利润	earn more profits
结果 3	这些收入可以用来支付维护这些建筑的费用	maintain these buildings

大家看一下下面的回答，自己再练习，说到熟练为止。

立场：I think it is necessary to spend money protecting **historic buildings**.

原因 1：It can **attract tourists** and **create revenues**.

原因 2：These buildings can become famous **cultural attractions with unique architectural styles**.

举例：Some **pagodas** in some cities in China are very popular with visitors from western countries.

结果 1+ 结果 2：Local communities can **charge admission fees** and the businesses in some industries such as hospitality can also **earn more profits**.

结果 3：Their revenues can be used to cover the cost of **maintaining these buildings**.

雅思作文相关真题

The restoration of old buildings in major cities in the world costs enormous government expenditure. This money should be used in new housing and road development. To what extent do you agree or disagree? (考试日期：20130727)

出国留学、工作、经商等也是雅思作文口语常考的话题。

百搭观点 39

A 出国留学
B 学习外语
C 旅游
D 看电影和电视节目
E 阅读报纸杂志
F 阅读书籍
G 和不同背景的朋友交流

可以熟悉各种文化，开拓视野，更容易找工作。

Study Abroad 相关词伙

1. go overseas 到国外
2. study abroad 出国学习
3. in a globalised world 在全球化的世界中
4. from diverse backgrounds 来自不同背景
5. master another language 精通另一门语言
6. pick up a foreign language 学习一门外语
7. fluent in the first language 母语流利
8. immerse themselves in a foreign language 将他们自己浸泡在一门外语里
9. language skills 语言能力
10. multinational enterprises 跨国企业
11. prestigious universities 著名大学
12. expand horizons 开阔视野
13. have a broader view of life 人生的视野更加开阔
14. experience the world 感受世界

口语 Part 3 练习题目

Question: Why do many students study abroad now?

大家先看着中文思路自己回答一次，然后使用词伙再回答一次。

结构	思路	词伙
直接回答	这是很显然的，当今许多年轻人都很热衷于出国，因为他们相信外国求学经历能打开工作的大门	go overseas, open the door to job opportunities
观点 1	通常来说，他们更可能上国外的著名大学	attend a prestigious university
举例	如果他们得到海外学位，他们能更容易在一个跨国企业找到工作	complete a degree, multinational enterprise
观点 2	此外，他们能泡在外语环境中	immerse themselves in a foreign language

结果	这能帮助他们精通另一种语言，从而能帮助他们在未来找到工作，因为在这个全球化的世界，你要和来自不同国家的人交流	master another language, in the globalised world, from diverse backgrounds

大家看一下下面的回答，自己再练习，说到熟练为止。

直接回答：It is clear that many young people today are keen to **go overseas** because they believe that the experience of studying abroad can **open the door to job opportunities**.

观点 1：In general, they are more likely to **attend a prestigious university** in other countries.

举例：If they **complete a degree** overseas, they can find a job easily in a **multinational enterprise**.

观点 2：In addition, they can **immerse themselves in a foreign language**.

结果：This can help them **master another language**, which can help them **find a job** in the future, because **in this globalised world**, you expect to **communicate with people from diverse backgrounds**.

全球化次话题 2：商品和钱的流通

从经济角度来说，全球化很多时候带来的是积极的影响。

百搭观点 40

A 游客去发展中国家消费

B 外商在世界不同地方投资

C 国际组织为发展中国家提供各种援助

D 国际组织带来的技术支持

E 有技术的劳动力移民去外国工作

有助于发展经济，减少贫困，提高生活水准。

注意：这个观点也可以反过来说。外商投资和进口商品导致本地企业倒闭，造成经济后退。外国的移民和劳工占用本地人的工作机会，也会造成经济影响。此外，国际的援助让本国没有动力去创新，发展经济。

Charity 相关词伙

1. charitable organisations 慈善组织
2. raise funds 筹钱
3. mobilise resources 调拨资源
4. international aid 国际援助
5. medical aid 医疗救助
6. needy people 有需要的人
7. people in need 有需要的人
8. basic necessities 日常生活用品
9. live in poverty 生活贫穷的人
10. get rid of poverty 摆脱贫穷
11. impoverished countries 贫穷国家
12. Third World countries 第三世界的国家

口语 Part 3 练习题目

Question: How do charitable organisations help people?

大家先看着中文思路自己回答一次，然后使用词伙再回答一次。

结构	思路	词伙
直接回答	我认为那些非盈利组织可以做两件事	not-for-profit organisations
观点 1	提供钱和医疗救助给那些需要帮助的人，这可以防止不必要的死亡	needy people, dying needlessly
举例	当那些人遭遇健康问题，或者无法负担基本的必需品时，这些是非常重要的	suffer from poor health, afford basic necessities
观点 2	可以筹集资金和调动资源来帮助那些生活在贫困国家的弱势群体	raise funds, mobilise resources, disadvantaged people living in impoverished countries
举例	国际组织可以在第三世界国家建立学校，或者引进技术来帮助农民去改善农业科技	international organisations, Third World countries, improve farming techniques
结果	帮助当地人摆脱贫穷，改善生活	get rid of poverty, improve their lives

大家看一下下面的回答，自己再练习，说到熟练为止。

直接回答：I think these **not-for-profit organisations** can do two things.

观点 1：Firstly, They can provide money or **medical care** to those **needy people** and this can prevent these people from **dying needlessly**.

举例：This is very important when these people **suffer from poor health** or cannot **afford basic necessities**.

观点 2：Secondly, I believe that these organisations can also **raise funds** and **mobilise resources** to help those **disadvantaged people living in impoverished countries**.

举例：For example, some **international organisations** may run **schools** in those **Third World countries** or introduce technology to help farmers to **improve farming techniques**.

结果：It can possibly help locals **get rid of poverty** and **improve their lives**.

雅思作文相关真题

Rich countries often give financial aid to poor countries, but it does not solve poverty, so rich countries should give other types of help to the poor countries rather than financial aid. To what extent do you agree or disagree? (考试日期：20090207)

全球化对环境也会有一定影响，主要体现在空航和空运的增加。

百搭观点 41

全球化增加了

A 货物在全世界的运输

B 人们去不同地方旅游、出差、学习和工作

这些都会促进空航和空运，造成尾气排放和石油消耗的增加。

Air Travel 相关词伙

1. travel by air 坐飞机出行
2. air travel 空航
3. air transport 空运
4. transport...by air 通过飞机运输
5. make non-essential trips 进行非必要的旅行
6. price war 价格战
7. in the airline industry 在航空业
8. air fares 机票费用
9. travel expenses 差旅费
10. on holiday 度假
11. tourist attractions 旅游景点
12. a source of pollution 污染源
13. greenhouse gases 温室气体
14. build up in the atmosphere 聚集在大气中
15. trap heat from the sun 从太阳吸收热量
16. extreme weather conditions 极端天气
17. unusually warm conditions 异常温暖的气候

口语 Part 3 练习题目

Question: Do you think it is necessary to restrict air travel to reduce pollution?

大家先看着中文思路自己回答一次，然后使用词伙再回答一次。

结构	思路	词伙
观点	同意	
解释 1	很多人因为航空业的价格战，已经进行了不必要的旅行	price war, make non-essential trips
解释 2	航空票价已经持续下跌，旅行费用已经比之前任何时候都低	air fares, travel expenses
举例	他们倾向于去其他城市或国家度假，而不是参观当地的旅游景点	local tourist attractions
结果 1	飞机排放物成为一种污染源	emissions from aircrafts
结果 2	温室气体在大气层形成，阻止了太阳的热量。这导致了极端天气，包括一些地区异常温暖的状况	greenhouse gases, build up, trapping, extreme weather conditions, unusually warm conditions

大家看一下下面的回答，自己再练习，说到熟练为止。

观点：Yes, I agree.

解释 1：Many people today have **make non-essential trips** because of the **price war** in the **airline industry**.

解释 2：**Air fares** have dropped continuously and **travel expenses** have been lower than ever before.

举例：They tend to go to other cities or countries on holiday rather than visiting **local tourist attractions**.

结果 1：**Emissions from aircrafts** have become a **source of pollution**.

结果 2：**Greenhouse gases** have **built up in the atmosphere, trapping heat from the sun**. This has led to **extreme weather conditions**, including **unusually warm conditions** in some areas of the world.

雅思作文相关真题

Some people suggest that a country should try to produce all the food for its population and import as little food as possible. To what extent do you agree or disagree? (考试日期：20110226)

全球化次话题3：文化交流

全球化的一个主要问题就是对文化的影响。主要是体现在西方国家的语言(也就是英语)，还有各种产品，包括媒体信息在全世界变得越来越普及和强大，影响着世界的文化。正面是使我们能接触不同的文化。反过来说，很多小国家的文化和语言会慢慢消失。

百搭观点42

全球化会影响全球的文化，包括

A 音乐　　B 电影

C 建筑　　D 食品

E 衣服　　F 价值观

G 语言

这些可能会慢慢变得单一，影响文化多样性，影响人们的文化认同感，世界会变得乏味，我们的思想也越来越单一，对文化、历史、传统的理解更浅薄。

注意：这个观点也可以反过来说。外国商品的增加，让我们有更加丰富的选择，甚至会激发市场的竞争，导致商品价格下降，质量上升，对经济和生活标准都有好的影响。

Music 相关词伙

1. folk songs 民族歌曲
2. pop songs 流行歌曲
3. rock music 摇滚音乐
4. classical music 古典音乐
5. hit songs 热门歌曲
6. pop stars 流行歌手
7. music lover 音乐爱好者
8. musical instruments 乐器
9. integrate musical styles 综合各种音乐风格
10. cultural differences 文化差异
11. differ from culture to culture 文化和文化之间的差异
12. western countries 西方国家

口语 Part 3 练习题目

Question: What are the differences between music nowadays and in the past?

大家先看着中文思路自己回答一次，然后使用词伙再回答一次。

结构	思路	词伙
观点	我认为在过去音乐反映了文化的差异	cultural differences
解释	对好音乐的理解在不同文化间是不同的	from culture to culture
举例	我清楚地记得小时候学的一些著名的民族歌曲。我的一些朋友也学习传统乐器	folk songs, musical instruments

对比	但是今天，我们每天听的很多歌似乎都来自西方国家。许多音乐人在他们的作品中融合了不同的音乐风格	western countries, integrated different musical styles in
举例	流行音乐、摇滚音乐在中国非常流行，然而中国的传统音乐已经不太流行了	pop songs, rock music, classical music

大家看一下下面的回答，自己再练习，说到熟练为止。

观点：I think the music in the past reflected **cultural differences**.

解释：The perception of good music differed **from culture to culture**.

举例：I do remember some famous **folk songs** I learned when I was a child. Some of my friends also learned **traditional musical instruments**.

对比：But today, it seems that a lot of songs we listen to every day are from **western countries**. Many musicians have **integrated different musical styles in** their works.

举例：**Pop songs**, **rock music** have been popular in China, while **classical music** of China has lost popularity.

Language 相关词伙

1. international language 国际语言
2. global language 全球性的语言
3. less spoken language 很少人说的语言
4. minority language 少数民族语言 / 小语种
5. endangered language 濒临消失的语言
6. mother tongue 母语
7. a means of communication 交流方式
8. cultural identity 文化认同
9. preserve traditions 保护传统
10. preserve language diversity 保护语言多样性
11. protect languages 保护语言
12. cultural diversity 文化多样性
13. celebrate festivals 庆祝节日
14. traditional food 传统食物

口语 Part 3 练习题目

Question: What would be the disadvantages of having a global language?

大家先看着中文思路自己回答一次，然后使用词伙再回答一次。

结构	思路	词伙
观点	使用国际语的最大缺点是一些小语种会消失	less spoken languages, die out
解释	偏远地区的年轻人学英语或其他主流语音，导致他们迟早忘记母语	remote communities, dominant languages, mother tongue, sooner or later
背景	语言不仅是交流方式，也是文化特性的重要组成部分	a means of communication, cultural identity
结果	如果一种语言消失了，传统、习俗、行为也会消失	

举例	如果语言消失，我们可能不知道一些文化中如何庆祝节日，也不知道人们会为节日准备什么传统食物	celebrate festivals, cook traditional food
拓展结果	我们无法保持传统并维护文化多样性	preserve traditions, cultural diversity

大家看一下下面的回答，自己再练习，说到熟练为止。

观点：The main disadvantage of having an **international language** is that some **less spoken languages** will die out.

解释：Many young people in some **remote communities** will study English and other **dominant languages** in the world, so they forget their **mother tongue sooner or later**.

背景：A language is not simply **a means of communication**, and it is an **important part of our cultural identity**.

结果：If a language disappears, some traditions, customs and behaviours will also disappear.

举例：For example, we might not know how **festivals are celebrated** in some cultures, and the **traditional food people normally cook** for these festivals, if their language were lost.

拓展结果：We're unlikely to **preserve traditions** and **cultural diversity**.

雅思作文相关真题

> ***Some people think governments should spend money on measures to save languages with few speakers from dying out completely. Others think this is a waste of financial resources. Discuss both views and give your opinion.***（考试日期：20110305）

3.4.10 常考写作和口语话题 10：教育

简单来说，教育类话题主要包括两大类：

第一类是关于儿童教育。这一类题目主要是关注影响儿童成长的不同因素，包括父母、亲戚、幼儿园、小伙伴、老师、邻居、社区、媒体等。

第二类是关于中学和大学教育。这一类题目主要是关注学校的各种活动和课程，是否能够影响年轻人的学习成绩、学习能力（包括阅读能力和数学能力）、动手能力、交流能力、团队能力、解决问题能力、辩证能力、想象力、运动能力等。

教育次话题 1：儿童教育

儿童教育很多的题目都是关于父母在小孩成长中扮演的角色的。

百搭观点 43

父母可以通过

A 和小孩一起旅游

B 一起做体育运动和户外活动

C 一起看电视和玩游戏

D 一起读书

E 一起吃饭和走亲戚

F 接送孩子

G 辅导孩子做作业

来增加和孩子的互动，改善关系，灌输知识，为孩子树立榜样，影响小孩的行为。

Behavioural Problems 相关词伙

1. good role models 好的榜样
2. first educators 第一个老师（启蒙老师）
3. copy behaviour 模仿行为
4. domestic violence 家庭暴力
5. behave badly 表现得很差
6. poor behaviour 不良的行为
7. behavioural problems 行为问题
8. show aggression 有暴力倾向
9. show good manners 表现出礼貌的行为
10. social norms 社会规范
11. show respect to (somebody) 表现出尊敬
12. speak in a friendly manner 说话有礼貌
13. send/take children to school 送孩子去学校
14. pick up children 接孩子

口语 Part 3 练习题目

Question: what are the benefits of reading stories to small children?

大家先看着中文思路自己回答一次，然后使用词伙再回答一次。

结构	思路	词伙
观点 1	一个好处是和孩子一起读书可以影响孩子的行为	have an impact on kids' behaviour
解释 1	在家中就可以培养孩子对阅读的喜爱，帮助孩子发展为了乐趣而读书的兴趣	foster the love of reading
解释 2	父母是孩子好榜样，孩子倾向于模仿父母的行为	good role models for children, copy the behaviours
对比	接触过家庭暴力的孩子会在学校的表现很差，并展现出好斗的特点	domestic violence, behave badly, show aggression
观点 2	此外，读书还可以教会孩子好的礼仪和社会规范	good manners, social norms
举例	有些书告诉孩子如何尊重老师，如何得体地讲话	show respect to teachers, speak in a friendly manner
结果	这可以防止他们在学校有不良行为	poor behaviour

大家看一下下面的回答，自己再练习，说到熟练为止。

观点 1：One benefit is that reading books with children can **have an impact on kids' behaviour**.

解释 1：It can **foster the love of reading** at home and help children **develop an interest** in **reading for pleasure**.

解释 2：Parents are **good role models for children**, and children tend to **copy the behaviours** of adults.

对比：In contrast, children exposed to **domestic violence** will also **behave badly** at school and **show aggression**.

观点 2：Reading books can also teach children **good manners and social norms**.

举例：Some books give children a good idea of how to **show respect to teachers**, how to **speak in a**

friendly manner.

结果：This can help **prevent poor behaviour** at school.

雅思作文相关真题

> ***Maintaining public libraries is a waste of money since computer technology is now replacing their functions. To what extent do you agree or disagree?*** (考试日期：20070210)

除此之外，还会经常考查老师的角色、学校的重要性、图书馆的重要性、书本的重要性等话题，这时候的观点和教育的功能差不多。

百搭观点 44

教育的提供和老师的教育有助于

A 小孩增加知识，以后方便找工作，社会失业率降低

B 年轻人懂得道德和社会规范

C 小孩学会如何和人交流

D 增加学生对不同科目的认识，以后大学做研究，甚至进行产品创新

E 不同的校内和校外活动塑造年轻人的性格和品质

F 培养人们的技能并提高他们的能力，方便他们不断学习，最终实现自己的梦想

G 人们掌握知识和技术，提高工作的效率和产出

Teachers/Schools 相关词伙

1. teach courses 教课
2. teach subjects 教课
3. the school system/the education system 教育系统
4. receive a well-rounded education 学习全面的知识
5. start school 上学
6. school curriculum 学校课程 / 课程大纲
7. core subjects 主科
8. attend university 上大学
9. enter university 上大学
10. lively and stimulating 生动又新颖的
11. engage children 激励孩子们
12. class activities 课堂活动
13. attend school 上学
14. curriculum content 课程内容
15. learning outcomes 学习效果

口语 Part 3 练习题目

Question: Who do you think will play a bigger role in a child's development, teachers or parents?

大家先看看中文思路自己回答一次，然后使用词伙再回答一次。

结构	思路	词伙
直接回答	小孩开始上学后，老师更重要	start school

观点 1	老师能够教小孩比较全面的知识	receive a well-rounded education
原因	老师受过培训，熟悉课程大纲	undergo specialised training, school curriculum
举例	他们会教小孩一些主科，如数学和英语	core subjects
结果	小孩获得这些基本的技能和知识，以后可以继续读大学	academic skills, enter university
对比	父母对教学大纲内容的认识不够，小孩很难提升	curriculum content, an in-depth knowledge of...
观点 2	老师也熟悉教学的方法	teaching methods
举例 1	他们会设计练习和课堂的活动，知道如何让课堂活跃，去吸引学生	design drills, class activities, lively and stimulating, engage students
举例 2	他们也会设计测试，检查学生的进步，达到要求的学生后来进入大学的可能性更大	design quizzes, monitor progress, go to university
对比	父母可能无法提升小孩的学习效果	improve learning outcomes

大家看一下下面的回答，自己再练习，说到熟练为止。

直接回答：Teachers are more influential once children **start school**.

观点 1：Teachers can teach a broad range of courses to ensure that children **receive a well-rounded education**.

原因：This is because teachers have **undergone specialised training** and they are familiar with **the school curriculum**.

举例：For instance, they can teach some **core subjects** to students, such as maths and English.

结果：Students who acquire relevant **academic skills** in these courses will possibly be able to **enter university** afterwards.

对比：In contrast, parents who **lack an in-depth knowledge** of **curriculum content** may not be able to help their children.

观点 2：It is also worth remembering that teachers are familiar with teaching methods as well.

举例 1：They can **design** some **drills** and **class activities**, and also understand how to make every **lesson lively and stimulating** to **engage children**.

举例 2：For example, they can **design some quizzes** to **monitor** students' **process**, and those students who meet the requirements are more likely to **go to university** afterwards.

对比：By contrast, parents may lack the ability to **improve children's learning outcomes**.

雅思作文相关真题

Some think that children should start school as early as possible, while others believe that they should start schools at the age of seven. Discuss both views and give your own opinion. (考试日期：20110310)

教育次话题 2：中学和大学教育

中学和大学教育主要是针对年轻人的就业问题，讨论的是如何能够设计各种不同的课程来帮助他们更好地就业。

百搭观点 45

A 中学做义工
B 中学毕业后工作或者旅游一年
C 大学打工
D 大学实习
E 直接开始工作，而不是继续读大学

有利于增强实际工作能力，熟悉公司运作，有助于择业，更好地为就业做准备。

Practical Work 相关词伙

1. do practical work 做实际工作
2. hands-on experience 实践经验
3. prepare for working lives 为工作做准备
4. practical experience 实践经验
5. work placements 实习
6. pursue a career 从事一份工作
7. well-suited to a job 很适合一份工作
8. improve practical skills 提高实践能力
9. do part-time work 做兼职工作
10. adapt to the workplace 适应职场
11. graduate from university 大学毕业
12. finish high school 高中毕业
13. leave school 毕业
14. take a gap year 高中毕业后的间隔年

口语 Part 3 练习题目

Question: Do you think working or traveling for a year after a student leaves school, instead of starting university directly, is a good choice?

大家先看着中文思路自己回答一次，然后使用词伙再回答一次。

结构	思路	词伙
观点 1	是的，我觉得花一年的时间去工作是一个好主意	take one year off, practical work
原因	你可以增加实践经验，为以后的工作生活做准备	increase hands-on experience, working lives
举例	例如，你可以学习如何处理文件，如何使用办公软件和办公设备，如何在一个团队中工作等	process documents, office equipment, work as part of a team

对比	没有这些实践经验，你不太可能从大学毕业后就适应工作场合	practical experience, adapt to the workplace
观点 2	调整一年的另一个好处是你更容易发现自己的天赋	taking a gap year, discover talents
原因	除了提高实践能力，你还会明白你适合什么工作，这可以帮助你选择未来大学里要学的科目，并决定未来你要追求的事业	improve practical skills, well-suited to a job, choose subjects, pursue a career
对比	实习和做兼职的功能差不多	work placements, do part-time work

大家看一下下面的回答，自己再练习，说到熟练为止。

观点 1：Yes, I suppose it is a good idea to **take one year off to do practical work**.

原因：You can **increase hands-on experience** and **prepare for working lives**.

举例：For example, you learn how to **process documents**, use **office software and equipment** and **work as part of a team**, etc.

对比：Without such **practical experience**, you are unlikely to **adapt to the workplace** when you **graduate from university**.

观点 2：Another benefit of **taking a gap year** is that you may **discover your talents** more easily.

原因：Apart from **improving practical skills**, you will see which **job you are well-suited to**. This can help you **choose the subjects** you study at university and the **careers you pursue** in the future.

对比：**Work placements** and **doing part-time work** have similar functions.

雅思作文相关真题

Some people think university education should prepare students for employment. Other people think the university has other functions. Discuss both views and give your opinion. （考试日期：20091024）

大学教育的另外一个常见话题就是选专业和选课程。

百搭观点 46

选专业和选课需要考虑

A 个人的兴趣和爱好

B 专业的就业前景

C 个人的财政和家庭情况

D 是否能够提升技能，并增加知识

E 大学的声誉和排名

F 国家的支持和政策

G 学习的时间和精力

University Subjects 相关词伙

1. offer employment possibilities 提供就业机会
2. complete degree courses 完成学业
3. an investment of time and money 投入时间和金钱
4. take subject courses 上专业课
5. fill knowledge gap 填补（劳动力市场上的）知识空白
6. pursue a career 从事一份工作
7. vocational courses 职业课程
8. academic courses 学术课程
9. areas of knowledge 领域知识
10. preferred areas of study 偏爱的学习领域
11. match interests 符合兴趣
12. passionate about 对……有热情
13. study with enthusiasm 有兴趣去学习
14. develop talents 发掘天赋
15. career success 事业上的成功
16. financial circumstances 财政情况

口语 Part 3 练习题目

Question: In your country, what factors would people consider when choosing a subject at university?

大家先看着中文思路自己回答一次，然后使用词伙再回答一次。

结构	思路	词伙
观点 1	就业前景	offer greater employment possibilities
原因	读大学需要花很多钱和时间	complete a degree, an investment of time and money
举例	如学医，往往要学习 5 年	practice medicine, take subject courses
结果	人们希望自己的专业在劳动力市场上填补一定的空缺，能够找到工作，收入高	fill knowledge gaps, pursue a career, high pay
拓展	这就是为什么很多人现在选择职业型的课程	vocational courses
观点 2	知识的领域是否符合个人的兴趣和爱好	areas of knowledge, match interests
原因 1	年轻人需要自己真正喜欢的科目，这样才可以有热情	passionate about, study with enthusiasm
原因 2	这样可以在自己喜欢的学习领域开发自己的潜力	preferred areas of study, develop talents
结果	可能成为专家，以后更加有可能成功	become professionals, achieve success

大家看一下下面的回答，自己再练习，说到熟练为止。

观点 1：I think most young people would consider whether the subject can **offer greater employment possibilities**.

原因：**Completing a degree** is **an investment of time and money**.

举例：For instance, graduates who want to **practice medicine** have to **take different subject courses** for five years.

结果：This is why they hope that what they learn can **fill the knowledge gaps** in the **labour market**, and they can **pursue a career** which leads to **high pay** and an improved standard of living.

拓展：This also explains why many people tend to choose **vocational courses**.

观点 2：Some people may also consider whether the **areas of knowledge match their interests**.

原因 1：They need to choose the subjects they **are passionate about**, so that they can **study with enthusiasm**.

原因 2：They can also **develop their talents** in their **preferred areas of study**,

结果：and they are likely to **become professionals** afterwards and **achieve success** in their careers.

雅思作文相关真题

> ***Some people believe that teenagers should concentrate on all school subjects, while others claim that students should focus on the subject that they are best at or that they find interesting. Discuss both views and give your opinion.*** (考试日期：20090509)

3.5 思考观点的角度

之前我们在总结十大话题的时候，说了很多不同话题的背景知识，方便大家了解雅思考试大概考什么题目，知道不同题目常用的观点是什么。

在教学过程中，我发现学生有另外一个问题：他们本身对话题有很多的认知，但是他们在考场上记不起来这些知识和观点，因为他们思考观点的时候，没有固定的方向。

因此，我大概总结了雅思作文思考观点时的常见角度，大家可以看看。我将话题分成教育类话题和非教育类话题。这两种题目思考观点的角度各有不同。

3.5.1 非教育类话题讲解

非教育类话题的思路大致如下：

- Culture（文化）：

A 生活方式和行为方式（衣食住行等） B 文化多样性

- Health（健康）：

A 身体 B 心理和情感

- Economy （经济）：

A 经济的发展 B 生活的成本 / 收入增加 C 求职和就业

- Society（社会）：

A 社会和家庭生活 B 社会价值观（社会平等、诚实、无私等） C 生活标准和满意度

- Technology（科技）：

A 科技革新和进步 B 教育和知识

• Law（法律）：

A 法律和政府的政策 B 道德和行为规范

• Environment（环境）：

A 环境保护 B 生活环境

按照这些单词的首字母，我将它们归纳成 **CHESTLE**，下面我会逐一解释雅思作文和口语一般会以这些角度考什么，会用到什么常见观点，有什么相关词伙，并且提供一些题目作为练习。

思考的观点角度 1：Culture（文化）

百搭观点 47

A 电脑网络　　B 阅读

C 看电影或者照片

虽然省钱省力，但是未必能够取代亲自去游览一个地方（包括古建筑）或者是看一个艺术品（包括绘画等）的方式，因为视觉感受不同，而且文化遗产的形成或制作过程实属不易，值得亲眼一见。

Architecture 相关词伙

1. historic building 历史建筑
2. historic site 历史遗址
3. heritage building 古建筑
4. cultural attraction 文化胜地
5. cultural site 文化遗址
6. architectural landmark 建筑地标
7. architectural treasure 建筑瑰宝
8. worth a visit 值得去看看
9. make a trip 进行一次旅行
10. a memorable experience 一次难忘的经历
11. in ancient times 在古时候
12. visual experience 视觉体验
13. cultural heritage 文化遗产

口语 Part 3 练习题目

Question: Would you like to view historic buildings online or visit these buildings in person?

大家先看着中文思路自己回答一次，然后使用词伙再回答一次。

结构	思路	词伙
支持的观点	在我看来，一方面，在网上搜索关于历史遗址的信息能节约金钱和时间	searching the web for information about
结果	在你出发之前，你会知道什么建筑是值得参观的	make the trip
相反的观点	另一方面，参观一个重要的文化场所能给你一次难忘的体验	a memorable experience

解释	近距离地看地标建筑是不同于在屏幕上看的	architectural landmarks
结果	你更可能体会到这些建筑珍品的价值	architectural treasures
举例	你会被古代建筑者的技能惊艳到	be amazed by

大家看一下下面的回答，自己再练习，说到熟练为止。

支持的观点：In my opinion, on the one hand, **searching the web for information about** historic sites can save money and time.

结果：You can have a good idea of what building is **worth a visit**, before you **make the trip**.

相反的观点：On the other hand, visiting an important cultural site can give you **a memorable experience**.

解释：Watching **architectural landmarks** closely is different from watching them **on screen**.

结果：You are more likely to appreciate these **architectural treasures**.

举例：You'll **be amazed by** the skills of builders in ancient times.

文化不只是 cultures，还包括 values，社会的价值观。

百搭观点 48

现代社会人们越来越注重公平，体现在

A 男女平等

B 教育平等

C 贫富差距缩小

D 消除年龄歧视

E 减少种族歧视

Reduce Poverty 相关词伙

1. reduce poverty 减少贫穷
2. break the cycle of poverty 打破贫穷的恶性循环
3. needy people 贫困的人
4. afford tuition fees 能支付学费
5. charitable organisations 慈善组织
6. maintain a basic standard of living 维持基本的生活水平
7. die needlessly 不必要的死亡
8. people with disabilities 残疾人
9. suffer from poor health 生病
10. afford basic necessities 买得起基本生活必需品
11. receive vocational training 接受职业培训
12. improve job skills 提高工作能力
13. close the gap between haves and have-nots 减少贫富差距
14. racial discrimination 种族歧视

口语 Part 3 练习题目

Question: How do charitable organizations help people?

大家先看着中文思路自己回答一次，然后使用词伙再回答一次。

结构	思路	词伙
直接回答	我认为这些组织可以做两件事	
观点 1	第一，提供钱或者医疗救助给需要帮助的人，这可以帮助那些人维持基本的生活，防止那些人无辜死去	needy people, dying needlessly
举例	这对没有工作的、无家可归的和残疾的人非常重要，他们可能身体状况很差或者负担不起基本的生活必需品	suffer from poor health, cover basic needs
观点 2	第二，我觉得那些组织可以向那些来自贫困背景的年轻人提供职业培训	vocational training, from less well-off backgrounds
解释	那些人负担不起学费，所以他们应该接受免费的培训去提升工作的技能	improve job skills
结果	这可以帮助他们脱贫	break the cycle of poverty

大家看一下下面的回答，自己再练习，说到熟练为止。

直接回答：I think these organisations can do two things.

观点 1：Firstly, they can give money or provide **medical care** to those **needy people** and this can help these people **maintain a basic standard of living**, and prevent these people from **dying needlessly**.

举例：This is very important to the unemployed, the homeless and **those with disabilities**, which can **suffer from poor health** or cannot even have money to **cover basic needs**.

观点 2：Secondly, I believe that those organisations can also provide **vocational training** for those young people **from less well-off backgrounds**.

解释：Those people cannot **afford tuition fees**, so they should receive free training to **improve job skills**.

结果：This can help them **break the cycle of poverty**.

思考观点的角度 2：Health（健康）

健康的角度包括生理和心理的健康。

百搭观点 49

A 工作太忙

B 学习太忙

C 玩游戏和看电视太久

D 玩电脑和手机

E 住在城市，没有运动的设施和空间

F 使用各种电器做家务

G 工业自动化和机械化

导致每天的运动时间很少，对健康不好。

Work Overtime 相关词伙

1. work unsocial hours 非正常时间上班
2. work overtime 加班工作
3. work long hours 长时间工作
4. high-stress jobs 压力大的工作
5. lack of sleep 缺乏睡眠
6. sleep deprivation 缺乏睡眠
7. suffer from insomnia 失眠
8. do exercise 运动
9. physical activity 身体锻炼
10. in poor health 身体状况不好
11. health problems 健康问题

口语 Part 3 练习题目

Question: What effects does working overtime have on the lives of employees, especially women?

大家先看着中文思路自己回答一次，然后使用词伙再回答一次。

结构	思路	词伙
观点 1	我认为女性要克服一些问题	overcome problems
举例 1	过度忙碌，非正常时间上班，缺乏睡眠	work unsocial hours, a lack of sleep
举例 2	没有时间运动	free time for exercise
结果	身体状况不好	health problems
观点 2	女性没有时间照顾家人	look after family
举例	做家务	do domestic work
结果	这些也属于体力活动，对健康有实际的影响	physical activity, affect their health

大家看一下下面的回答，自己再练习，说到熟练为止。

观点 1：I think there will be a couple of **problems women have to overcome**.

举例 1：Firstly, if they have to **work unsocial hours**，**a lack of sleep** will become a problem.

举例 2：They do not have **free time for exercise**.

结果：As a consequence, they are in poor health. For example, they may have **health problems** such as obesity.

观点 2 + 举例：Another problem is that they do not have time to **look after family, do domestic work, take care of** their children.

结果：These are also **physical activity** which can **affect their health**.

我们再练习一道题。

Lifestyle 相关词伙

1. lead a hectic life 过着忙碌的生活
2. live a healthy life 过健康的生活
3. live an active life 喜欢运动
4. live an inactive life 不喜欢运动
5. exercise regularly 经常运动
6. play sport 做运动（美式常用）
7. do sport 做运动（英式常用）
8. indoor activities 室内活动
9. access to exercise equipment 有健身设备
10. green space 绿地
11. make way for modern buildings 被现代建筑取代

口语 Part 3 练习题目

Question: Do children today enjoy watching sports rather than do sport themselves? Why?

大家先看着中文思路自己回答一次，然后使用词伙再回答一次。

结构	思路	词伙
直接回答	是的	
原因 1	首先，他们的父母树立了一个坏的榜样	set a bad example
举例	他们过着紧张忙碌的生活，不经常锻炼	lead a hectic life
结果	所以他们的孩子从小也没有体育运动的习惯	from an early age, playing sport, the habit of
原因 2	另一个原因是城市人口过密	overpopulated
举例	为了腾出地方给摩天大楼，绿地、公园、花园被毁坏了	make way for
结果 1	父母找不到合适的场所让孩子做运动	do sport
结果 2	室内活动已经主导了孩子的业余时间	spare time

大家看一下下面的回答，自己再练习，说到熟练为止。

直接回答：Yes.

原因 1：First of all, their parents have **set a bad example**.

举例：They **lead a hectic life**, and do not **exercise regularly**.

结果：So their children do not **have the habit of playing sport from an early age**.

原因 2：Another reason is that cities **are overpopulated**.

举例：Green space, parks, gardens have been destructed to **make way for** modern buildings.

结果 1：Parents cannot find the right place for children to **do sport**.

结果 2：**Indoor activities** have dominated children's **spare time**.

百搭观点 50

A 公园

B 花园

C 绿色的地方

D 乡村地区

E 海边

空气更好，让人心情舒爽，空旷的地方也方便运动，从而让我们更加健康。

Greenspaces 相关词伙

1. public gardens 公共花园
2. do outdoor activities 做户外运动
3. go for a jog 慢跑
4. feel relaxed 感觉放松
5. reduce stress 减轻压力
6. keep fit 保持身材
7. flowering plants 开花植物
8. evergreen trees 常青树
9. beautiful landscape 美丽的风景
10. enjoy the scenery 欣赏风景
11. take in the scenery 领略风光
12. admire the scenery 赞美景色
13. stunning scenery 极好的景色

口语 Part 3 练习题目

Question: Why do people who live in cities like public gardens?

大家先看着中文思路自己回答一次，然后使用词伙再回答一次。

结构	思路	词伙
观点 1	城市居民把花园看作可以做户外运动的地方	places for doing outdoor activities
举例 1	他们可能和家人或者朋友散步，享受这里的风景	take a walk
举例 2	对我来说，这是能让我慢跑的好地方	go for a jog
结果	提供了一个能保持身材和放松的绝佳机会	keep fit, wind down
对比	否则，城市生活就非常有压力了	urban life
观点 2	在花园里，接触开花的植物和常青树能让你感到放松	be exposed to, flowering plants
结果	它是一个减压的轻松途径	reduce stress

大家看一下下面的回答，自己再练习，说到熟练为止。

观点 1：I suppose the main reason is that urban dwellers regard gardens as **places for doing outdoor activities**.

举例 1：They may **take a walk** with family or friends and enjoy the scenery there.

举例 2：In my case, this is a wonderful place where I can **go for a jog**.

结果：It is a great opportunity to **keep fit and wind down**.

对比：Otherwise, **urban life** can be very stressful.

观点 2：Another reason is that whenever you **are exposed to flowering plants, evergreen trees** in public gardens, you will feel relaxed.

结果：It is an easy way to **reduce stress**.

百搭观点 51

A 医生的建议　　B 政府的宣传和指引

C 老师的教导　　D 父母的榜样行为

E 政府的法律　　F 书籍和杂志的健康类文章

都可以让人养成好的生活习惯，包括

A 健康饮食　　B 多运动

C 少坐车或自己开车　　D 少抽烟喝酒

Government Intervention 相关词伙

1. government intervention 政府介入
2. government action 政府行为
3. launch awareness campaigns 发起宣传活动
4. introduce laws 颁布法律
5. make laws 制定法律
6. tighten regulations on 加紧监管
7. impose a tobacco tax on 征收烟草税
8. curb smoking 控制吸烟
9. stay healthy 保持健康
10. prevention is more important than the cure 预防比治疗重要
11. fall ill 生病

口语 Part 3 练习题目

Question: Do you think doctors should be responsible for teaching people on how to be healthy?

大家先看着中文思路自己回答一次，然后使用词伙再回答一次。

结构	思路	词伙
观点 1	是的，预防比治疗更重要	
解释	建议患者过一个健康的生活是医生的责任	advise patients to live a healthy life
举例	应该告诉人们有哪些疾病与生活方式有关	lifestyle-related diseases
对比	如果他们不锻炼也不健康饮食，他们会很容易生病	exercise regularly, healthy eating, fall ill easily

观点 2	政府也能起很大的作用，政府干预有时候比医生的建议更有用	government intervention
解释	政府可以提供一些健康指南并且举行一些宣传活动去告知公众如何保持健康	health guidelines, launch awareness campaigns stay healthy
阐述	政府可以在必要的时候颁布法律改变人们的生活方式	introduce laws
举例	政府可以颁布烟草税来控制抽烟	curb smoking

大家看一下下面的回答，自己再练习，说到熟练为止。

观点 1：Yes, prevention is more important than the cure.

解释：It is the doctors' responsibility to **advise patients to live a healthy life**.

举例：People should be told that there are many **lifestyle-related diseases**.

对比：For example, if they don't **exercise regularly** and pay attention to **healthy eating**, they can **fall ill easily**.

观点 2：Of course, the government also has an important role to play, and **government intervention** is sometimes more effective than health professionals' advice.

解释：They can offer some **health guidelines** and **launch awareness campaigns** to tell the public what they do to **stay healthy**.

阐述：If necessary, they can **introduce laws** to change people's lifestyles.

举例：For example, the government can impose a tobacco tax to **curb smoking**.

思考观点的角度 3：Economy（经济）

在经济方面，我们一般会考虑三个方向：

- 经济是发展还是倒退，如商业活动是否增加了。
- 人们的收入是上升还是下降，人们是否可以负担得起生活的成本。
- 人们是否可以求职和就业，还是有失业的风险。

百搭观点 52

人们需要

A 很勤奋地工作　　B 接受培训

C 提高文凭　　D 丰富自己各方面的技能

才可以找到工作，适应竞争，保证收入。

Job Seeking 相关词伙

1. labour market 劳动力市场
2. intensely competitive 竞争激烈
3. intense competition 激烈的竞争
4. improve job security 提高工作的稳定性
5. find work 找到工作
6. lose jobs 失业
7. steady income 稳定的收入
8. increase earnings 增加收入
9. cover living expenses 支付生活费
10. undergo training 接受培训
11. complete a degree 获得一个学位
12. meet requirements 符合要求
13. sharpen skills/add to the skill set 丰富技能

口语 Part 3 练习题目

Question: Have people become busy in recent years or have they had more free time?

大家先看着中文思路自己回答一次，然后使用词伙再回答一次。

结构	思路	词伙
观点	人们变得比以前更忙了	than before
解释	劳动力市场竞争变得更激烈了，失业率一直在不断上升	labour market, intensely competitive unemployment rate
结果	很多人不得不非常努力地工作来获得工作保障	job security
举例	或者他们不得不接受培训去提升他们的技能，以满足雇主的要求	undergo training, upgrade skills
对比	否则，他们会失去工作，无法支付他们的生活开销	lose jobs, cover living expenses

大家看一下下面的回答，自己再练习，说到熟练为止。

观点：I'd say that people have **become busier than before**.

解释：**The labour market** has become **intensely competitive**, and **the unemployment rate** has been rising constantly.

结果：Many people have to **work very hard** to **improve job security**.

举例：Or they have to **undergo training** to **upgrade their skills** to meet the requirements of employers.

对比：Otherwise, they can **lose their jobs** and **fail to get the money to cover their living expenses**.

百搭观点 53

公司需要

A 注意客户的需要，设计有竞争力的产品　　B 产品性价比高

C 提供准时、快捷、贴心的服务，处理客户投诉很快捷

D 有激情、接受过培训、有创造力的员工

E 好的理财能力，控制好成本　　F 足够的资金

G 好的商业计划　　H 好的管理能力，增加效率

才能够赚取利润并获得成功。

Business 相关词伙

1. competitive advantages 竞争优势
2. intense competition 激烈的竞争
3. satisfy the needs 满足需求
4. serve a niche market 服务小众市场
5. stand out from the crowd 脱颖而出
6. set up a company 创立一个公司
7. run a successful business 经营一个成功的生意
8. running cost 运营成本
9. make profits 赚取利润
10. make ends meet 收支相抵
11. go bankrupt 破产
12. go bust 破产（口语）
13. good value for money 性价比很高
14. cost reduction measures 减少成本的措施
15. business plans 商业计划
16. handle complaints 处理投诉

口语 Part 3 练习题目

Question: What factors can affect a company's development?

大家先看着中文思路自己回答一次，然后使用词伙再回答一次。

结构	思路	词伙
观点 1	产品或者服务要有竞争力	competitive advantages
原因	竞争很激烈	intense competition
结果	你的产品需要满足客户的需要，可能还要找到一个细分市场，才可以脱颖而出	satisfy the needs, serve a niche market, stand out from the crowd
观点 2	需要有一定资金去开公司	set up a company
原因	去支付运营上的开销，直到产品盈利，商业收支平衡	running cost, make profits, make ends meet
结果	否则，公司会倒闭	go bankrupt

大家看一下下面的回答，自己再练习，说到熟练为止。

观点 1：A successful business should focus on its **competitive advantages**.

原因：It is because **competition is intense** in the market.

结果：You should make sure that your products can **satisfy the needs of customers** and possibly **serve a niche market**. Your products can thus **stand out from the crowd**.

观点 2：You also need to **have adequate capital** to **set up a company**.

原因：You should have money to **cover the running cost**, until your products can **make profits** and the whole business can **make ends meet**.

结果：Otherwise, the company can **go bankrupt**.

思考观点的角度 4：Society（社会）

在社会方面，我们要考虑三个角度：

- 社会和家庭生活：人们是否注意社会生活，如朋友的聚会、家庭生活等。
- 社会价值观：我们是不是还尊重社会平等、诚实、无私、节约等社会价值。
- 生活标准和满意度：人们是否快乐，是否对生活满意。

百搭观点 54

通过

A 社交网站　　B 手机和电话

C 视频　　D 飞机旅行

使人们可以保持和朋友、家人以及同事的联系，不管距离多远都可以维持感情。

Telecommunications 相关词伙

1. telecommunications technology 电信技术
2. use a mobile phone 使用移动电话
3. mobile devices 移动设备
4. text messaging 短信
5. instant messaging 即时消息
6. via email 通过电子邮件
7. on the phone 在手机上
8. on the computer 在电脑上
9. fax machines 传真机
10. online services 在线服务
11. the access to Internet services 接入互联网服务
12. travel by air 乘飞机旅行
13. maintain a lifelong relationship 保持终身的关系
14. forge a strong relationship 形成牢固的关系
15. stay in touch with 和……保持联系

口语 Part 3 练习题目

Question: How can people maintain the relationship with friends they have had for a long time?

大家先看着中文思路自己回答一次，然后使用词伙再回答一次。

结构	思路	词伙
观点 1	依靠电信科技	telecommunications technology
原因	人们现在为了工作生活在不同城市	employment opportunities
举例	发信息写 email	text messaging
结果	可以保持联系	stay in touch with
观点 2	坐飞机去看朋友	visit friends
结果	保持友谊	maintain a lifelong relationship

大家看一下下面的回答，自己再练习，说到熟练为止。

观点 1：I think the most effective way to achieve this is to make the most of **telecommunications technology**.

原因：People today live in different cities for **employment opportunities**.

举例：They have little choice but communicate with friends by **text messaging or via email**.

结果：They can **stay in touch with** each other wherever they are, as long as they have mobile phones and have **Internet connections**.

观点 2：Another method is to **visit friends** on holiday, as the cost of travelling by air has become more affordable than ever.

结果：This can also help **maintain a lifelong relationship**.

百搭观点 55

A 做义工

B 社区组织社区活动和比赛

C 邻居交朋友

D 多推广社区的文化活动，如音乐表演

有助于促进人和人的交流，大家能相互帮助，关系也会更加密切，更有社区的感觉。

Community 相关词伙

1. charity work 慈善工作
2. charity groups 慈善团体
3. community cohesion 社区凝聚力
4. give a helping hand 给予帮助
5. needy people 有需要的人
6. experience difficult times 经历困难时期
7. gain support 获得帮助
8. members of community 社区的成员
9. part of community 社区的一分子
10. bring people together 让人们聚在一起
11. a sense of community 社区的感觉
12. musical shows 音乐表演
13. raise funds 筹款

口语 Part 3 练习题目

Question: Do you think everyone should do charity work?

大家先看着中文思路自己回答一次，然后使用词伙再回答一次。

结构	思路	词伙
观点 1	慈善工作有助于增强社区凝聚力	community cohesion
原因	帮助有需要的人	needy people
结果	每个参与的人都觉得自己以后困难的时候会得到别人的帮助，他们有归属感	experience difficult times, gain support, feel part of community
观点 2	慈善工作也会让人凝聚在一起	bring people together
举例	有些慈善团体通过音乐表演筹款，这能促进人与人之间的交流，帮助他们建立牢固的关系	charity groups, musical shows, raise funds, develop a strong relationship

大家看一下下面的回答，自己再练习，说到熟练为止。

观点 1：I think all people should be involved in charity work because it can contribute to **community cohesion**.

原因：Charity work can give **a helping hand** to **needy people**.

结果：Participants will feel that if they **experience difficult times** in the future, they're likely **to gain support from** other **members of community**. They'll feel **part of community**.

观点 2：Charity work can also **bring people together**.

举例：Some **charity groups** have chosen to **raise funds** by **musical shows**. This can **promote communication** between people involved and help them **develop a strong relationship**.

百搭观点 56

A 参加体育运动

B 关注时尚和服饰

C 阅读新闻

D 看体育比赛

E 发展一些兴趣和爱好

F 参加聚会

G 上网聊天和使用社交网站

H 用手机 APP 交友

可以增加和朋友的话题，丰富了社会活动，能认识更多朋友。

Social Activities 相关词伙

1. keep fit 保持身材
2. lead a healthy life 过健康的生活
3. social activity 社会活动
4. gather together 聚一起
5. make new friends 交新的朋友
6. go out for a meal 外出聚餐
7. eat out 外出就餐
8. have a coffee 喝咖啡
9. talking points 话题
10. sports fans 体育迷
11. watch soccer games 看足球比赛
12. live events 直播赛事

口语 Part 3 练习题目

Question: Why do you think some people are so enthusiastic about sport?

大家先看着中文思路自己回答一次，然后使用词伙再回答一次。

结构	思路	词伙
观点 1	我认为人们做运动为了保持身材和过健康的生活。但是运动也是一种社会活动	keep fit, a social activity
举例	例如人们在一起打篮球，踢足球和打板球，他们会交新朋友	play basketball, soccer and cricket, make new friends
结果	比赛之后，他们可能一起外出吃饭或者喝咖啡	go out for a meal, have a coffee
观点 2	另外，这些体育迷可以谈论体育明星。这些都是聊天话题	talking points
举例	他们可能一起看足球比赛和直播赛事	watch soccer games, live events
结果	这些是他们社会生活的一部分	part of their social life

大家看一下下面的回答，自己再练习，说到熟练为止。

观点 1：I suppose that people **play sport** in order to **keep fit** and **lead a healthy life**. But sport can be **a social activity** as well.

举例：For example, people **gather together** to **play basketball, soccer and cricket**. They **make new friends**.

结果：After games, they may **go out for a meal** together or **have a coffee**.

观点 2：In addition to this, **sports fans** can talk about **sports personalities**. These are **talking points**.

举例：They may **watch soccer games** together and some **live events**.

结果：These can be **part of their social life**.

百搭观点 57

扩大朋友圈，可以

A 获得信息

B 获得朋友的建议

C 获得金钱的支持

D 获得工作或者生意的机会

E 和朋友一起消磨时间、解压

Friends 相关词伙

1. circle of friends 朋友圈
2. make good friends 成为好朋友
3. build up a network of contacts 建立关系网
4. form a good relationship 形成良好的关系
5. develop a lifelong friendship 发展一段终生的友谊
6. a lasting friendship 持续的友谊
7. peer pressure 同辈的压力
8. hang out with friends 与朋友出去玩
9. socialise with neighbours 与邻居交往
10. close friends 亲密的朋友
11. gain financial support 获得经济支持
12. business opportunities 商业机会

口语 Part 3 练习题目

Question: Do parents in your country teach their children how to make friends?

大家先看着中文思路自己回答一次，然后使用词伙再回答一次。

结构	思路	词伙
观点 1	中国的父母非常关注孩子和谁做朋友，他们认为朋友圈很重要	circle of friends
原因	中国社会竞争很厉害	highly competitive
结果	父母希望孩子交上好的朋友，甚至从小就发展关系网	make good friends, build up a network of contacts
观点 2	父母也不放心小孩的交友选择，特别是异性	friends of the opposite sex
原因	他们担心同龄人的影响	peer pressure
结果	他们希望小孩和表现好的小孩建立好的关系	form a good relationship

大家看一下下面的回答，自己再练习，说到熟练为止。

观点 1：Yes, parents in China want to **keep an eye on** what friends their children make. They think **the circle of friends** is very important.

原因：I suppose it is because the country is **highly competitive**.

结果：Parents want their children to **make good friends** and even **build up a network of contacts** from a young age.

观点 2：Parents are also not very confident in the choices their children make, especially when their children hang out with **friends of the opposite sex**.

原因：They are worried about **peer pressure**.

结果：They want their children to **form a good relationship** with those **well-behaved children**.

百搭观点 58

人们

A 购买昂贵的家具　　B 购买复杂的电子产品

C 购买名牌衣服　　D 购买昂贵的汽车

E 去海外旅游　　F 甚至学外语

会觉得自己有面子，觉得能在社会上有地位，也就更加开心和满足。

Materialistic World 相关词伙

1. material possessions 物质财产
2. live in a materialistic world 生活在物质的社会
3. up-to-date equipment 时尚的设备
4. hi-tech products 高科技产品
5. purchase the advanced model 买最先进的版本
6. status symbol 身份的象征
7. the middle class 中产阶级
8. buy more than they need 买的东西多过自己需要的
9. in a consumer culture 消费社会
10. improve self-esteem 提升自信
11. find contentment 开心和满足
12. behind the times 过时
13. out of touch with the world 与世隔绝

口语 Part 3 练习题目

Question: Why do some people enjoy buying hi-tech products?

大家先看着中文思路自己回答一次，然后使用词伙再回答一次。

结构	思路	词伙
原因 1	很多人对高科技产品感兴趣，包括最新的产品，因为这些产品可以提高他们的自尊心	hi-tech products, up-to-date equipment improve self-esteem
原因 2	我们生活在一种消费文化里，我们被广告商们劝说买一些我们实际上不需要的东西	a consumer culture
举例	很多消费者倾向于购买最先进的手机	the most advanced model of
结果 1	他们喜欢炫耀这些产品，因为他们想让人觉得他们很时尚	show off, be seen as
结果 2	他们可以通过买这些产品获得满足感	find contentment
对比	如果不买，他们会觉得自己落伍了	behind the times

大家看一下下面的回答，自己再练习，说到熟练为止。

原因 1：I suppose that many people are interested in **hi-tech products**, including **up-to-date equipment** because these products can **improve their self-esteem**.

原因 2：We live in **a consumer culture**, where we are persuaded by advertisers to buy something we don't actually need.

举例：For example, many consumers tend to purchase the **most advanced model** of mobile phones.

结果 1：They would love to **show off** these products because they want to **be seen as** fashionable.

结果 2：They can **find contentment** in buying these products.

对比：Otherwise, they may feel that they are **behind the times**.

思考观点的角度 5：Technology（科技）

科技有好有坏。一方面提高了效率，增加了产量。另外一方面让人变懒、变笨。

因为我们之前很详细地说过了各种科技变化对我们生活的影响，所以这个部分我们不再赘述。

百搭观点 59

A 坐飞机出行　　B 开车上下班

C 坐地铁　　D 使用 APP 叫车

让人们出行更加方便，提高了效率。

Transportation 相关词伙

1. drive cars 开车
2. travel by car 开车旅行
3. travel by air 坐飞机
4. travel by tube 坐地铁
5. private car use 私家车的使用
6. means/modes of travel 旅行方式
7. ways to get around 出行的方式
8. use public transport 使用公共交通工具
9. get to and from work 上下班
10. daily commuters 上班族
11. travel a long distance 走很长的路程
12. suburban commuters 郊区的上班族
13. travel to the central office 去中心办公区

口语 Part 3 练习题目

Question: Why do you think many people have chosen to drive cars, rather than travel by bus?

大家先看着中文思路自己回答一次，然后使用词伙再回答一次。

结构	思路	词伙
观点	开私家车比公共交通更方便、更快	drive private cars, use public transport
举例	郊区上班族不得不长途跋涉去上班，一些居民区没有公交站或其他公共交通方式 如果他们有私家车，就可以节省通勤时间	suburban commuters, travel a long distance commuting time
结果	对上班的人来说很重要	working people

大家看一下下面的回答，自己再练习，说到熟练为止。

观点：I think the primary reason is that **driving private cars** is more convenient and faster than **using public transport**.

举例：For example, **suburban commuters** have to **travel a long distance to work**, and some **residential areas** may not have **bus stations** or any access to public transport. If they have a private car, it can save daily **commuting time**.

结果：This is important for **working people**.

思考观点的角度 6：Law（法律）

在法律方面，雅思主要涉及的话题是社会的法律，还有就是社会规范和社会公德（属于前面第四类话题：文化和价值观里面）。

百搭观点 60

A 贫穷
B 缺乏教育
C 法律不够严厉
D 政府执法不严，警察人手不够
E 人们自私和贪婪
F 对政府政策不满
G 不同文化种族的人有矛盾

导致犯罪行为增加。

Laws 相关词伙

1. commit crimes 违法
2. make fast money 快速赚钱
3. break the law 触犯法律
4. violate laws 违反法律
5. obey laws 遵守法律
6. comply with laws 遵守法律
7. face any punishment 面对惩罚
8. a prison sentence 监禁
9. severe consequences 严重后果
10. youth crime 青少年犯罪
11. juvenile delinquency 青少年犯罪
12. young offenders 年轻的罪犯
13. petty crimes 轻微的犯罪
14. serious crimes 严重的犯罪
15. racial tensions 种族矛盾

口语 Part 3 练习题目

Question: Why do you think some people break the law?

大家先看着中文思路自己回答一次，然后使用词伙再回答一次。

结构	思路	词伙
观点 1	主要原因是很多人缺钱	lack money
解释	他们没有工作，所以他们没有钱来满足基本需求并养家糊口	cover basic needs, raise a family
结果	他们做违法的事来快速赚钱	commit crimes, make fast money
观点 2	另一个原因是他们受教育程度低	poorly educated
举例	他们不明白触犯法律的严重后果	break the law, severe consequences
结果	有时他们违反法律仅仅是因为他们觉得很刺激，并且不知道要面临惩罚，例如监禁	violate laws, face any punishment, a prison sentence

大家看一下下面的回答，自己再练习，说到熟练为止。

观点 1：I think the main reason is that many people **lack money**.

解释：They do not have jobs, so they do not have money to **cover basic needs** and **raise a family**.

结果：They **commit crimes** to **make fast money**.

观点 2：Another reason is that they may be **poorly educated**.

举例：They do not realise the **severe consequences** of **breaking the law**.

结果：Sometimes they **violate laws** simply because they think it is exciting and they don't know they have to **face any punishment** such as **a prison sentence**.

百搭观点 61

A 在公共地方遵守秩序
B 使用礼貌语言
C 在公共场合不抽烟
D 在公共场合遵守手机使用的社会规则
E 开会和赴约要准时
F 遵守穿衣的标准
G 诚实
H 平时尽量不要制造噪声
I 要遵守餐桌礼仪

属于社会规范和标准，体现了人们在意别人、体贴别人。

Social Norms 相关词伙

1. conform to social norms 遵守社会规范
2. follow social rules 遵守社会规则
3. show good manners 有礼貌
4. show respect to others 尊重他人
5. complete work on time 准时完成工作
6. arrive punctually 准时到
7. handle enquiries politely 礼貌地处理咨询
8. late for work 上班迟到
9. good work ethic 好的职业道德
10. build good working relationships 建立好的工作关系
11. a sense of responsibility 责任感

口语 Part 3 练习题目

Question: Is it important to be punctual in the industrialised world?

大家先看着中文思路自己回答一次，然后使用词伙再回答一次。

结构	思路	词伙
立场	是的，现代社会非常欣赏守时	in modern societies
观点 1	准时会影响工作表现	workplace performance
原因	你可以准时完成工作	complete work on time
举例	你可以及时处理顾客的咨询	customers' enquiries
结果	顾客对你的服务更加满意	customer satisfaction
对比	迟到会影响效率	
观点 2	准时有助于建立好的工作关系	build good working relationships
原因	别人会觉得你很敬业，有责任感	a good work ethic，a sense of responsibility
结果	他们会更加愿意和你合作	

大家看一下下面的回答，自己再练习，说到熟练为止。

立场：Yes, punctuality is always appreciated in **modern societies**.

观点 1：It can have a direct impact on your **workplace performance**.

原因：If you **go to work on time** every day, you are very likely to **complete your work on time**.

举例：For instance, you can **handle customers' enquiries** more efficiently.

结果：This can increase the level of **customer satisfaction**.

对比：In contrast, lateness can affect productivity and put you or your company **at a disadvantage**.

观点 2：Punctuality can also help you **build good working relationships**.

原因：Other people will see you as a person who has **a good work ethic**. They believe that you have **a sense of responsibility**.

结果：They are more willing to work with you. This can be important to your **career success**.

思考观点的角度 7：Environment（环境保护）

百搭观点 62

A 政府的宣传
B 提供设施
C 增加环保宣传
D 进行法律制裁
E 投资环保科技
F 补助使用环保科技的个人和公司

有助于提升人们和企业的环保意识。

Environmental Protection 相关词伙

1. go green 环保
2. environmentally friendly 环保的
3. environmental protection 环境保护
4. environmental benefits 环境效益
5. live a sustainable life 过环保的生活
6. environmental impacts 环境的影响
7. launch massive campaigns 开始大规模的宣传活动
8. environmental awareness 环境意识
9. educate the public about 给大众提供……方面的教育
10. impose heavy fines 大额罚款
11. recycle waste 回收垃圾
12. rubbish bins 垃圾箱
13. household waste/rubbish 家庭垃圾
14. energy conservation 节能

口语 Part 3 练习题目

Question: In your country, is recycling considered to be important?

大家先看着中文思路自己回答一次，然后使用词伙再回答一次。

结构	思路	词伙
观点	不，我不这样认为。在中国，回收垃圾还没有受到人们的重视	attached with importance

举例	我们没有很多垃圾桶帮助大家分类垃圾，让人们将可回收的东西放到合适的垃圾桶里	categorise waste, put recyclable items
结果	金属、纸和瓶子不能被有效地循环利用	reused effectively
转折	政府发起大规模的宣传运动，增强市民的环保意识，我们可以做得比现在更好	launch massive campaigns, environmental awareness
原因	我们明白，垃圾能对环境造成危害，我们会更环保	cause damage to the environment, go green

大家看一下下面的回答，自己再练习，说到熟练为止。

观点：No, I don't think so. **Recycling waste** has not yet been **attached with importance** in China.

举例：As you may have noticed, we do not have many rubbish bins to help people to **categorise waste** and **put recyclable items** in the right bins.

结果：As a consequence, metals, paper and bottles cannot be **reused effectively**.

转折：If the government had **launched some massive campaigns** to raise citizens' **environmental awareness**, we could have done much better than now.

原因：We understand that waste can **cause damage to the environment**. We are more likely to **go green**.

百搭观点 63

A 汽车数量的增加

B 各种电器的使用

C 电能的消耗

D 不注意节约和回收

E 将机器用于农业和工业

都会让我们更加依赖化石资源，它们会增加温室气体的排放，污染环境，危害动植物和人的健康。

Car Emissions 相关词伙

1. curb car use 限制汽车的使用
2. car emissions 汽车尾气
3. create exhaust fumes 产生废气
4. dangerous to our health 对我们的健康产生危害
5. cause air pollution 引起空气污染
6. tackle pollution 解决污染问题
7. suffer from poor health 忍受身体不适
8. poor air quality 空气质量差
9. mitigate problems 缓解问题
10. a bad harvest in agriculture 农业收成不好
11. increase the health cost 增加医疗费用
12. global warming 全球变暖
13. climate change 气候变化

口语 Part 3 练习题目

Question: Do you think that governments should control the number of private cars that are on the road?

大家先看着中文思路自己回答一次，然后使用词伙再回答一次。

结构	思路	词伙
观点	是的，很有必要去限制汽车的使用	curb car use
原因 1	因为汽车能产生废气，引起空气污染，这对我们健康是有危险的	create exhaust fumes
结果	城市雾霾会越来越严重，很多人因为糟糕的空气质量忍受着健康问题。如果政府限制私家车的使用，这个问题可以得到缓解	increasingly smoggy, suffer from poor health, poor air quality, be mitigated
原因 2	汽车尾气排放也是全球变暖和气候变化的一个主要原因	car emissions, global warming, climate change, a primary cause
结果	气候变化对经济有负面影响，因为这会导致农业收成不好，也增加了健康成本	have a negative effect on a bad harvest, health cost

大家看一下下面的回答，自己再练习，说到熟练为止。

观点：Yes, I agree that it is necessary to **curb car use**.

原因 1：It is because cars can **create exhaust fumes**, and it’s a primary source of **air pollution**, which is **dangerous to our health**.

结果：cities will become **increasingly smoggy**. Many people today have **suffered from poor health** because of **poor air quality**. This problem can **be mitigated** if the government curbs private car use.

原因 2：**Car emissions** are also **a primary cause** of **global warming and climate change**.

结果：Climate change can **have a negative effect on** the economy because it can lead to **a bad harvest** in agriculture and also **increase the health cost**.

百搭观点 64

A 旅游业发展　　B 城市发展

导致人口增加，带来很多环境后果，包括

A 垃圾增加　　B 自然风景被破坏

C 汽车增加，空气污染和噪声污染

Environmental Problems 相关词伙

1. environmental problems 环境问题
2. environmental issues 环境议题
3. environmental impacts 环境的影响
4. environmental destruction 环境的破坏
5. cause damage to the environment 对环境造成破坏
6. drop litter 扔垃圾
7. awash with rubbish 充满了垃圾
8. clear forest 清理森林
9. destroy wetlands 破坏湿地
10. damage the beautiful landscape 破坏美好的风景

口语 Part 3 练习题目

Question: What are the problems caused by tourism to some communities?

大家先看着中文思路自己回答一次，然后使用词伙再回答一次。

结构	思路	词伙
直接回答	旅游业繁荣带来两个问题	tourism boom
观点 1	环境问题	environmental problems
举例	很多游客意识不到他们对环境的责任，乱扔垃圾	environmental responsibilities, drop litter
结果	旅游景点充斥着垃圾	tourist destinations, awash with rubbish
观点 2	社区建设了更多设施，例如酒店、餐厅、度假村来迎合游客的需求	construct facilities, cater for the needs of travellers
结果	森林被砍伐，风景被破坏	clear forests

大家看一下下面的回答，自己再练习，说到熟练为止。

直接回答：There are two problems which arise from a **tourism boom**.

观点 1：The first issue is that it may cause some **environmental problems**.

举例：Many travellers are not conscious of their **environmental responsibilities**, so they **drop litter**.

结果：Many **tourist destinations** are **awash with rubbish**, which can **harm wildlife and natural flora**.

观点 2：Another problem is that some communities **have constructed more facilities** such as hotels, restaurants, **holiday resorts**, to **cater for the needs of** travellers.

结果：This means that **forest has been cleared** and the beautiful **landscape has been damaged**.

3.5.2 教育类话题讲解

教育类话题主要是从我们中国教育系统比较提倡的德、智、体、美、劳五个角度去讨论。细致来说：

德，包括：道德、品质和行为。道德主要是指能否分辨对错和遵守行为规范，品质指人成功的一些素质，包括勤奋、坚韧不拔等。另外就是学生是否守规矩，懂得礼貌。

智，包括：（1）智力和学习技能的发展；（2）考试和学习成绩；（3）使用知识进行创新。

体，包括：身体发育和身体健康。这一点和非教育类的 health 差不多。

美，包括：审美能力和业余爱好。主要涉及学生非学术能力和活动能力。这一点和政府类题目下面的文化活动差不多，这里就不赘述。

劳，包括：教育是否能够全方面提高学生的能力，包括交流能力和团队工作能力。

另外还要考虑到一个角度：小孩对学习的热情和动力。

思考观点的角度 1：道德、品质和行为

百搭观点 65

学校通过

A 道德课
B 军训
C 阅读
D 实习
E 校外活动
F 树立模范

等来提高学生的品质，包括

A 责任感
B 勤奋好学
C 不放弃

等精神。

Qualities 相关词伙

1. the education system 教育系统
2. the school system 学校系统
3. higher education 高等教育
4. receive a university education 接受大学教育
5. receive training 接受培训
6. moral principles 道德准则
7. a sense of responsibility 责任感
8. instill virtues into 向……灌输美德
9. productive members of society 对社会有贡献的人
10. build character 塑造个人品质
11. develop qualities 培养素质
12. in difficult situations 在恶劣的环境下
13. show determination to win 必胜的决心
14. show perseverance 坚韧不拔

口语 Part 3 练习题目

Question: What are advantages of the education system in your country?

大家先看着中文思路自己回答一次，然后使用词伙再回答一次。

结构	思路	词伙
观点	中国教育体制的一个主要优势是关注学生的素质发展	qualities of students
原因	我们的课程设置包含一些体现道德观和价值观的课程，老师关注于灌输美德给下一代	moral principles and values, focus on, instill virtues into
举例 1	教育学生要努力学习，即使考试成绩没那么好	
举例 2	大学甚至要求学生接受军训来培养人格、发展素质能力	receive training in the military facilities, build character, develop qualities

结果	相信学生可以通过这种方式可以了解在困境中坚持不懈的价值	in difficult situations, the value of perseverance

大家看一下下面的回答，自己再练习，说到熟练为止。

观点：I think one major advantage of **the school system** in China is it pays attention to **the qualities of students**.

解释：Our curriculum **contains some lessons** about **moral principles and values**. Teachers **have focused on instilling virtues into** the next generation,

举例 1：for example, teaching children to study hard, even though they do not **perform well in exams**.

举例 2：Our universities can even require students to **receive training in the military facilities** to **build character** and **develop some positive qualities**.

结果：We believe that students in this way can learn **the value of perseverance in difficult situations**.

百搭观点 66

父母和老师可以通过

A 规则
B 惩罚（如罚站、留堂）
C 减少一些福利（如看电视和打游戏）
D 自身的榜样
E 书上的例子
F 奖励

等方式来影响小孩的是非感和行为，这些方式决定了是否喜欢学习、如何与人相处、生活的习惯等。

Discipline 相关词伙

1. do some activities 做一些活动
2. develop positive habits 培养良好的习惯
3. from an early age 从幼年开始
4. improve literacy 提高文学素养
5. start school 开始上学
6. maintain discipline 维持纪律
7. parenting styles 父母管教的方式
8. behavioural problems 行为问题
9. impose sanctions on 施加惩罚
10. impart a clear code of conduct 传授明确的行为规范
11. act as acceptable members of society 成为社会的好公民
12. good manners 有礼貌
13. grounding and detention 罚站和留堂

口语 Part 3 练习题目

Question: In your country, how do parents teach children different things at home?

大家先看着中文思路自己回答一次，然后使用词伙再回答一次。

结构	思路	词伙
观点 1	一起做一些活动，帮助孩子从小培养好习惯	do some activities, develop some positive habits from an early age

举例	阅读	read books
结果	在小孩上学前，提高小孩的读写能力	improve literacy, children start school
观点 2	管教	maintain discipline
解释	如果小孩有行为问题，父母要惩罚孩子	behavioural problems
结果	这可以很好地向孩子灌输行为规则，告诉孩子如何成为好公民，教他们有礼貌	impart a clear code of conduct, good manners

大家看一下下面的回答，自己再练习，说到熟练为止。

观点 1：Normally, parents can **do some activities** together with their children, and this can help children **develop some positive habits from an early age**.

举例：For example, parents can **read books** for their children such as stories before the bedtime.

结果：This can help **improve literacy** even before **children start school**.

观点 2：**Maintaining discipline** is also important.

解释：If children have **behavioural problems**, parents should possibly impose some sanctions on them.

结果：This can help **impart a clear code of conduct** to children and teach them how to act as acceptable members of society and how to show **good manners**.

我们再看看关于校规的一些词伙。

Rules 相关词伙

1. obey rules 遵守规则
2. comply with rules 遵守规则
3. break/violate rules 破坏规则
4. establish/set rules 建立规则
5. ground rules 基本的规则
6. follow golden rules 遵守黄金准则
7. break school rules 破坏校规
8. violate norms 不遵守社会规范
9. adhere to cultural norms 遵守文化规范
10. show good behaviour 讲礼貌
11. develop positive habits 形成好的习惯
12. company regulations 公司的规定

口语 Part 3 练习题目

Question: Do you think it is important to obey rules?

大家先看着中文思路自己回答一次，然后使用词伙再回答一次。

结构	思路	词伙
观点 1	遵守校规，为成年生活做准备	follow school rules, prepare for adulthood
解释	培养学生好的行为习惯有利于成年后的人生	good behaviour, develop positive habits, come of age
举例	穿校服，以后工作也会习惯穿着正式，还有遵守公司其他的规定	wear uniform, dress formally

观点 2	遵守规则让小孩成为一个好公民，因为他们要遵纪守法	obey rules, an acceptable member of society comply with laws
举例	禁止说坏话 / 说谎	use bad language, forbid cheating
结果	如果没有规则去规范孩子的行为，坏的行为会变成暴力，而小孩成年后会通过欺骗获得钱	regulate behaviour, bad behaviour enter adulthood

大家看一下下面的回答，自己再练习，说到熟练为止。

观点 1：I think if we require children to **follow school rules**, it can **prepare children for adulthood**.

解释：Actually these school rules can help children understand what constitutes **good behaviour**, and also help them **develop positive habits**, which can benefit them when they **come of age**.

举例：For instance, if they are required to **wear uniform** and have got used to that, possibly in the future, when they work for companies, they will also be comfortable with **dressing formally** in the company and also follow other company policies.

观点 2：**Obeying rules** is also a part of the requirement of being an **acceptable member of society** because in society, you have to obey rules and **comply with laws**.

举例：For instance, schools usually forbid children to **use bad language** and **forbid cheating**.

结果：If there is no rule to **regulate children's behaviour**, **bad behaviour** can evolve into violence and frauds when they **enter adulthood**.

百搭观点 67

除了家长和老师之外

A 名人

B 电影和电视里的角色

C 身边的小伙伴

D 邻居和亲戚

E 社区

都会影响小孩的想法和行为，小孩会模仿这些行为，因为他们觉得这些行为是好的或是值得推崇的。

Celebrities 相关词伙

1. the younger generation 年青一代
2. famous sportspeople 著名运动员
3. sports stars 体育明星
4. inspire the next generation 激励下一代
5. develop skills 培养技能
6. develop talents 发展天赋
7. become world famous 变得世界闻名
8. emulate idols 模仿偶像
9. role models 楷模
10. a good influence 积极的影响
11. demonstrate determination 表现出决心
12. encounter difficulties 遇到问题
13. achieve success 获得成功

口语 Part 3 练习题目

Question: Do you think famous people have a strong influence on young people?

大家先看着中文思路自己回答一次，然后使用词伙再回答一次。

结构	思路	词伙
支持的观点	对年轻人有影响	the younger generation
原因	名人的成功经历能激励年轻人	career success
举例	体育明星成功靠努力提高自己	sports stars, apply themselves to develop skills and abilities
结果 1	很多小孩也会模仿偶像，遇到困难的时候展现出决定	emulate idols, encounter difficulties demonstrate determination
结果 2	最后也会成功	achieve success
相反的观点	有些名人可能会追求奢侈的生活方式	lead a lavish life
举例	他们会被药物滥用和其他问题毁了	misuse of drugs
结果	他们给年轻人树立的是错误的榜样	set bad examples

大家看一下下面的回答，自己再练习，说到熟练为止。

支持的观点：Yes, celebrities can be an influence on **the younger generation**.

原因：These famous people's **career success** can **inspire young people**.

举例：For example, many **sports stars** have **applied themselves to develop skills and abilities** until they become **world famous**.

结果 1：Many children may try to **emulate these idols**. They **demonstrate determination** when they **encounter difficulties**.

结果 2：They could **achieve success** themselves.

相反的观点：On the other hand, some celebrities may **lead a lavish life**.

举例：They are destroyed by problems such as the **misuse of drugs** and gambling.

结果：They've basically **set bad examples** for young people.

思考观点的角度 2：智力

百搭观点 68

A 上不同的课程

B 接触不同的文化

C 和不同阶层的人交流

D 通过各种渠道增加知识和见闻

人可以更加有创造能力，体现在

A 可以将不同学科的知识很好地利用起来，找到新的解决方法

B 能从各个角度想问题

Creativity 相关词伙

1. attend courses 上课
2. improve job skills 提高工作能力
3. apply skills to work 将技能用于工作
4. increase productivity 增加产出
5. come up with creative ideas 想出有创意的点子
6. tackle problems creatively 有创造性地解决问题
7. unconventional measures 非常规手段
8. achieve creative potential 发挥创造力
9. use imagination 运用想象力
10. brain development 大脑发育
11. educational toy 益智玩具
12. have a good grasp of advanced technology 很好地掌握先进科技
13. foster innovation 促进创新
14. stifle creativity 扼杀创造力
15. make profits 创造利润

口语 Part 3 练习题目

Question: Do you think it is good for a company to send their employees for further education?

大家先看着中文思路自己回答一次，然后使用词伙再回答一次。

结构	思路	词伙
观点	这对一个公司非常重要	vitally important
解释 1	员工参加这些课程可以提升工作技能，并把这些技能应用到工作中。可以帮助公司提高生产力	attend courses, job skills, apply to, increase productivity
解释 2	受过良好教育的员工更有可能提出有创意的想法，因为他们熟练掌握先进技术，可以用不同学科知识处理问题	come up with, have a good grasp of, tackle problems
举例	他们懂得如何设计手机软件去提升公司的产品和服务	design mobile phone apps
结果	员工可以实现他们的创意潜能，公司也可以获得更多利润	achieve their creative potential, make more profits

大家看一下下面的回答，自己再练习，说到熟练为止。

观点：Yes, I believe that this is **vitally important** for a company.

解释 1：It is because employees who **attend some courses** can **improve job skills** and **apply these skills to their work**. This can help company to **increase productivity**.

解释 2：Another benefit is that well-educated employees are more likely to **come up with some creative ideas** because they **have a good grasp of advanced technology** and they can **tackle problems** with knowledge **from different disciplines**.

举例：For example, they may understand how to **design mobile phone apps** to promote the company's products and services.

结果：Employees can **achieve their creative potential** and companies can **make more profits**.

百搭观点 69

通过

A 阅读书籍，包括电子书
B 看新闻
C 看教育类的电视节目和电影
D 看网络教育视频
E 和朋友、父母、老师交流
F 旅游
G 通过手机看信息

人们可以不断增加知识。

Knowledge 相关词伙

1. read books 读书
2. read articles online 在线阅读文章
3. knowledge-based economy 知识型经济
4. acquire knowledge 获得知识
5. increase knowledge 增长知识
6. a vital source of knowledge 一个重要的知识来源
7. digital books 数字图书
8. broaden horizons 开阔眼界
9. broaden minds 开阔思路
10. keep up to date with what is happening 了解最新发生的事情
11. keep well-informed about 对……保持消息灵通
12. educational programmes 教育类电视节目

口语 Part 3 练习题目

Question: Do Chinese people enjoy reading?

大家先看着中文思路自己回答一次，然后使用词伙再回答一次。

结构	思路	词伙
观点 1	取决于如何定义阅读	
解释	提到读书，人们今天倾向于关注那些有利于自己事业发展的书籍	career advancement
举例	例如读有关电脑技能、软技能以及和职业相关的技能的书籍	computer skills, soft skills, skills related to occupations
对比	在知识型经济下，如果他们不每天获取知识，他们很难生存	knowledge-based economy, acquire knowledge
观点 2	另一方面，很多人也喜欢通过其他方式获得知识，这些也是重要的知识来源	vital sources of knowledge
举例	很多人上网阅读文章	read articles on the Internet

结果	通过网上新闻和电子书籍，他们可以及时了解整个世界的动态	online news, digital books, keep up to date with
拓展	他们希望了解事情	well-informed

大家看一下下面的回答，自己再练习，说到熟练为止。

观点 1：It depends on how you define reading.

解释：When it comes to reading books, people in my country today tend to focus on books which can benefit their **career advancement**.

举例：They may read books about **computer skills**, **soft skills** and also **skills related to their occupations**.

对比：China has been interested in developing **a knowledge-based economy**, so many people know they cannot survive if they did not **acquire knowledge** every day.

观点 2：On the other hand, of course, people also **gain knowledge** in other ways, there are many other **vital sources of knowledge**.

举例：For example, they read **articles on the Internet**.

结果：By reading **online news** and **digital books**, they can **keep up to date with** what is happening throughout the world.

拓展：They are keen to become **well-informed** about everything.

思考观点的角度 3：各方面的能力

百搭观点 70

A 玩游戏

B 参加团队活动和团体运动项目

C 和邻居交往

D 参加社区活动

E 参加俱乐部和兴趣小组的活动

需要小孩和别人交流，倾听别人，从而提高交流能力。

Skills 相关词伙

1. educational games 教育游戏
2. outdoor games 户外运动
3. set rules 设定规则
4. express ideas 表达观点
5. good listening skills 良好的倾听技巧
6. improve soft skills 改善软技能
7. communication skills 交流能力
8. interpersonal skills 人际技能
9. leadership skills 领导能力
10. physical skills 运动技能
11. life skills 生活技能
12. basic skills 基本技能
13. young players 年轻球员

口语 Part 3 练习题目

Question: Should children only play games that teach them something?

大家先看着中文思路自己回答一次，然后使用词伙再回答一次。

结构	思路	词伙
观点	其他游戏也能帮助孩子，而不只是教育类游戏	educational games
举例 1	室外活动教孩子怎么交流，小孩从小就知道沟通的重要性	outdoor games
结果 1	小孩可以讨论如何设计规则，如何表达自己的看法，如何倾听别人	set rules, express ideas, show good listening skills
结果 2	提高交流能力	improve communication skills
举例 2	有些电脑游戏可以帮助小孩提高领导能力，因为小孩需要懂得怎么去领导一个队伍	leadership skills, lead a team

大家看一下下面的回答，自己再练习，说到熟练为止。

观点：I believe that other games can also be helpful, and children should not play **educational games** only.

举例 1：For example, some **outdoor games** may give children opportunities to communicate with others and children will understand how important communication can **be from a young age**.

结果 1：In these games, they will talk about how to **set rules**. They will also have to **express their ideas**. And sometimes they need to **show good listening skills**.

结果 2：This can **improve communication skills**.

举例 2：Some video games can help young players to **develop leadership skills** because they need to learn how to **lead a team** to **win a game**.

百搭观点 71

A 团队运动项目

B 合作学习

C 义工

D 参加乐队和合唱团

E 玩一些团队游戏

可以提高小孩的团队合作能力。

Teamwork 相关词伙

1. work collaboratively 一起工作
2. work closely with 和……密切合作
3. work as a team 一个团队一起工作
4. team projects 团队项目
5. team assignments 团队作业
6. team sport 团队运动
7. raising money for charity 为慈善机构筹款
8. collaborative teamwork 团队合作
9. save/shorten time 节省时间
10. divide the effort 分担任务
11. complete a project 完成项目
12. embark on another team project 开始一个团队项目
13. uncover benefits 发现（别人的）贡献
14. make decisions as a group 团队一起做决定

口语 Part 3 练习题目

Question: Do you think schools should promote group activities?

大家先看着中文思路自己回答一次，然后使用词伙再回答一次。

结构	思路	词伙
观点 1	孩子可以从团体活动中获益	group activities
解释	他们可以知道如何和其他人合作去实现共同的目标	work collaboratively with others, achieve shared targets
举例	他们可以和同龄人一起密切工作去为慈善筹钱	work closely together with their peers, raise money for charity
结果	他们可以明白团队合作不仅节省时间，还比独自工作效率更高	collaborative teamwork, save time
观点 2	他们会学会尊重他人	
举例	当进行团队运动时，孩子们可以发现其他人的优点	
结果	所以无论何时当他们从事一个团队项目，他们将试着欣赏每个参与者的努力	embark on a team project, appreciate the effort of every participant
拓展	他们会学会作为一个整体去做决定，而不是将自己的观点强加给他人	impose their opinions on others

大家看一下下面的回答，自己再练习，说到熟练为止。

观点 1：Yes, I strongly believe that children can benefit from **group activities**.

解释：First of all, they can learn how to **work collaboratively with others** to **achieve shared targets**.

举例：For example, they may **work closely together with their peers** to **raise money for charity**.

结果：They can see how **collaborative teamwork** can **save time** and achieve more than they can do when they work alone.

观点 2：Secondly, they will learn to respect others.

举例：For example, when **playing team sports**, children can uncover strengths and talents of other members.

结果：So whenever they **embark on a team project**, they would try to **appreciate the effort of every participant**.

拓展：They will learn to **make decisions as a group**, rather than **impose their opinions on others**.

百搭观点 72

读大学能够提高年轻人的

A 领导能力	B 组织能力(包括管理实践和资源的能力)
C 解决问题的能力	D 找信息的能力
E 写作能力	F 使用电脑的能力
G 思辨能力和分析能力	H 实际工作能力的能力
I 团队能力和交流能力，包括演讲能力	J 控制情绪的能力

有时候，作文会考查“人成功的因素”的文章，也可以用这个百搭观点。

Academic Skills 相关词伙

1. research skills 研究能力	2. academic skills 学术能力
3. analytical skills 分析能力	4. problem-solving skills 解决问题的能力
5. search the web for information 上网找资料	6. gather information 收集信息
7. do research 做调查	8. critical thinking skills 思辨能力
9. leadership skills 领导能力	10. computer literacy 电脑能力
11. leadership qualities 领导的素质	12. practical skills 实际工作的能力
13. organisational skills 组织能力	14. sharpen skills/add to the skill set 丰富技能

口语 Part 3 练习题目

Question: Are you good at solving problems?

大家先看着中文思路自己回答一次，然后使用词伙再回答一次。

结构	思路	词伙
直接回答	取决于碰到什么问题	encounter problems
观点 1	如果是上网找资料，对我来说很简单	searching the web
原因	网上有很多强大的搜索引擎，我可以通过网络搜索信息	search engines
观点 2	另一方面，我可能不能够解决一些实际问题，例如如何组织一场大型会议	practical problems
原因	因为我没有很多实际经验	practical experience
对比（虚拟语气）	如果我在大公司工作很多年，我可能会拥有组织能力，能够更容易地处理那些问题	organisational skills

大家看一下下面的回答，自己再练习，说到熟练为止。

直接回答：Well, it depends on **what problems I will encounter**.

观点 1：If you are talking about **searching the web for information**, it is quite easy for me.

原因：There are many powerful **search engines** online. I can **gather information** by **doing research** online.

观点 2：On the other hand, I might not be able to **handle some practical problems**, such as how to organize a large meeting.

原因：It is because I do not have much **practical experience**.

对比：（虚拟语气）If I had worked for a large company for many years, I could have developed **organisational skills** and dealt with these problems more easily.

雅思作文相关真题

Some people think that the interview is an unreliable way for a company to recruit new staff, and there are better selection methods. To what extent do you agree or disagree?（考试日期：20151203）

思考观点的角度 4：学习兴趣

百搭观点 73

A 就业前景

B 专业是否符合自己的天赋

C 课程是否能提升实际能力

D 老师上课的方式是否有趣

E 老师是否注意和学生的互动

决定了某些学生对专业、学业的兴趣。

Talent 相关词伙

1. specialise in a subject 专注于一个学科
2. study a subject 学习一门学科
3. career prospects 职业前景
4. well-paid jobs 待遇优厚的工作
5. career opportunities 工作机会
6. develop a talent 发展特长
7. bright students 聪明的学生
8. academically gifted 学习上有天赋
9. a natural talent in 在……方面天生的才能
10. mathematical talents 数学才能
11. do calculations 做计算
12. build expertise 建立专业知识
13. put...in an advantageous position 把……放在有利位置
14. a tedious job 一个乏味的工作

口语 Part 3 练习题目

Question: Do you like your major? Why?

大家先看着中文思路自己回答一次，然后使用词伙再回答一次。

结构	思路	词伙
直接回答	是的，学习经济学感觉很好。这是我想专攻的学科	specialise in
观点 1	中国拥有强大的经济，我相信如果学习经济学，我会有一个好的就业前景	a good career prospect

结果	我想在银行或金融机构工作，这些地方提供很多高薪的职位	financial institutions, well-paid jobs
观点 2	另一个原因是我认为我在数学方面有天赋	natural talent in
原因	学习经济学需要我每天做大量的计算	calculation
结果	帮助我提升专业才能，让我处于有利的位置	build expertise, put me in an advantageous position
对比	很多人觉得这是一份无趣的工作，但是我喜欢	tedious job

大家看一下下面的回答，自己再练习，说到熟练为止。

直接回答：Yes, it is a great feeling to study economics. This is a subject I want to **specialise in**.

观点 1：China has a strong economy and I believe that I have **a good career prospect** if I study economics.

结果：I want to work in banks or **financial institutions**, because these places offer many **well-paid jobs**.

观点 2：Another reason is that I think I have a **natural talent in** mathematics.

原因：Studying economics requires me to **do a lot of calculation** every day.

结果：This can help me **build expertise** very easily and **put me in an advantageous position**.

对比：It is a **tedious job** for many, but I enjoy doing it.

百搭观点 74

A 老师有针对性的指导

B 小班教学

C 父母在作业上提供帮助

D 有好的同学做榜样

E 从学龄前提高学习能力

F 在取得进步后给予学生一定奖励

都有助于增加学生的信心，克服困难，获得好成绩。

Motivated Students 相关词伙

1. traditional classroom 传统的教室
2. study independently 独立学习
3. provide instruction 提供指导
4. on a one-on-one basis 在一对一的基础上
5. build confidence 建立信心
6. maintain enthusiasm for studies 保持对学习的热情
7. develop a serious interest in 培养强烈的兴趣
8. keep students interested 保持学生的兴趣
9. stay self-motivated 保持热情
10. a negative attitude towards schooling 对于学业的负面态度
11. lack self-discipline 缺乏自制力
12. get distracted 分心

口语 Part 3 练习题目

Question: Do you think teachers will be replaced by technology in the future?

大家先看着中文思路自己回答一次，然后使用词伙再回答一次。

结构	思路	词伙
观点 1	我觉得传统的教学不会消失	traditional classroom
原因	很多学生缺乏自学能力	study independently
结果	需要老师的一对一辅导，这样他们才有信心和兴趣	provide instruction on a one-to-one basis build confidence, maintain enthusiasm for studies
观点 2	这些学生缺乏自制力	lack self-discipline
结果	需要老师的指导	direction from teachers
对比	否则，他们很容易分散注意力	get distracted

大家看一下下面的回答，自己再练习，说到熟练为止。

观点 1：I don't think the **traditional classroom** will disappear in the future.

原因：Many students don't have the skills to **study independently**.

结果：That's why teachers sometimes have to **provide instruction on a one-to-one basis**.This can help students **build confidence** and **maintain enthusiasm for studies**.

观点 2：Many students also **lack self-discipline**, especially those at primary or middle school.

结果：They need **direction from teachers**, and teachers sometimes have to punish **unruly children**.

对比：Otherwise, they can **get distracted**.

百搭观点 75

A 只关注考试，而且作业太多

B 死记硬背

C 缺乏课外活动

D 只关注理论知识，不注重实践

E 选课不符合自己的天赋

都会导致学生失去兴趣，没有学习的动力。

Exams 相关词伙

1. devote time 付出时间
2. prepare for exams 准备考试
3. revise for exams 复习备考
4. exam factories 考试工厂（只是关注考试的地方）
5. exam grades/exam results 考试成绩
6. workload increases 工作量增加
7. do homework 做家庭作业
8. learn facts by heart 背东西
9. rote learning 死记硬背
10. find enjoyment 发现乐趣
11. extra-curricular activities 课外活动
12. pursue a hobby 追求一种爱好
13. combine work with pleasure 劳逸结合

口语 Part 3 练习题目

Question: Do children in China enjoy their childhoods?

大家先看着中文思路自己回答一次，然后使用词伙再回答一次。

结构	思路	词伙
观点 1	不，现在很多中国的孩子不得不花大量时间去准备考试	prepare for exams
原因	学校已经变成考试工厂，学习任务增加	exam factories
结果	很多孩子不得不每天花费数小时做家庭作业，然后通过死记硬背学知识	learning many things by heart
拓展	他们不能在学校生活中找到乐趣	find enjoyment in school lives
观点 2	另一个问题是他们没有足够的时间去进行课外活动	extra-curricular activities
举例	他们很难去追求自己的爱好，例如打篮球和学音乐	pursue a hobby
结果	不能劳逸结合	combine work with pleasure

大家看一下下面的回答，自己再练习，说到熟练为止。

观点 1：No, many children in China today have to devote their time to **preparing for exams**.

原因：Schools have become **exam factories**, and the **workload has increased**.

结果：Many children have to spend hours **doing homework** every day and **learning many things by heart**.

拓展：They cannot **find enjoyment in school lives**.

观点 2：Another problem is that they don’t have much time for **extra-curricular activities**.

举例：It’s difficult for them to **pursue a hobby**, such as playing basketball and learning music.

结果：They cannot **combine work with pleasure**.

3.6 词伙在作文的应用

我们之前说过，雅思大作文的主体段和口语 Part 3 的回答有很多类似之处，都要注意扣题、拓展、连接等。当然，也有一些不同之处：

不同 1：作文非常正式，不能用缩写，如 I’m, there’s, they’re 等。

不同 2：作文对语法要求很高，语法越准确分越高，而口语的语法相对来说，重要性低一点。

不同 3：作文的每个观点拓展更应该具体一点（毕竟有充足的时间考虑），而口语如果一个观点拓展不多，可以再说 1~2 个观点，关键是源源不断地说。

因为大作文在《顾家北手把手教你雅思写作》一书中已经有非常详细的介绍，我们这里就举几个例子说说百搭观点的使用。

例 1：雅思 Task 2 作文的题目

Advertising encourages consumers to buy in quantity rather than promoting quality. To what extent do you agree or disagree?

题目大意： 广告鼓励消费者买东西时重量不重质。你是否同意？

百搭观点

人们

A 购买昂贵的家具

B 购买复杂的电子产品

C 购买名牌衣服

D 购买昂贵的汽车

E 去海外旅游

F 甚至学外语

觉得自己有面子，在社会上有地位，更加开心和满足。

主体段的思路、词伙和段落

结构	思路	段落
观点	广告让人们觉得一些产品很流行	Advertisements sometimes suggest that some products are in fashion and also in great demand, so many fashion-conscious consumers rush to buy these products in large quantities.
结果	人们觉得买这些产品会有面子，会有满足感	They experience happiness from these buying habits, believing that these products show their status.
举例	他们买新的手机	For example, they tend to purchase a new generation of mobile phones and take pleasure from the ownership of these up-to-date devices, whether or not these products are functional.
对比	否则，他们会觉得自己落伍了	Otherwise, they may feel that they are behind the times.

例 2：雅思 Task 2 作文的题目

It is said that work is the most important thing of people's life. Without the success of career, life will become meaningless. To what extent do you agree or disagree with the opinion?

题目大意： 人们说工作是人生命重要的事。没有职业的成功，人生会失去意义。你是否同意这个看法。

百搭观点

人们

A 赚大量的钱变得富裕

B 事业上功成名就

C 捐钱让社会其他人更加开心

D 陪伴家人，或者享受家人的陪伴

E 自己生活得很自由和独立

F 享受朋友、邻居和同事的陪伴

G 大手大脚花钱购物

H 存钱为退休时过稳定的生活做准备

I 注意减少压力，保持健康

都会感到快乐。

主体段的思路、词伙和段落

结构	思路	段落
观点	有了令人满意的事业，生活会更开心	A fulfilling career has a profound impact on the living standards of people, and for this reason, the importance of work can hardly be exaggerated.
原因	人们可以购买很多商品	With steady income, people can cover basic needs and even afford other expenses that can contribute to a decent quality of life.
举例	他们可以买得起房子，给孩子提供好的环境	For example, they can buy their own homes and provide their children with a comfortable home environment.
对比	没有工作的人生活很拮据	In contrast, those who do not achieve success in working lives may live on a tight budget and suffer ill-health because of poverty.

例 3：雅思 Task 2 作文的题目

In many cities, planners tend to arrange shops, schools, offices, and homes in specific areas and separate them from each other. Do you think the advantages of this policy outweigh the disadvantages?

题目大意 在很多城市，城市规划者将商店、学校、办公室和住宅安排在特定的地方，相互分开。你觉得这个政策的好处是否多过坏处？

百搭观点

A 政府提供房屋补助

B 政府提供福利房

C 拆旧房建新房

D 鼓励人们移居小城镇或者郊区

E 建高楼

F 减少公园和公共场所多建房子

解决城市的住房问题。

主体段的思路、词伙和段落

结构	思路	段落
立场	功能区减少生活成本	Zoning can benefit many city dwellers because the cost of living can be lower.
原因	城市拥挤，中心地带房价飙升	Cities are overcrowded because a large number of people flock to these economically advanced areas for job opportunities, and for this reason, the housing price of the central area soars.
结果 1	在城市的外围建造学校和住宅可以缓解这个问题	This situation can be improved if new schools and apartment blocks are built in some specific areas outside of the city centre.
结果 2	环境更好，价格更低	The cost of home ownership in these less populated areas is lower, and they can also enjoy improved living conditions.

例 4：雅思 Task 2 作文的题目

Money should be spent on creating new public buildings such as museums or conference halls rather than repairing existing ones. To what extent do you agree or disagree?

题目大意： 钱应该用于建设新的公共建筑（如博物馆和会议厅），而不是用来修现有的建筑。你是否同意？

百搭观点

全球化会影响全球的文化，包括

A 音乐　　B 电影

C 建筑　　D 食品

E 衣服　　F 价值观

G 语言

这些可能会慢慢变得单一，影响文化多样性，影响人们的文化认同感，世界会变得乏味，我们的思想也越来越单一，对文化、历史、传统的理解更浅薄。

主体段的思路、词伙和段落

结构	思路	段落
中心句	老建筑一般都有文化价值，老建筑能让大家了解到城市的历史和文化	Old buildings are normally of cultural significance and can tell people a lot about the history and culture of cities.

解释	有些建筑见证了城市的重大事件	Some of these buildings have witnessed some landmark events of a city.
结果	人们会知道过去的事件是如何影响城市的文化、传统和特点的	Those who visit these buildings can understand the impact of past events on the culture, traditions and character of this city.
举例	有殖民风格的建筑能体现出人们注意殖民时期外国侵略者的文化对当地人生活的影响	Colonial architecture in some cities may show how foreign invaders' culture influenced the local community during the era of colonialism.
对比	这些建筑如果被拆了，后人就没那么容易记住历史，这也削弱了他们的历史认同感	If these buildings were demolished and replaced by new ones, future generations would be less likely to remember history and this could erode the sense of identity.

3.7 如何加强词伙的记忆和增加有用的词汇？

很多同学的 active vocabulary（主动词汇，或叫可用词汇）远远比 passive vocabulary 少。也有很多同学平时学范文，单词都懂，但是自己一写作、一交流，就记不起来用，这都是 active vocabulary 缺乏的表现。

他们每天都看 *Economist*，BBC，语言考试的阅读分数很高，但是到了写作和口语的时候，来来回回都是老掉牙、比较中式的几个表达。

主要的原因是这么一些：

原因 *1*：他们听和读的资料太多太杂，和口语写作联系不大。

原因 *2*：听和读的材料没有很好地利用起来，他们只是泛泛地学习，而不是有针对性地学习，关注可以用的单词和词伙。

那么如何提升自己的 active vocabulary？进行下面 4 步就可以：

步骤 *1*：阅读相关的材料；

步骤 *2*：用“地道的中文”翻译主要观点；

步骤 *3*：按照中文记录匹配的词伙；

步骤 *4*：使用词伙自己重新写一次。

3.7.1 阅读相关的材料

如果你真想有效提高自己的 active vocabulary, 你不能随便阅读材料。如“奥巴马的厕所”“特朗普的情妇”等，这些材料有趣，但是和生活工作的交流联系不大。

在选择阅读材料的时候，你可以选定某个和写作或者口语常见话题的特定话题。如你今天写的一篇雅思作文是关于 Antarctica 游客增加的影响，那么就阅读一下相关的文章。

我们看一下下面这篇 BBC 的文章，Antarctica 的游客人数增加的原因。

The reasons for the increase in tourist numbers include:

Tourism is a growing industry.

Media has made people more aware of extreme environments.

There are more flexible patterns of work.

Air travel is more economically viable, and can be booked more conveniently over the Internet.

There has been a trend towards ecotourism or adventure tourism.

People have more disposable income.

3.7.2 用“地道的中文”翻译主要观点

我相信大部分同学看懂这几个句子都不会有什么困难，而且能很快看完，但是可能这些句子里的一些表达，以后永远不会用。

因为大家不知道这些表达事实上是自己经常有可能用的。

更深层的原因是不管中翻译英，还是英翻译中，大部分同学都喜欢字字翻译。

the increase in tourist numbers 游客数量的增加

a growing industry 一个正在成长的行业

flexible patterns of work 灵活的工作模式

economically viable 经济上可行的

a trend towards adventure tourism 探险旅游的趋势

disposable income 可支配收入

如果这么翻译，你以后很难想起来用，因为你的中文表达里很少会说到这些表达，你也就很难将目前阅读的材料和自己的作文联系一起。

3.7.3 按照中文记录匹配的词伙

下面我用“地道的中文”来翻译上面的那些表达，我会尽可能思考这些英文怎么翻译成我们中文经常说的一些表达：

the increase in tourist numbers 游客数量的增加

a growing industry 一个不断发展的行业

flexible patterns of work 灵活的工作模式

economically viable 便宜

a trend towards adventure tourism 喜欢探险的人越来越多

disposable income 有钱，有更多闲钱

大家有没有觉得很多表达非常接地气?

在考口语的时候，如果介绍家乡游客很多，我们可以说 There has been an increase in tourist numbers.

如果介绍自己现在读的专业很有前景，我们可以说 I have chosen this subject because it's a growing industry.

如果别人问电脑对我们的影响是什么，我们可以说 Computers have made our lives easier. We can enjoy flexible patterns of work with the advent of the computer.

如果别人问为什么很多人不买电力车，我们可以回答 Because for most people, buying an electric car is not economically viable.

这样的例子很多。大家有没有发现，只有将有用的词伙摘录出来，然后将英文词伙和我们常用的中文表达联系起来，最后不断使用，才很容易掌握!

3.7.4 使用词伙自己重新写一次

现在，自己想几句中文，将上面的表达迅速地串起来写成一个作文的段落，从而加深记忆。

中文：旅游行业不断发展，游客数量越来越多，包括去 Antarctica 的人，原因 1，人们现在有钱了，机票也便宜了。原因 2，他们工作灵活，有时间。原因 3，他们喜欢冒险。

英文：Tourism is a growing industry, and tourist numbers have increased considerably, including those visiting Antarctica. They have more disposable income now, while air travel is more economically viable. In addition, they have more free time to travel because of flexible patterns of work. Furthermore, they are becoming adventurous, and there has been a trend towards adventure tourism.

最后，找机会不断使用这些表达，这些表达就会变成自己的 active vocabulary。

最后的最后，有些同学会问怎么去寻找相关的文章？

方法 1：上谷歌，输入关键词和你喜欢的杂志，如 *Economist*, BBC, *Times* 寻找。

方法 2：阅读一些比较靠谱的作文书。像我在写书的时候，也借鉴了很多 BBC 的文章中的词伙。这些表达不仅地道，也是比较常用和高频的。先从这些词伙积累起来，比较省力省时。

第 4 章

词伙在 G 类信件中的应用

在普通类 (General Training) 中，作文的第一部分是写信，如你要去参加一个课程、你要去辞退工作等，往往需要考生想一个场景或者故事，去解释上什么课程、为什么辞掉工作等。很多考生遇到的问题就是不能在考场上那么短的时间内想到很好的故事，或者想到故事后不知道用什么单词表达。

在这个方面，G 类信件和口语 Part 2 非常类似，涉及“编故事”。使用词伙逆袭法可以帮助大家解决这个问题。我们可以围绕一些词伙去想故事，这样不仅故事想得快，而且想出来也可以很好地用词伙表达。

关于书信写作的整个流程，注意事项，常用的句子和表达，我们都在《顾家北手把手教你雅思写作》一书上有清晰的指引，这里就不重复。

我们主要关注怎么思考回答每个书信的三个小问题。

我翻阅了过去 5 年的书信，按照常考话题分成了五类，分别是：(1) 媒体；(2) 工作；(3) 地点；(4) 服务和商品；(5) 庆祝仪式和社会活动。

4.1 第一类题目：媒体

和口语 Part 2 的媒体类题目一样，书信经常会考参加的课程、阅读的报刊、要出席的会议、要做的演讲、电视节目等。

正如之前我在口语 Part 2 的媒体类话题所说的一样，媒体类的题目是最容易用词伙逆袭法的，只要是熟悉的话题，稍微改变，都可以套上去。

以下题为例，关于参加一个培训课程：

Write a letter to your manager because you will take a three-day training course, and in the letter, you

- ***suggest when the course begins***
- ***describe what you can learn***
- ***tell the manager who will take over your work.***

关于课程，你可以套用很多话题的词伙，包括：

如果你熟悉政府关于艺术投资的话题，那么你可以说参加一个艺术课程。

如果你熟悉科技类手机或者网络的话题，那么你可以说参加电子商务的课程。

如果你熟悉城市化的题目，你可以说参加绿化的课程。

如果你熟悉文化和价值观的题目，你可以说参加礼仪的课程。

如果你熟悉工作类的题目，你可以说参加工作培训课程等。

下面的表格是我回答三个小问题的思路和相关词伙。

三个小问题	中文思路	词伙
Suggest when the course begins	课程在一所语言学校举行 我请三天假，应该不会严重影响公司运行	language school take three days off the operation of our department
Describe what you can learn	课程给我提供了学西班牙语的机会 让我对西班牙人风俗、习惯和信仰有更深的了解 我们公司准备在西班牙建办事处 我感觉有必要掌握这门外语	pick up a language deepen my understanding of run an office master this language
Tell the manager who will take over your work	Anderson 可以接管在我离开期间我的工作 我们一起工作很多年了，他很清楚我的工作任务和责任	take over on leave tasks and responsibilities

下面是范文。

Dear John,

I am writing this letter to apply for three days' leave, during which time I hope I can attend a class about Spanish.

The course will be available in a local **language school** next month. It will coincide with a relatively short **working week** of our company, so I am sure that if I take **three days off**, it would not affect **the operation of our department** seriously.

This course provides me with opportunities to **pick up** Spanish and, more importantly, **deepen my understanding of** customs, traditions and beliefs of Spanish people. As our company is about to **run an office** in Spain, I feel the need to **master this language**.

I believe that Anderson can **take over** when I am **on leave**. He has been working with me for a couple of years and familiar with all my **tasks and responsibilities**.

I would be grateful if you approve my plan, because I have to **enroll in this course** as soon as possible.

Yours sincerely,

Adam

不难看到，我用了雅思大作文常考的全球化话题中关于“学习外语”的一些词伙，这封信件就很轻松写出来了。

这是口语逆袭法的另外一个应用。

4.2 第二类题目：工作

书信经常涉及工作会议、工作相关课程、申请工作、出差、公司介绍等话题，考生往往可以用自己大学专业或者职业来写（因为熟悉相关词汇），这样书信就很容易写完。

考生平时备考的过程中可以阅读一些外文书籍或者网络上找到的关于自己专业的一些文章，积累一些相关的词伙，然后遇到工作相关的题目就可以使用了。

例如，如果你是做会计工作的，你可以在谷歌上找一些关于会计的 cover letter，找出相关的词伙。

Cover Letter 的相关词伙

1. a master's degree in accounting 会计硕士
2. accounting competencies 会计能力
3. manage financial records 处理财务记录
4. manage budgets 处理预算问题
5. in the accounting field 在会计领域
6. accounting programmes 会计软件
7. an extensive accounting background 深厚的会计背景
8. accounting principles 会计准则
9. the accountant position 会计职位
10. in the accounting profession 会计专业
11. bottom line 盈亏底线

然后我们可以看看以前的 G 类信件，

我们看看下面这个题目：

A new international hotel has posted various job vacancies. In the letter to the hotel, you suggest

- ***what position you want to apply***
- ***why it interests you***
- ***what qualification and experience you have.***

这是关于求职的。我们可以使用很多会计相关的词伙来完成这封求职信，虽然我们本身不一定是读会计的。

下面的表格是我回答三个小问题的思路和相关词伙。

三个小问题	中文思路	词伙
What position you want to apply	应聘会计职位 看职位介绍以后，我觉得能胜任，因为有 8 年的相关工作经验，还有好的时间管理能力和团队协作能力	accountant position reviewing the job description in the accounting field time management skills ability to work as a good team player

Why it interests you	这个职位是为对管理账目和预算、还有对税务有深入了解的人准备的 只有能够很好运用会计软件的人才能胜任	manage financial records taxation-related issues accounting programmes accounting processes
What qualification and experience you have	我有很多的经验，我曾在一个国企工作 我有会计相关学位也有会计证	extensive accounting background an accredited holder the accounting profession

下面是范文。

Dear Sir or Madam,

I am writing to express my interest in the **accountant position** that is advertised on *New Zealand Herald*. After **reviewing the job description**, I strongly believe that I am a well-qualified candidate for the job since I have more than eight years of experience **in the accounting field**, strong **time management skills** and **ability to work as a good team player**.

I understand that the position is open to those who have an in-depth knowledge of how to **manage financial records**, **manage budgets** and deal with **taxation-related issues**. Apart from this, only those who familiar with up-to-date **accounting programmes** can thrive in this position and design highly productive **accounting processes** for the hotel.

With my **extensive accounting background**, primarily in state-owned enterprises, I have been seeking challenges in the private sector, especially a well-established company whose accountants have to deal with enormous amounts of accounting work on a daily basis. I am willing to see my **accounting competencies** contribute significantly to the **bottom line** of the company.

I am **an accredited holder** of **a Master's degree in Accounting** and also obtained several well-recognised certificates of **the accounting profession**. I would welcome the opportunity to meet with you to discuss my qualifications, and learn more about the hotel and the vacancy.

Yours faithfully,

Jennifer Liang

在雅思书信中，还有一些题目是关于你不能出席一些会议、不能去看球赛和音乐会、不能参加一个派对或者是家庭的聚会、不能去旅游等，遇到这些题目，也可以用和工作相关的词伙编故事。

例如，一个做会计的人可以说自己要准备会计表格，要分析财务数据，工作很忙，所以无法去旅游。

4.3 第三类题目：地点

书信写作经常涉及地点一类的话题，这个和口语 Part 2 也很类似。只是书信写作关于地点的描述更为单一，主要是两类：(1) 搬家；(2) 旅游。

前者主要是和城市化题目有联系，涉及城市生活的便捷度和生活质量问题，主要考虑因素就是(1) 交通；(2) 学校；(3) 购物和其他设施；(4) 社区是否安全；(5) 空气质量；(6) 绿化和公园；(7) 房价和租金；(8) 房子是否宽敞和装修是否好等。

旅游主要是涉及对不同地方的描述，包括 (1) 古建筑；(2) 景点；(3) 博物馆；(4) 艺术馆；(5) 公园；(6) 海滩；(7) 森林；(8) 购物中心；(9) 标志建筑物；(10) 饭店和美食；(11) 演唱会和一些文化活动等。

这些话题的很多词伙之前在复习口语 Part 3 的时候出现过，这里我们找个题目练习就好。

下面这个题目是关于朋友来你的家乡旅游，那么你就可以在上述的那些地方选几个，然后在信件中出现，就好了。

You want your friend to visit your hometown. In your letter to your friend, you

- ***explain why you want your friend to stop by***
- ***recommend the places you want your friend to visit***
- ***give advice about how your friend prepares for the trip***

下面的表格是我回答三个小问题的思路和相关词伙。

三个小问题	中文思路	词伙
Explain why you want your friend to stop by	我听说您马上要来广州参加一个国际会议 谢谢您去年我和妻子去新西兰度假时的热情招待	an international conference took a vacation
Recommend the places you want your friend to visit	我的家乡有很多保护很好的世纪建筑 我知道您对中国南方的建筑风格很感兴趣，您将会大开眼界 我们会在当地一些传统的粤菜馆吃饭	century-old heritage buildings architectural heritage feast for your eyes Cantonese food
Give advice about how your friend prepares for the trip	告诉我您什么时间方便过来，我会查一下城际列车的时间，然后给您买票 您也可以带上泳衣，我们可以去海里游泳	make the trip check the timetable take a dip

下面是范文。

Dear John,

Mary told my wife that you're about to attend **an international conference** in Guangzhou, and I wonder whether you can make time to visit my city. Thanks for your hospitality in the last year when my wife and I **took a vacation** in New York, and it's our turn to organise an **unforgettable trip** for you!

My hometown has been known for many well-preserved, **century-old heritage buildings**. I know you have been fascinated by **architectural heritage** of Southern China, and these buildings will be a **feast for your eyes**. Apart from this, we can also have meals in local restaurants which specialise in cooking **traditional Cantonese food**, and this is something a gourmet like you wouldn't miss.

If you give me the go-ahead, I'd like you to tell me when you are available to **make the trip**. I can **check the timetable** of the intercity bus for you, so I can buy the ticket online. You may also bring swimsuits, if you want to **take a dip** in the sea.

With love,

Donald Chen

4.4 第四类题目：对服务和商品不满意

书信写作有一个常考场景就是你坐飞机、坐车、旅游、去酒店、去饭店吃饭、参加俱乐部、去购物等，觉得服务不好或者对买的东西不满意，写信去投诉，希望对方有所赔偿，或者改进服务等。

当然，有些时候如果是满意对方的服务，也会写感谢信。

遇到这种题目，只要使用关于商业的一个百搭观点就差不多了。

百搭观点

公司需要

A 注意客户的需求，设计有竞争力的产品　　B 产品性价比高

C 提供准时快捷贴心的服务，处理客户投诉很快捷

D 有激情、接受过好培训、有创造力的员工

E 好的理财能力，控制好成本　　F 足够的资金

G 好的商业计划　　H 好的管理能力和高效率

才能够赚取利润并获得成功。

你可以说服务不够贴心，性价比不够高，员工不够好，产品质量不好等。

我们看看下面的例子：

You had a long business flight, but you were not happy with the service. In a complaint letter to the airline company, you

- ***give information about when and where you took the flight***
- ***explain why you were not satisfied with the service***
- ***suggest what the airline company can do to improve the service.***

下面的表格是我回答三个小问题的思路和相关词伙。

三个小问题	中文思路	词伙
Give information about when and where you took the flight	我对2016年9月16日早上飞去奥克兰的经历很不满意。我订了一张票并且起得很早去赶早班机	booked a flight catch the morning flight arrived at the airport

Explain why you were not satisfied with the service	当我到机场的时候，飞机晚点了，我等了两个小时才登机 服务质量也不好，机舱内温度很低。乘务人员也没给我饮料和饼干，因为他们人手不足	flight was deladyed boarded the flight standards of service flight attendants ignored my request
Suggest what the airline company can do to improve the service	我希望你们能补偿我飞机晚点的损失并且加强员工培训	flight delays staff training

下面是范文。

To whom it may concern,

I used to be a **loyal customer** of your company, but I had an **unpleasant experience** on September 16, 2016, when I **flew to** Auckland. It was not a **scheduled trip**, but my aunt was **taken to hospital** because of a heart attack and wanted to see me.

I **booked a flight** immediately and left home early to **catch the morning flight** (flight number: AKL 372). When I **arrived at the Christchurch airport**, I was told that the **flight was delayed**. After waiting for two hours (during which time I received no messages about when the plane was ready), I eventually **boarded the flight**.

Apart from this, the **standards of service** were also disappointing. **Flight attendants** told me that they did not have any blanket when I complained about the low **cabin temperature**. They also constantly **ignored my request** to refill orange juice and offer some biscuits, and their excuse was that they were understaffed to answer all requests.

I am kindly asking that your company compensate me for the **flight delay** and also upgrade **staff training** to ensure that they provide services consistent with your company's image. I believe your prompt response to my concerns can convince me and other potential passengers that our interests are taken seriously.

Yours faithfully,

4.5 第五类题目：庆祝仪式和社会活动

书信写作还经常涉及邀请朋友和同事等来参加派对、婚礼、结婚纪念日宴会或者聚餐等，这些话题非常像口语 Part 2 关于描述事件的话题。

备考这些话题的时候，大家要注意积累相关的词伙，如派对、食物、饮料、装修场地、音乐、表演等。平时找些真题练习一下这些词伙，直到熟悉为止，这样考场上就可以用上去。

如关于生日宴会，我们有下面这么一些常用词伙。

Partying 相关词伙

1. throw a party 举办宴会
2. host a party 举办宴会
3. go to a party 出席宴会
4. attend parties 出席宴会
5. office party 公司里举行的宴会
6. dinner party 家里举行的聚餐
7. birthday party 生日宴会
8. birthday cake 生日蛋糕
9. blow out candles 吹蜡烛
10. refreshing drinks 很好喝的饮料(或者酒)
11. housewarming party 入伙聚餐
12. serve drinks 提供酒水
13. karaoke party k 歌的宴会
14. farewell party 告别宴会

下面我们看看这个信件题目，尝试写一下。

You friend's birthday is coming, and you want to organise a party for him or her. In a letter to your friend, you

- ***describe the place you want to celebrate it***
- ***explain the exact day of the party***
- ***give details of what you want to do for his or her birthday.***

下面的表格是我回答三个小问题的思路和相关词伙。

三个小问题	中文思路	词伙
Describe the place you want to celebrate it	在我房子的后院举行晚宴，享受自然公园的风光并在一个令人愉快的环境中享受我们的晚餐	dinner party enjoy a good view of the natural park in a pleasant setting
Explain the exact day of the party	不确定你会不会在生日那天工作，因为你告诉我你有兼职 女生独自在国外要克服思家情绪很难，告诉我你下班的时间，我去接你	overcome homesickness get off work
Give details of what you want to do for his or her birthday	我妻子会准备一些中国晚餐和饮料，我们可以在吹蜡烛前美餐一顿	prepare a Chinese meal refreshing drinks a decent meal blowing out candles

下面是范文。

Dear Jane,

I haven't seen you for a long time. How is everything? I understand that your birthday is coming and if you do not have any arrangement, I wonder whether you would like to drop by and celebrate it with us?

You know my house has a big backyard where we can have a barbeque **dinner party**. We can **enjoy a good view of the natural park** and enjoy the dinner **in a pleasant setting**.

I am not sure whether you need to work on your birthday, as you told me that you have a part-time job now. It is not easy for a girl to **overcome homesickness** alone in a foreign country. Just tell me when you **get off work** or when you are available, I will pick you up.

My wife will **prepare a Chinese meal** as well as some **refreshing drinks**. We will have **a decent meal** before **blowing out candles**. Thanks a lot for helping my kid study English and my wife has always been wanting to **return this favour**. Please accept this invitation!

With love,

Ken

附录

附录 *1*：全书词伙分类列表

Academic Skills

research skills 研究能力
academic skills 学术能力
analytical skills 分析能力
problem-solving skills 解决问题的能力
search the web for information 上网找资料
gather information 收集信息
do research 做调查
critical thinking skills 思辨能力
leadership skills 领导能力
computer literacy 电脑能力
leadership qualities 领导的素质
practical skills 实际工作的能力
organisational skills 组织能力
sharpen skills/add to the skill set 丰富技能

Air Travel

travel by air 坐飞机出行
air travel 空航
air transport 空运
transport...by air 通过飞机运输
make non-essential trips 进行非必要的旅行
price war 价格战
in the airline industry 在航空业
air fares 机票费用
travel expenses 差旅费
on holiday 度假
tourist attractions 旅游景点
a source of pollution 污染源
greenhouse gases 温室气体
build up in the atmosphere 聚集在大气中
trap heat from the sun 从太阳吸收热量
extreme weather conditions 极端天气
unusually warm conditions 异常温暖的气候

Animal Testing

animal tests 动物实验
animal experiments 动物实验
conduct experiments 做实验
animal welfare groups 动物权益团体
develop a new drug 研发一种新药
show promising results 有好结果
side effect 副作用
exposed to abuse 受到虐待
medical tests 药物实验
alternative methods of research 可代替的研究方法
medical products 医用品
skincare products 护肤品

Architecture

historic building 历史建筑
historic site 历史遗址
heritage building 古建筑
cultural attraction 文化胜地
cultural site 文化遗址
architectural landmark 建筑地标

architectural treasure 建筑瑰宝
make a trip 进行一次旅行
in ancient times 在古时候
cultural heritage 文化遗产
worth a visit 值得去看看
a memorable experience 一次难忘的经历
visual experience 视觉体验

Behavioural Problems

good role models 好的榜样
copy behaviour 模仿行为
behave badly 表现得很差
behavioural problems 行为问题
show good manners 表现出礼貌的行为
show respect to (somebody) 表现出尊敬
send/take children to school 送孩子去学校
first educators 第一个老师(启蒙老师)
domestic violence 家庭暴力
poor behaviour 不良的行为
show aggression 有暴力倾向
social norms 社会规范
speak in a friendly manner 说话有礼貌
pick up children 接孩子

Business

competitive advantages 竞争优势
satisfy the needs 满足需求
stand out from the crowd 脱颖而出
run a successful business 经营一个成功的生意
make profits 赚取利润
go bankrupt 破产
good value for money 性价比很高
business plans 商业计划
intense competition 激烈的竞争
serve a niche market 服务小众市场
set up a company 创立一个公司
running cost 运营成本
make ends meet 收支相抵
go bust 破产(口语)
cost reduction measures 减少成本的措施
handle complaints 处理投诉

Car Emissions

curb car use 限制汽车的使用
create exhaust fumes 产生废气
cause air pollution 引起空气污染
suffer from poor health 忍受身体不适
mitigate problems 缓解问题
increase the health cost 增加医疗费用
climate change 气候变化
car emissions 汽车尾气
dangerous to our health 对我们的健康产生危害
tackle pollution 解决污染问题
poor air quality 空气质量差
a bad harvest in agriculture 农业收成不好
global warming 全球变暖

Celebrities

self-made celebrities 依靠自己努力而出名的人
lead a life of luxury 过奢侈的生活
designer clothes 名牌的衣服
extravagant parties 奢华的派对
start from scratch 白手起家
live a frugal life 过节约的生活
drive prestigious cars 开豪车
set a bad example 树立坏的榜样

pursue material goods 追求物质的东西
admire celebrities 羡慕名人
pop singers 摇滚歌手
famous entertainers 有名的娱乐圈人士
movie stars 电影明星
achieve fame 成名
positive role models 正面的榜样
devoted fans 忠实粉丝
the younger generation 年青一代
famous sportspeople 著名运动员
sports stars 体育明星
inspire the next generation 激励下一代
develop skills 培养技能
develop talents 发展天赋
become world famous 变得世界闻名
emulate idols 模仿偶像
role models 楷模
a good influence 积极的影响
demonstrate determination 表现出决心
encounter difficulties 遇到问题
achieve success 获得成功

Charity

charitable organisations 慈善组织
raise funds 筹钱
mobilise resources 调拨资源
international aid 国际援助
medical aid 医疗救助
needy people 有需要的人
people in need 有需要的人
basic necessities 日常生活用品
live in poverty 生活贫穷的人
get rid of poverty 摆脱贫穷
impoverished countries 贫穷国家
Third World countries 第三世界的国家

Clothes

follow a dress code 遵守着装要求
wear uniforms 穿制服
dress formally 穿着正式
casual dress 休闲服装
present a professional image 展现专业形象
make a good impression 留下好印象
social rules 社会规则
social norms 社会规范
social etiquette 社交礼仪
public places/spaces 公共场所

Communication

face-to-face communication 面对面交流
communication skills 交流能力
human interaction 人际交往
interpret messages 解释信息；翻译信息
facial expression 面部表情
body language 肢体语言
avoid misunderstandings 避免误解
a sign of respect 以示尊敬
listen to others 倾听别人
a good listener 一个好的听众
a good communicator 良好的沟通能力；出色的沟通者
form strong relationships 形成牢固的关系
live alone 独居
live far away from family 住得离家很远
social activity 社交活动
family life 家庭活动

Community

charity work 慈善工作
charity groups 慈善团体
community cohesion 社区凝聚力
give a helping hand 给予帮助
needy people 有需要的人
experience difficult times 经历困难时期
gain support 获得帮助
members of community 社区的成员
part of community 社区的一分子
bring people together 让人们聚在一起
a sense of community 社区的感觉
musical shows 音乐表演
raise funds 筹款

Computers

computer games 电脑游戏
educational games 教育类游戏
computer skills 电脑技能
computer literacy 计算机素养
connect to the Internet 联网
download software 下载软件
use online communication tools 使用在线交流工具
store information 存储信息
process documents 处理文件
edit photos 编辑照片
produce videos 制作视频

Consumer Society

consumer societies 消费型社会
buy more than they need 买的东西多过自己需要的
spend more than they earn 入不敷出
excess shopping 过度购物
the latest gadgets 最新的电子设备
get into debt 负债
pay off debts 还清债务
financial problems 经济问题
low income families 低收入家庭
economic pressure 经济压力

Cover letter

a master's degree in accounting 会计硕士
accounting competencies 会计能力
manage financial records 处理财务记录
manage budgets 处理预算问题
in the accounting field 在会计领域
accounting programmes 会计软件
an extensive accounting background 深厚的会计背景
accounting principles 会计准则
the accountant position 会计职位
in the accounting profession 会计专业
bottom line 盈亏底线

Creativity

attend courses 上课
improve job skills 提高工作能力
apply skills to work 将技能用于工作
increase productivity 增加产出
come up with creative ideas 想出有创意的点子
tackle problems creatively 有创造性地解决问题
unconventional measures 非常规手段
achieve creative potential 发挥创造力
use imagination 运用想象力
brain development 大脑发育
educational toy 益智玩具

have a good grasp of advanced technology 很好地掌握先进科技
foster innovation 促进创新
stifle creativity 扼杀创造力
make profits 创造利润

Crime

a deterrent effect 威慑作用
escape punishment 逃避惩罚
think twice 再三考虑
prevent crime 阻止犯罪
curb crime 遏制犯罪
combat crime 打击犯罪
commit a crime 犯罪
break laws 违反法律
violate laws 触犯法律
catch criminals 抓捕罪犯
an escaping criminal 在逃罪犯
armed police 武装警察
carry weapons 携带武器
pay a fine 支付罚款
serve a prison term 服刑
work as a volunteer 作为志愿者
reduce poverty 减少贫穷
vocational/job training 职业培训
surveillance cameras 视频监控

Discipline

do some activities 做一些活动
develop positive habits 培养良好的习惯
from an early age 从幼年开始
improve literacy 提高文学素养
start school 开始上学
maintain discipline 维持纪律
parenting styles 父母管教的方式
behavioural problems 行为问题
impose sanctions on 施加惩罚
impart a clear code of conduct 传授明确的行为规范
act as acceptable members of society 成为社会的好公民
good manners 有礼貌
grounding and detention 罚站和留堂

Educational Equality

from less well-off backgrounds 来自贫穷的家庭
disadvantaged students 贫穷的学生
children from poor homes 来自贫穷家庭的孩子
children from deprived backgrounds 贫穷的孩子
from less well-off families 来自普通家庭
exempted from tuition fees 免除学费
drop out of school 辍学
educational equality 教育的公平
the equal access to education 教育公平
study at university 在大学学习
free-interest loans 无息贷款
financial support 财政支持
the cost of learning 学习的成本
break the cycle of poverty 摆脱贫穷
reduce poverty 减少贫穷
vocational/job training 职业培训
bridge the gap between rich and poor 减少贫富差距
close the economic divide 减少贫富差距
the education system 教育系统
the school system 学校系统
higher education 高等教育
receive a good education 接受好的教育
a well-educated workforce 受过良好教育的劳动力队伍
public schools 公立学校
set scholarships 设立奖学金

student loans 学生贷款
free education 免费教育
free access to knowledge 免费获取知识
broadband internet services 宽带服务

Energy Consumption

alternative energy sources 可替代能源
clean energy 清洁能源
renewable resources 可再生资源
energy conservation 能源保护
energy consumption 能源消耗
generate electricity 发电
natural light 自然光
sustainable materials 可持续材料
electric cars 电动汽车
hybrid cars 混合能源汽车
car giants 汽车业巨头
traditional fossil fuels 传统化石燃料
environmentally friendly materials 环保材料
energy-saving technology 节能科技
energy efficiency 节能

Environmental Problems

environmental problems 环境问题
environmental issues 环境议题
environmental impacts 环境的影响
environmental destruction 环境的破坏
cause damage to the environment 对环境造成破坏
drop litter 扔垃圾
awash with rubbish 充满了垃圾
clear forest 清理森林
destroy wetlands 破坏湿地
damage the beautiful landscape 破坏美好的风景

Environmental Protection

go green 环保
environmentally friendly 环保的
environmental protection 环境保护
environmental benefits 环境效益
live a sustainable life 过环保的生活
environmental impacts 环境的影响
launch massive campaigns 开始大规模的宣传活动
environmental awareness 环境意识
educate the public about 给大众提供……方面的教育
impose heavy fines 大额罚款
recycle waste 回收垃圾
rubbish bins 垃圾箱
household waste/rubbish 家庭垃圾
energy conservation 节能

Exams

devote time 付出时间
prepare for exams 准备考试
revise for exams 复习备考
exam factories 考试工厂（只关注考试的地方）
exam grades/exam results 考试成绩
workload increases 工作量增加
do homework 做家庭作业
learn facts by heart 背东西
rote learning 死记硬背
find enjoyment 发现乐趣
extra-curricular activities 课外活动
pursue a hobby 追求一种爱好
combine work with pleasure 劳逸结合

Family

family life 家庭生活
spend quality time 度过宝贵时光
achieve a work-life balance 实现工作和生活的平衡
family commitments 家庭责任
family dinners 家庭聚餐
family ties 家庭关系
family activities 家庭活动
a loving family 一个有爱的家庭
feel lonely 感到孤独
a sense of loneliness 孤独感
a sense of isolation 孤立感
emotional support 情感上的支持

Film

the film industry 电影行业
top-grossing films 最卖座的电影
go to the cinema 去电影院
big-budget films 大预算电影
special effects 特技效果
star famous actors 由巨星主演
the box office 票房
talented filmmakers 有天赋的电影人（制片人）
produce high-quality films 制作高质量的电影
domestically produced films 国产电影
locally produced films 当地制作的电影

Food

cook a meal 做饭
cooking skills 做饭技能
life skills 生活技能
prepare meals 准备饭菜
fruits and vegetables 水果和蔬菜
a healthy diet 健康的饮食
a balanced diet 均衡的饮食
eat fatty food 吃脂肪过多的食物
fast food 快餐
fish and chips 鱼和薯条
fizzy drinks 碳酸饮料
high in salt and sugar 高盐高糖的
fresh ingredients 新鲜的食材
combat obesity 对抗肥胖问题

Food Technology

increase yields 增加产量
food production 食品生产
grow crops 种庄稼
cultivate crops 种庄稼
a good harvest 收成很好
chemical fertilisers 化肥
apply pesticides 使用杀虫药
pest disease 病虫害
food prices 食品价格
GM food 转基因食品
genetic engineering 基因工程
high-yield crops 高产量的庄稼
resistant to pests 抗虫害
intensive farming 高密度农场
use preservatives 使用防腐剂
mechanised farming 机械化种植
grow faster 生长得更快
food shortage 食物短缺

Friends

circle of friends 朋友圈
make good friends 成为好朋友
build up a network of contacts 建立关系网
form a good relationship 形成良好的关系

develop a lifelong friendship 发展一段终生的友谊
a lasting friendship 持续的友谊
peer pressure 同辈的压力
hang out with friends 与朋友出去玩
socialise with neighbours 与邻居交往
close friends 亲密的朋友
gain financial support 获得经济支持
business opportunities 商业机会

Gender Discrimination

gender discrimination 性别歧视
discrimination on the grounds of sex 性别歧视
gender bias 性别偏见
gender equality 性别平等
the equal access to education 教育公平
gender differences 性别差异
gender gap narrows 缩小性别差距
managerial skills 管理技能
business leaders 商业领袖
members of the board 董事会成员
shatter the glass ceiling （女性）打破职位提升的障碍
enter the workforce 进入职场
close the gender gap 减少男女歧视
raise a family/start a family 养家糊口

Global Warming

global warming 全球变暖
climate change 气候变化
greenhouse gases 温室气体
build up in the atmosphere 聚集在大气中
trap heat from the sun 存储来自太阳的热量
extreme weather conditions 极端天气条件
unusually warm conditions 异常温暖的气候条件

Government Intervention

government intervention 政府介入
government action 政府行为
launch awareness campaigns 发起宣传活动
introduce laws 颁布法律
make laws 制定法律
tighten regulations on 加紧监管
impose a tobacco tax on 征收烟草税
curb smoking 控制吸烟
stay healthy 保持健康
prevention is more important than the cure 预防比治疗重要
fall ill 生病

Greenspaces

public gardens 公共花园
do outdoor activities 做户外运动
go for a jog 慢跑
feel relaxed 感觉放松
reduce stress 减轻压力
keep fit 保持身材
flowering plants 开花植物
evergreen trees 常青树
beautiful landscape 美丽的风景
enjoy the scenery 欣赏风景
take in the scenery 领略风光
admire the scenery 赞美景色
stunning scenery 极好的景色

Happiness

achieve happiness 获得幸福（结果）
experience happiness 感受幸福（过程）
find enjoyment 找到乐趣
find joy 找到乐趣
cover basic needs 满足基本需求
improve living standards 改善生活水平
a higher standard of living 更高的生活水平
live comfortably 过上舒适的生活
feel stressed out 感到紧张
non-financial factors 非经济因素
family life 家庭生活
social life 社会生活
feel lonely 感到孤独
earn a decent income 有体面的收入
earn money 挣钱
achieve career success 实现职场成功
enjoy a happy retirement 享受快乐的退休时光
donate money 捐钱

Health

stay healthy 保持健康
a sedentary lifestyle 一个久坐的生活方式
endanger health 危害健康
harmful to health 对健康有危害
concentrate on work 专注于工作
suffer from heart diseases 患上心脏病
improve physical health 促进身体健康
sick leave 病假
prone to health problem 容易有健康问题
see doctors 看医生
achieve ambitions 实现自己的梦想
attain goals 实现自己的目标
economic value 经济价值

Housing

housing shortage 住房短缺
urban planning 城市规划
densely populated cities 人口很多的城市
redevelop run-down urban areas 重新开发破旧城区
make room for 为……腾出空间
residential buildings 住宅楼
the housing market 住房市场
provincial towns 乡镇
state housing 国家房，即有政府补贴的“公租房”，福利房
pay a mortgage 付按揭款
housing developers 房产开发商
high-rise buildings 高层建筑
accommodate people 容纳人
low-density neighbourhoods 低建筑密度的社区
land-scarce cities 土地稀缺城市
meet the growing demand for housing 满足对住房日益增长的需求
demolish old buildings 拆除老房子

Internet

web-based technology 网络科技
work from home 在家里工作
teleworking, telecommuting, work at home 远程办公
shop online 上网购物
attend online courses 上网课
travel to work 去公司
travel a long distance to work 上班路程远
save time 省时间
face-to-face communication 面对面的交流
attend meetings 开会

avoid rush-hour traffic 避开交通高峰时段

watch videos online 在网上看视频

social networking websites/social media 社交媒体网站

video chat programme 视频聊天软件

in a formal setting 正式的场合

Job Creation

lose jobs 失去工作

the jobless rate 失业率

create jobs 创造就业机会

make a living 谋生 / 维持生计

earn money 赚钱

live comfortably 生活得好 / 过上好日子

population ageing 老龄化

out of work 失业

reduce unemployment 减少失业问题

provide job opportunities 提供就业机会

earn salaries 赚取薪水

feed family 养家

economic recession/an economic crisis 经济危机

foreign brands 外国产品

Job Satisfaction

well-motivated employees 很积极的员工

improve motivation 提高积极性

live a comfortable life 过舒服的生活

pay rise 加薪

a good working environment 一个好的工作环境

inspire loyalty 让员工更加忠诚

the atmosphere in the workplace 工作环境

flexible patterns of work 灵活的工作模式

a steady career 稳定的职业

a good motivator 一个好的激励因素

a sense of progress 进步感

raise a family 养家糊口

a sense of belonging 归属感

obtain job satisfaction 获得工作满意度

achieve ambition 实现个人的野心

working conditions 工作条件

working relationship 工作关系

Job Seeking

labour market 劳动力市场

intense competition 激烈的竞争

find work 找到工作

steady income 稳定的收入

cover living expenses 支付生活费

complete a degree 获得一个学位

sharpen skills/add to the skill set 丰富技能

intensely competitive 竞争激烈

improve job security 提高工作的稳定性

lose jobs 失业

increase earnings 增加收入

undergo training 接受培训

meet requirements 符合要求

Knowledge

read books 读书

knowledge-based economy 知识型经济

increase knowledge 增长知识

read articles online 在线阅读文章

acquire knowledge 获得知识

a vital source of knowledge 一个重要的知识来源

digital books 数字图书
broaden horizons 开阔眼界
broaden minds 开阔思路
keep up to date with what is happening 了解最新发生的事情
keep well-informed about 对……保持消息灵通
educational programmes 教育类电视节目

Language

international language 国际语言
global language 全球性的语言
less spoken language 很少人说的语言
minority language 少数民族语言 / 小语种
endangered language 濒临消失的语言
mother tongue 母语
a means of communication 交流方式
cultural identity 文化认同
preserve traditions 保护传统
preserve language diversity 保护语言多样性
protect languages 保护语言
cultural diversity 文化多样性
celebrate festivals 庆祝节日
traditional food 传统食物

Laws

commit crimes 违法
make fast money 快速赚钱
break the law 触犯法律
violate laws 违反法律
obey laws 遵守法律
comply with laws 遵守法律
face any punishment 面对惩罚
a prison sentence 监禁
severe consequences 严重后果
youth crime 青少年犯罪
juvenile delinquency 青少年犯罪
young offenders 年轻的罪犯
petty crimes 轻微的犯罪
serious crimes 严重的犯罪
racial tensions 种族矛盾

Lifestyle

lead a hectic life 过着忙碌的生活
live a healthy life 过健康的生活
live an active life 喜欢运动
live an inactive life 不喜欢运动
exercise regularly 经常运动
play sport 做运动（美式常用）
do sport 做运动（英式常用）
indoor activities 室内活动
access to exercise equipment 有健身设备
green space 绿地
make way for modern buildings 被现代建筑取代

Living Standards

steady jobs 稳定的工作
steady income 稳定的收入
a well-paid job 收入很高的工作
cover living expenses 支付生活费
live comfortably 过很舒适的生活
afford tuition fees 支付学费
pay bills 支付生活杂费
pay off the mortgage 还清房贷
lead a happy life 过快乐的生活
financial difficulties 经济困难

Materialistic World

material possessions 物质财产
live in a materialistic world 生活在物质的社会
up-to-date equipment 时尚的设备
hi-tech products 高科技产品
purchase the advanced model 买最先进的版本
status symbol 身份的象征
the middle class 中产阶级
buy more than they need 买的东西多过自己需要的
in a consumer culture 消费社会
improve self-esteem 提升自信
find contentment 开心和满足
behind the times 过时
out of touch with the world 与世隔绝

Mechanisation

improve productivity 提高生产力
improve efficiency 提高效率
do repetitive tasks 执行重复任务
replace human labour 取代人类劳动力
reduce the workforce 减少劳动力
mechanise tasks 机械化任务
mechanised assembly lines 机械化装配线
mechanised farming 机械化耕作
automate the process 过程自动化
done by hand 手工完成
computerise the service 服务电脑化
industrial robots 工业机器人
reduce the labour cost 减少劳动力成本
grow the economy 促进经济

Medical Services

easier access to medical services 更加容易接触医疗服务
public hospitals 公办医院
medical equipment 医疗设备
clinical experience 临床经验
receive medical treatments 接受医疗
contract an illness 患病
high medical expenses 高医疗费用
a long waiting list 排长队
medical research 医疗调查
improve our health 促进我们的健康
in the pharmacy industry 在医药行业
invent new drugs 发明新药物
cure diseases 治愈疾病
previously incurable diseases 以前不可治疗的疾病
waste management 垃圾管理
spread of diseases 传播疾病
infectious/ contagious diseases 传染病
healthy living 生活健康
improve life expectancy 延长寿命
boost public health 提升大众健康

Motivated Students

traditional classrooms 传统的教室
study independently 独立学习
provide instruction 提供指导
on a one-on-one basis 在一对一的基础上
build confidence 建立信心
maintain enthusiasm for studies 保持对学习的热情
develop a serious interest in 培养强烈的兴趣
keep students interested 保持学生的兴趣

stay self-motivated 保持热情
a negative attitude towards schooling 对于学业的负面态度
lack self-discipline 缺乏自制力
get distracted 分心

Museums

art museums 艺术博物馆
war museums 战争博物馆
exhibit artefacts 展览文物
organise an exhibition 举办一个展览
a connection to the past 连接历史
cultural heritage 文化遗产
enrich cultural lives 丰富文化生活
admission fees 门票
open to the public 对公众开放
free admission 免费入场
free entry 免费进入

Music

folk songs 民族歌曲
pop songs 流行歌曲
rock music 摇滚音乐
classical music 古典音乐
hit songs 热门歌曲
pop stars 流行歌手
music lover 音乐爱好者
musical instruments 乐器
integrate musical styles 综合各种音乐风格
cultural differences 文化差异
differ from culture to culture 文化和文化之间的差异
western countries 西方国家

News

news reports 新闻报道
news outlets 新闻机构
news organisations 新闻组织
news media 新闻媒体
professional reports 专业报道
gather first-hand information 收集第一手资料
broadcast news 播放新闻
a reliable source of information 一条有可靠来源的信息
increase ratings 提高收视率
expand the readership 拓展读者群体
sensationalise crimes 夸大犯罪事实
cover up political scandals 掩盖政治性的丑闻
mislead the public 误导公众
fake news 虚假新闻
political pressure 政治压力
in an opinionated way 带有主观看法
on the spot 现场
conceal the truth 隐瞒真相

Older People

older people 老人
the elderly 老者
senior citizens 年长者
the older generation 老一辈
out of touch with the world 跟不上时代
resistant to change 抵触改变
old-fashioned ideas 过时的观念
fit into the modern world 适应现代社会

adopt advanced technology 采用高科技
life experience 生活经历
make a rash decision 做轻率的决定
out of touch with the world 与世界脱节
hold back social progress 阻碍社会进步
sensible advice 明智的意见
take risks 冒险
risk averse 风险规避
a source of income 收入来源
a financial burden on 财政负担

Online News

read news online 在网上看新闻
check online news 阅读网上新闻
read news stories 看新闻
have free time 空闲时间
keep up to date with what is happening 了解最近发生的事情
watch videos online 看网络视频
have faster access to news in real time 更快了解到实时新闻
the live coverage of 实况转播
TV news 电视新闻
the delivery of visual information 视频信息的呈现
news programmes 新闻节目

Online Shopping

run an online business 经营网络商务
online shops 网店
an online auction website 竞买的网站
the cost of operation 运营成本
place an order 下单
offer a replacement 换货
in the comfort of my home 在家里
fake products 假货
shoddy goods 不好的产品
consumer rights 消费者权益
a code of practice 行业规范
a business owner 公司老板
e-commerce websites 电商网站
retail outlets 零售店
answer enquiries 回答问题
make a payment 付款
grow business 扩大业务
fit into my schedule 融入自己的日程表
faulty goods 有问题的产品
genuine brands 真货
buying decisions 购买的决定

Partying

thow a party 举办派对
go to a party 出席派对
office party 公司里举行的派对
birthday party 生日宴会
birthday present 生日礼物
refreshing drinks 很好喝的饮料(或者酒)
serve drinks 提供酒水
farewell party 告别宴会
host a party 举办派对
attend parties 出席派对
dinner party 家里举行的聚餐
birthday cake 生日蛋糕
blow out candles 吹蜡烛
housewarming party 入伙聚餐
karaoke party k歌的派对

Photos

take photos 拍照
take pictures 拍照
take a selfie 拍自拍照
a photo album 相册
portable device 可移动设备
capture special moments 捕捉特别的瞬间
relive experiences 重温一些（美好的瞬间或者日子）
upload photos 上传相片
social networking websites 社交网站
digital cameras 数码相机
edit images 编辑相片
brighten colours 让颜色更加鲜艳
make slow motion movies 制作慢动作电影

Practical Work

do practical work 做实际工作
hands-on experience 实践经验
prepare for working lives 为工作做准备
practical experience 实践经验
work placements 实习
pursue a career 从事一份工作
well-suited to a job 很适合一份工作
improve practical skills 提高实践能力
do part-time work 做兼职工作
adapt to the workplace 适应职场
graduate from university 大学毕业
finish high school 高中毕业
leave school 毕业
take a gap year 高中毕业后的间隔年

Qualities

the education system 教育系统
the school system 学校系统
higher education 高等教育
receive a university education 接受大学教育
receive training 接受培训
moral principles 道德准则
a sense of responsibility 责任感
instill virtues into 向……灌输美德
productive members of society 对社会有贡献的人
build character 塑造个人品质
develop qualities 培养素质
in difficult situations 在恶劣的环境下
show determination to win 必胜的决心
show perseverance 坚韧不拔

Reduce Poverty

disadvantaged students 贫穷的学生
children from poor homes 来自贫穷家庭的孩子
exempted from tuition fees 免除学费
drop out of school 辍学
educational equality 教育的公平
study at university 在大学学习
free-interest loans 无利息贷款
financial support 财政支持
break the cycle of poverty 摆脱贫穷
bridge the gap between rich and poor 减少贫富差距
close the economic divide 减少贫富差距
public schools 公立学校
set scholarships 设立奖学金
student loans 学生贷款
free education 免费教育
free access to knowledge 免费获取知识

broadband internet services 宽带服务
break the cycle of poverty 打破贫穷的恶性循环
afford tuition fees 能支付学费
maintain a basic standard of living 维持基本的生活水平
die needlessly 不必要的死亡
suffer from poor health 生病
receive vocational training 接受职业培训
close the gap between haves and have-nots 减少贫富差距
racial discrimination 种族歧视
reduce poverty 减少贫穷
needy people 贫困的人
charitable organisations 慈善组织
people with disabilities 残疾人
afford basic necessities 买得起基本生活必需品
improve job skills 提高工作能力

Rules

obey rules 遵守规则
break/violate rules 破坏规则
ground rules 基本的规则
break school rules 破坏校规
adhere to cultural norms 遵守文化规范
develop positive habits 形成好的习惯
comply with rules 遵守规则
establish/set rules 建立规则
follow golden rules 遵守黄金规则
violate norms 不遵守社会规范
show good behaviour 讲礼貌
company regulations 公司的规定

Selfish People

give a helping hand 伸出援手
show compassion 同情
behave selfishly 做事自私
motivated by greed 出于贪婪
gain an unfair advantage over 获取不公平的优势
teach moral values 灌输道德观
with a heart of gold 有颗金子般美好的心
responsive to emotional needs 响应情感需求
driven by self-interest 受自身利益驱使
cheat in exams 在考试中作弊
make easy money 不劳而获
traditional values 传统的价值

Shopping

a strong appetite 需求很高
consumer goods 消费品
household appliances 家庭用具
online stores 网络商店
in the comfort of their homes 在舒适的家里
shopping malls 购物中心
buy...on impulse 冲动买……
consumer society 消费社会
pay by credit card 用信用卡付账
a growing demand 需求很高
electrical equipment 电子设备
shop online 网络购物
online retailers 网络零售商
on high streets 在购物街
shopping streets 购物街
steep discounts 大降价
consumer culture 消费文化

Skills

educational games 教育游戏
outdoor games 户外运动
set rules 设定规则
express ideas 表达观点
good listening skills 良好的倾听技巧
improve soft skills 改善软技能
communication skills 交流能力
interpersonal skills 人际技能
leadership skills 领导能力
physical skills 运动技能
life skills 生活技能
basic skills 基本技能
young players 年轻球员

Social Activities

keep fit 保持身材
lead a healthy life 过健康的生活
social activity 社会活动
gather together 聚一起
make new friends 交新的朋友
go out for a meal 外出聚餐
eat out 外出就餐
have a coffee 喝咖啡
talking points 话题
sports fans 体育迷
watch soccer games 看足球比赛
live events 直播赛事

Social Life

cultural activities 文化活动
do social activities 参加社会活动
social life 社会生活
mix with others 和他人来往
socialise with neighbours 和邻居来往
cut stress 减少压力
release stress 释放压力
tasks at hand 手边的工作
forget about work 忘记工作
reduce anxiety 缓解紧张情绪
join the choir 参加合唱团
a pleasurable experience 非常有趣的经历
visit art galleries 参观艺术馆
join a band 参加乐队

Social Norms

conform to social norms 遵守社会规范
follow social rules 遵守社会规则
show good manners 有礼貌
show respect to others 尊重他人
complete work on time 准时完成工作
arrive punctually 准时到
handle enquiries politely 礼貌地处理咨询
late for work 上班迟到
good work ethic 好的职业道德
build good working relationships 建立好的工作关系
a sense of responsibility 责任感

Space Technology

space missions 太空任务
space exploration 太空探索
space science 太空科学
advance knowledge 先进的知识

habitable planets 适合居住的星球
population explosion 人口增长
provide shelter for 为……提供避难所
sustain our civilisation 保护我们的文明
used commercially 商业化地使用
protective clothes 保护衣
in the hostile environment 在恶劣的环境里
on the ground 在地面上
travel in outer space 太空旅行
an immediate payoff 马上有回报

Sport

play sport 做运动
gentle physical exercise 温和的身体锻炼
moderate intensity activities 强度适中的运动
mild exercise 温和的锻炼（不刺激的运动）
go for a jog 去慢跑
take a brisk walk 去快跑
go for a swim 去游泳
burn calories 燃烧卡路里
increase blood circulation 促进血液循环
build strength 增强体力
keep a good body shape 保持好的身材
improve health 促进身体健康
lead an inactive life 不运动的生活
suffer injuries 受伤
extreme sports 极限运动
professional trainers 专业的教练

Stress

economic pressure 经济压力
financial difficulties 财政困难
combine work and family commitments 协调好工作和家庭之间的关系
work commitments 工作投入
a fight schedule 时间很紧
find time 找到时间
put a severe strain on 对……施加更大的压力
reduce stress 减少压力
cope with stress 应付压力
a source of stress 压力的来源
feel stressed 感到压力
feel relaxed 感到轻松
cost of living 生活费用
material goods 物质的东西
avoid procrastination 避免拖延
time management skills 时间管理

Study Abroad

go overseas 到国外
study abroad 出国学习
in a globalised world 在全球化的世界中
from diverse backgrounds 来自不同背景
master another language 精通另一门语言
pick up a foreign language 学习一门外语
fluent in the first language 母语流利
immerse themselves in a foreign language 将他们自己浸泡在一门外语里
language skills 语言能力
multinational enterprises 跨国企业
prestigious universities 著名大学
expand horizons 开阔视野
have a broader view of life 人生的视野更加开阔
experience the world 感受世界

Talent

specialise in a subject 专注于一个学科
study a subject 学习一门学科
career prospects 职业前景
well-paid jobs 待遇优厚的工作
career opportunities 工作机会
develop a talent 发展特长
bright students 聪明的学生
academically gifted 学习上有天赋
a natural talent in 在……方面天生的才能
mathematical talents 数学才能
do calculations 做计算
build expertise 建立专业知识
put...in an advantageous position 把……放在有利位置
a tedious job 一个乏味的工作

Teachers/Schools

teach courses 教课
teach subjects 教课
the school system/the education system 教育系统
receive a well-rounded education 学习全面的知识
start school 上学
the school curriculum 学校课程 / 课程大纲
core subjects 主科
attend university 上大学
enter university 上大学
lively and stimulating 生动又新颖的
engage children 激励孩子们
class activities 课堂活动
attend school 上学
curriculum content 课程内容
learning outcomes 学习效果

Teamwork

work collaboratively 一起工作
work closely with 和……密切合作
work as a team 一个团队一起工作
team projects 团队项目
team assignments 团队作业
team sport 团队运动
raising money for charity 为慈善机构筹款
collaborative teamwork 团队合作
save/shorten time 节省时间
divide the effort 分担任务
complete a project 完成项目
embark on another team project 开始一个团队项目
uncover benefits 发现（别人的）贡献
make decisions as a group 团队一起做决定

Technology

technological advances 科技的进步
state-funded scientific research 政府资助的科学研究
scientific institutions 科学机构
medical advances 医学进步
technological innovations 技术的创新
technological change 技术的改变
advanced technology 先进科技
new technology 新技术
state-of-the-art technology 最新技术
cutting-edge technology 高新技术
technological breakthroughs 技术突破
the hi-tech industry 高新技术产业
improve the environment 保护环境
reduce diseases 减少疾病

fight hunger 减少饥荒

space technology 太空技术

Telecommunications

telecommunications technology 电信技术

use a mobile phone 使用移动电话

mobile devices 移动设备

text messaging 短信

instant messaging 即时消息

via email 通过电子邮件

on the phone 在手机上

on the computer 在电脑上

fax machines 传真机

online services 在线服务

the access to Internet services 接入互联网服务

travel by air 乘飞机旅行

maintain a lifelong relationship 保持终身的关系

forge a strong relationship 形成牢固的关系

stay in touch with 和……保持联系

Teleworking

work from home 在家远程办公

work at home 在家工作（工作地点是自己的家）

paperless office 使用现代办公设备（如传真机和电脑）的办公室，也可以说“无纸办公室”

travel to and from work 上下班

show discipline 自律

stay self-motivated 保持积极性

show initiative 表现主动性

enter the workforce 参加工作

combine work and raising a family 兼顾工作和家庭

flexible working hours 灵活的工作时间

work commitments 工作的责任

sacrifice family life 牺牲家庭生活

Tourism

create revenues 产生收入

attract tourists 吸引游客

tourist attractions 旅游胜地

tourist destinations 旅游目的地

the tourist sector 旅游业

go sightseeing 去观光

a driver of economic growth 一个经济增长的驱动力

an important part of the economy 经济的重要组成部分

a source of income 收入来源

create jobs 创造就业机会

create employment/generate employment 创造就业机会

charge admission fees 收取门票

creative industry 创意产业

Traffic Congestion

reduce traffic congestion 减少交通阻塞

cope with traffic jams 处理交通阻塞

rush-hour traffic 高峰期的交通

cycle to work 骑自行车去上班

within walking distance 步行就可以到

driving test 驾照考试

driving license 驾驶执照

curb private car use 限制私人汽车的使用

car ownership 拥有汽车

fuel tax 汽油税

congestion tax 交通阻塞税

broaden roads 扩宽道路

build new roads 修路

use public transport 使用公共交通

car pooling 拼车

raise standards 提升标准

pedestrianised streets 步行街

reduce car emissions 减少汽车尾气

Transportation

drive cars 开车

travel by air 坐飞机

private car use 私家车的使用

ways to get around 出行的方式

get to and from work 上下班

travel a long distance 走很长的路程

travel to the central office 去中心办公区

travel by car 开车旅行

travel by tube 坐地铁

means/modes of travel 旅行方式

use public transport 使用公共交通工具

daily commuters 上班族

suburban commuters 郊区的上班族

Trees

plant trees 种树

tree-lined avenues 林荫大道

a view of nature 自然景观

provide the shade 提供阴凉

absorb dust 吸尘

plant life 植物

cut down trees 砍树

lined with trees (街道) 两边种满了树

feel close to nature 亲近自然

provide shelter 提供休憩处

ever-green trees 常青树

flower garden 花园

University Subjects

offer employment possibilities 提供就业机会

complete degree courses 完成学业

an investment of time and money 投入时间和金钱

take subject courses 上专业课

fill knowledge gap 填补（劳动力市场上的）知识空白

pursue a career 从事一份工作

academic courses 学术课程

preferred areas of study 偏爱的学习领域

passionate about 对……有热情

develop talents 发掘天赋

financial circumstances 财政情况

vocational courses 职业课程

areas of knowledge 领域知识

match interests 符合兴趣

study with enthusiasm 有兴趣去学习

career success 事业上的成功

Urbanisation

relocate to cities 搬去城市

keep pace with the demand 满足需求

afford home ownership 买得起房子

employment opportunities 就业机会

reduce the quality of life 影响生活质量

a growing population 不断增长的人口

population expansion 人口扩张
put pressure on 增加压力
public transport service 公共交通服务
transport costs 交通费用
population is mobile 人口流动大
valuable services/ essential services 和民生有关的服务

Waste

consumer goods 消费者商品
household goods 家庭用品
consumer products 消费者产品
end up in landfill sites 填埋在垃圾场
contaminate the environment 污染环境
household waste 家庭垃圾
industrial waste 工业浪费
household rubbish 家庭垃圾
drop litter 扔垃圾
dump waste 扔垃圾
incinerate waste 焚烧垃圾
dispose of waste 处理垃圾
enter the food chain 进入食物链
hazardous waste 有害的垃圾

Water

fresh water 淡水
tap water 自来水
a threat to public health 一个对公众健康的威胁
water pollution 水污染
contaminate water 污染水
underground water 地下水
heavily polluted 污染严重
boil water 开水
a clean water supply 一个干净水源
poor sanitation 恶劣的卫生状况
bottled water 瓶装水
water consumption 耗水量
soil erosion 水土流失
efficiency in water use 有效用水
untreated sewage 未经处理的废水

Wildlife Preservation

human activities 人类活动
poor farming practices 不好的耕种模式
destroy the forest 破坏森林
mine coal 开采煤田
oil drilling 开采石油
animal die out 动物灭绝
biodiversity loss 生物多样性下降
intensive farming 密集耕种
the loss of biodiversity 生物多样性的缺失
improve biodiversity 改善生物多样性
endangered species 濒危物种
rare animals 稀有物种
cause damage to the environment 对环境造成危害
toxic chemicals 有毒的化学品
habitat destruction 栖息地破坏
face a high risk of extinction 面临很高的灭绝风险
on the verge of extinction 濒临灭绝

Women in the Workforce

male-dominated industries 男性占主导地位的行业
clerical work 白领工作
juggle different roles 扮演不同的角色

balance work and family commitments 平衡工作和家庭责任的关系
domestic responsibilities 家庭责任
domestic work 家务活
child-rearing duties 抚养孩子的责任
raise children 抚养孩子
high-paying industries 高薪行业
advance one's career 发展某人的事业
a fulfilling career 令人满意的事业
career success 事业成功
maternity leave 产假
physically demanding jobs/manual work 体力活
career choices 职业选择

Work Overtime

work unsocial hours 非正常时间上班
work overtime 加班工作
work long hours 长时间工作
high-stress jobs 压力大的工作
lack of sleep 缺乏睡眠
sleep deprivation 缺乏睡眠
suffer from insomnia 失眠
do exercise 运动
physical activity 身体锻炼
in poor health 身体状况不好
health problems 健康问题

Zoo

animal in captivity 被关住的动物
locked in cages 被关在笼子里
lose freedom 失去自由
freedom is restricted 自由受到限制
natural behaviour 天生的行为
hunting instincts 狩猎的天性
fierce animals 猛兽
reintroduce species 将动物放回（野外）
in the wild 在野外
human-caused disturbances 人类（对动物造成）的干扰
manmade environment 人工环境
artificial environment 人工环境
illegal hunting 非法狩猎
exhibit animals 展出动物
animal testing 动物实验
kill animals for meat 杀动物来吃肉
raise pets 养宠物

附录2：百搭观点列表

政府类

1. (A 加大惩罚力度，如罚款 B 服刑 C 社区服务和做义工 D 加强法律教育 E 扶贫 F 提供职业培训，减少失业 G 增加警察，甚至是配枪警察 H 设置视频监控系统 I 政府教大家如何保护自己) 有助于减少犯罪。

2. (A 女性接受教育的机会增加 B 家庭经济压力增加导致男性的收入不够养家 C 企业注意女性的特质，如细心 D 女性对职业成就越发有追求 E 科技发展让很多职业都减少了体力和身体要求)，从而促进了女性进入职场，提升了女性的地位，减少了男女歧视，并且促进了性别平等。

3. 女性被认为是 (A 以家庭为重 B 生育影响事业 C 身体不能从事高强度工作 D 女性天生比较有同情心，没什么野心 E 比较多愁善感和情绪化) 都会影响其事业的发展和工作的选择。

4. 老年人被认为是 (A 保守 B 不愿意接受新的科技 C 和世界缺乏接触 D 身体不好 E 没有收入，比较节省)，所以被认为会 (A 阻碍创新 B 阻碍社会发展 C 和年轻人有矛盾 D 不适合继续工作 E 对家庭和社会产生经济负担)。

5. 政府对教育的支持主要体现在 (A 开设更多公立学校 B 提供社区的职业培训 C 给大学生提供奖学金、学生贷款，甚至减免学费 D 提高老师待遇 E 在社区设置图书馆，方便大家免费看书 F 提高宽带服务，让大家更容易从网络上获得知识)。

6. 政府的资金有限，钱应该多花在和普通民众生活直接相关的服务上 (A 教育 B 医疗 C 交通 D 养老金 E 住房等)，而不是花在一些本身有一定盈利能力的项目上 (A 音乐 B 电影 C 艺术 D 某些科学项目 (如医药) E 博物馆 F 古建筑和文化景点)，也不是在回报期比较长的项目 (如 A 太空科技 B 医药) 上。

7. (A 政府投资博物馆和艺术馆 B 资助艺术家 C 艺术展和博物馆免费入场 D 举办音乐会和参加音乐活动 E 看电影 F 上社区的艺术课 G 去图书馆看书) 可以丰富我们的文化生活，有助于文化产业的发展，有助于文化的多样性。

8. 政府可以通过 (A 资助公立医院 B 投资医药研究，发明新药 C 进行健康和防疫等方面的宣传 D 免费给居民打疫苗，防止传染病 E 加强城市卫生管理 (包括厕所、垃圾处理、用水等) F 增加房屋供应，避免高密度居住条件下产生的传染病蔓延 G 通过对烟酒、快餐食品加税等方式来引导人们注意生活健康) 提升大众健康，延长寿命等。

科技类

9. 科技的发展对我们有很多积极的影响，包括 (A 环保科技改善环境，减少污染 B 医疗科技减少疾病，延长寿命 C 农业科技增加产量，减少饥荒 D 电脑、机械、机器人、空航等提高效率 E 太空科技给我们提供了研究方向，促进各方面的技术发展)。

10. 电脑、网络和手机主要的好处是可以让信息的传递更加方便，允许人们 (A 在家里办公 B 通过手机和电脑看书和新闻 C 用手机来拍照和上传照片 D 在家里可以通过视频上课 E 通过社交网络发布新闻 F 在网络和手机上浏览网店可以更好地比价和选择产品 G 浏览网站即可，不用去博物馆和艺术馆 H 和家人朋友同事视频聊天）。

11. （A 过分使用社交网站 B 手机和电话交流 C 依赖电邮工作，不去见客户和同事 D 喜欢独居 E 生活在大城市或者国外，离家人和朋友很远 F 喜欢看电视和打游戏，不喜欢社交 G 工作狂，长时间工作）会减少面对面交流和社会活动以及家庭活动，导致交流水平的下降，使人和人之间缺乏情感联系。

12. （A 使用农药和化肥 B 密度种植 C 基因科技 D 使用防腐剂 E 机械化种植）都可以让农作物生长得更快，农田产量更多，减少食品短缺的问题。

13. （A 电脑化 B 机械化 C 机器人 D 自动化）让很多工作，特别是体力工作，变得更加有效率、更加有质量保证，还能减低成本，对经济有一定促进作用。

14. （A 机械化 B 电脑化 C 机器人的增加 D 经济危机，企业收入下降 E 外国进口货品的增加 F 老龄化趋势导致推迟退休）都会减少工作机会，影响人们的收入。

15. 私人企业很多时候不会投资（A 太空科技 B 新能源 C 道路和其他公共设施 D 传统艺术 E 老建筑的维护 G 老人院，学校 H 自然保护区），因为这些项目要么回报率很低，要么很久都没有回报。

城市化

16. 很多人去城市居住，因为（A 工作机会多 B 设施比较完备 C 教育好 C 思想比较先进），但是问题是（A 人口增加导致物价飞涨 B 房屋紧缺 C 交通堵塞 D 空气污染严重 E 基础设施和服务（如医疗）供不应求 F 城市的公园和绿地减少 G 很多人找不到工作，犯罪率提高 H 人口流动，人们没有社区的感觉）。

17. （A 拓宽马路并增加道路的数量 B 增加汽油税，鼓励大家不开车 C 增加路考难度，提高驾照发放标准 D 发展公共交通工具 E 鼓励大家移居市郊，同时公司也搬到市郊 F 设立步行街 G 鼓励大家走路或骑车上班 H 拼车 I 让人们在家里上班）都有助于减少交通堵塞，减少骑车量，减少尾气污染，也会提高效率，产出。

18. 城市人口增加导致（A 修路和拓展道路 B 修高楼），从而减少绿地、花园、树木等，导致（A 污染变得严重 B 人们看不到绿色植物心情不好 C 缺乏运动和室外活动的地方 D 人们没有乘凉的地方 E 缺乏一些能举办文化活动（如音乐节或赏花会）的场所 F 一些野生动物和鸟类不再栖息于城市）。

19. （A 政府提供房屋补助 B 政府提供福利房 C 拆旧房建新房 D 鼓励人们移居小城镇或者郊区 E 建高楼 F 减少公园和公共场所多建房子）解决城市的住房问题。

社会文化和价值观

20. 人们（A 赚大量的钱变得富裕 B 事业上功成名就 C 捐钱让社会其他人更加开心 D 陪伴家人，或者享受家人的陪伴 E 自己生活得很自由和独立 F 享受朋友、邻居和同事的陪伴 G 大手大脚花钱购物 H 存钱为退休时过稳定的生活做准备 I 注意减少压力，保持健康），都会感到快乐。

21. （A 学校重视学习好的学生 B 竞技体育鼓励年轻人战胜别人 C 媒体推崇那些暴富的人，强调金钱的重要性 D 学校和父母没有注意孩子进行道德和无私的教育 E 社会不注意无私和道德的公益宣传 F 工作竞争激烈）导致年轻人现在更加关注自己的成就和利益，而不去关心和体谅别人。

22.（A 在公共地方遵守秩序 B 使用礼貌语言 C 在公共场合不抽烟 D 在公共场合遵守手机使用的社会规则 E 开会和赴约要准时 F 遵守穿衣的标准 G 诚实 H 平时尽量不要制造噪音 I 要遵守餐桌礼仪 J 送礼物）属于社会规范和标准，体现了人们在意别人、体贴别人。

23.（A 物价飞涨 B 城市生活费用很高 C 大家现在喜欢买奢侈品，变得很物质 D 失业率高 E 经济波动大 F 人们对个人成就的追求提升了 G 电话和网络让人们在下班时间也可以工作 H 缺乏时间管理能力，而且还经常犯拖延症）都导致人们越来越忙，工作时间变长，忘记了家庭生活。

24. 社会活动（A 参加聚会 B 和朋友一起去旅游 C 聚餐 D 逛街）和文化活动（A 看电影 B 听音乐 C 参加乐队 D 看画展 E 去博物馆 F 参观古建筑）有助于释放一些不好的情绪，可以暂时不去思考工作，有利于消除疲惫，重燃活力。

25.（A 广告 B 信用卡付账 C 电子商务 D 经济发展导致收入增加 E 产品不断更新 F 某些商品的价格不断下降 G 追求时尚的名人不断在媒体上出现 H 人们追求物质享受）导致了消费文化的盛行：人们喜欢攀比，喜欢大手大脚花钱，喜欢买很多东西。

生活方式

26.（A 加强锻炼 B 走路上班 C 注意劳逸结合，减少工作时间 D 少吃快餐 E 不抽烟喝酒 F 好的作息习惯，不要熬夜看电视打游戏和工作 G 少发脾气 H 经常体检，生病得到及时救治 I 注意一些健康活动，如读书、旅游、解压 J 不要总是待在城市或者污染严重的地方 K 住通风好的、宽敞的房子）都有助于健康。

27. 健康的好处多多，包括（A 可以工作赚钱 B 享受生活，做各种各样的事情 C 实现事业的梦想 D 减少病假，劳动产出会更高，给企业和国家带来经济价值 E 减轻医疗系统的压力，政府可以投资到其他的民生项目上）。

28.（A 在家做饭 B 少吃快餐 C 多吃素菜，少吃肉类 D 少吃零食 E 少吃进口食品，多吃本地新鲜食品）会减少体重，减少得一些健康疾病，包括肥胖和心脏病等的概率。

工作类

29.（A 工作的收入 B 工作的稳定性 C 工作的升职和发展机会 D 和同事上司的关系 E 工作的环境 F 工作时间和放假时间的长短 G 工作的自由度 H 实现自己才华的机会）能够决定工作满意度。

环境类

30.（A 工厂使用节能科技 B 家庭使用节能设备 C 建筑使用节能材料 D 开发新能源，包括太阳能和风能，去发电 E 开发电动汽车和混合能源车）有助于减少化石资源的使用，更加环保。

31.（A 使用农药 B 工业排污 C 家庭污水 D 海洋垃圾 E 森林破坏导致水土流失 F 人口增长 G 不注意节约用水）都会导致水资源减少，或者水污染增加。

32.（A 广告和消费文化鼓励大家消费 B 城市没有垃圾回收设备 C 政府没有提高大家的垃

圾回收的意识 D 工厂没有垃圾处理的技术和设备 E 很多产品都是由不可降解的物质做成的）导致垃圾大量增加，从而（A 影响土壤和水源 B 垃圾的毒素影响我们的食物 C 动植物死亡）。

33. 人口增长，导致人类活动增加（A 过分耕种 B 过分放牧 C 砍伐树林 D 使用化肥 E 房地产开发 F 建厂发电 G 开矿和开采石油）会破坏环境，尤其是动植物栖息地，导致动物灭绝，影响生物多样性。

34. （A 偷猎 B 将动物用于表演 C 将动物关在动物园里 D 用动物做实验 E 吃动物的肉 F 养宠物）都会对动物造成伤害，不够人道。

媒体类

35. 新闻媒体不报道真实信息的主要原因是（A 要夸大坏信息来增加收视率 B 迫于政治或者经济压力去隐瞒和修改信息 C 无法去实地报道新闻，只能捏造 D 新闻工作者不够客观 E 为了迎合观众制造假新闻）。

36. 通过（A 网络 B 手机 C 听广播）获得信息，主要是（A 快捷 B 方便），而传统媒体（A 电视 B 杂志和报纸 C 书本）的优点是（A 有深度的分析 B 有更多的图像信息）。

37. 广告（A 告诉我们消费很快乐，不断鼓励我们花钱 B 通过明星代言来让我们购买奢侈品和不需要的东西 C 推广一些不好的生活方式，如吃快餐、喝酒、玩游戏等 D 夸大产品的功效，鼓励大家购买）导致大家乱花钱，影响生活质量，甚至使某些人债台高筑。

全球化

38. （A 保护城市的老建筑 B 维持一些传统文化和习惯 C 发展文化产业（包括艺术、音乐等）D 保护自然风景）可以吸引游客，这些游客的消费会为社区带来收入，工作机会增加。

39. （A 出国留学 B 学习外语 C 旅游 D 看电影和电视节目 E 阅读报纸杂志 F 阅读书籍 G 和不同背景的朋友交流）可以熟悉各种文化，开阔视野，更容易找工作。

40. （A 游客去发展中国家消费 B 外商在世界不同地方投资 C 国际组织为发展中国家提供各种援助 D 国际组织带来的技术支持 E 有技术的劳动力移民去外国工作）有助于发展经济，减少贫困，提高生活水准。

注意：这个观点也可以反过来说。外商投资和进口商品导致本地企业倒闭，造成经济后退。外国的移民和劳工占用本地人的工作机会，也会造成经济影响。此外国际的援助让本国没有动力去创新，发展经济。

41. 全球化增加了（A 货物在全世界的运输 B 人们去不同地方旅游、出差、学习和工作），这些都会促进空航和空运，造成尾气排放和石油消耗的增加。

42. 全球化会影响全球的文化，包括（A 音乐 B 电影 C 建筑 D 食品 E 衣服 F 价值观 G 语言）这些可能会慢慢变得单一，影响文化多样性，影响人们的文化认同感，世界会变得乏味，我们的思想也越来越单一，对文化、历史、传统的理解更浅薄。

注意：这个观点也可以反过来说。外国商品的增加，让我们有更加丰富的选择，甚至会激发市场的竞争，导致商品价格下降，质量上升，对经济和生活标准都有好的影响。

教育

43. 父母可以通过（A 和小孩一起旅游 B 一起做体育运动和户外活动 C 一起看电视和玩游戏 D 一起读书 E 一起吃饭和走亲戚 F 接送孩子 G 辅导孩子做作业）来增加和孩子的互动，改善关系，灌输知识，为孩子树立榜样，影响小孩的行为。

44. 教育的提供和老师的教育有助于（A 小孩增加知识，以后方便找工作，社会失业率降低 B 年轻人懂得道德和社会规范 C 小孩学会如何和人交流 D 增加学生对不同科目的认识，以后大学做研究，甚至进行产品创新 E 不同的校内和校外活动塑造年轻人的性格和品质 F 培养人们的技能并提高他们的能力，方便他们不断学习，最终实现自己的梦想 G 人们掌握知识和技术，提高工作效率和产出）。

45. （A 中学做义工 B 中学毕业后工作或者旅游一年 C 大学打工 D 大学实习 E 直接开始工作，而不是继续读大学）有利于增强实际工作能力，熟悉公司运作，有助于择业，更好地为就业做准备。

46. 选专业和选课需要考虑（A 个人的兴趣和爱好 B 专业的就业前景 C 个人的财政和家庭情况 D 是否能够提升技能，并增加知识 E 大学的声誉和排名 F 国家的支持和政策 G 学习的时间和精力）。

非教育类话题讲解

百搭观点（文化）：

47. （A 电脑网络 B 阅读 C 看电影或者照片）虽然省钱省力，但是未必能够取代亲自去游览一个地方（包括古建筑）或者是看一个艺术品（包括绘画等）的方式，因为视觉感受不同，而且文化遗产的形成或制作过程实属不易，值得亲眼一见。

百搭观点（文化）：

48. 现代社会人们越来越注重公平，体现在（A 男女平等 B 教育平等 C 贫富差距缩小 D 消除年龄歧视 E 减少种族歧视）。

百搭观点（健康）：

49. （A 工作太忙 B 学习太忙 C 玩游戏和看电视太久 D 玩电脑和手机 E 住在城市，没有运动的设施和空间 F 使用各种电器做家务 G 工业自动化和机械化）导致每天的运动时间很少，对健康不好。

百搭观点（健康）：

50. （A 公园 B 花园 C 绿色的地方 D 乡村地区 E 海边）空气更好，让人心情舒爽，空旷的地方也方便运动，从而让我们更加健康。

百搭观点（健康）：

51. （A 医生的建议 B 政府的宣传和指引 C 老师的教导 D 父母的榜样行为 E 政府的法律 F 书籍和杂志的健康类文章）都可以让人养成好的生活习惯，包括（A 健康饮食 B 多运动 C 少坐车或自己开车 D 少抽烟喝酒）。

百搭观点（经济）：

52. 人们需要（A 很勤奋地工作 B 接受培训 C 提高文凭 D 丰富自己各方面的技能）才可以找到工作，适应竞争，保证收入。

百搭观点（经济）：

53. 公司需要（A 注意客户的需要，设计有竞争力的产品 B 产品性价比高 C 提供准时、快捷、贴心的服务，处理客户投诉很快捷 D 有激情、接受过培训、有创造力的员工 E 好的理财能力，控制好成本 F 足够的资金 G 好的商业计划 H 好的管理能力，增加效率）才能够赚取利润并获得成功。

百搭观点（社会）：

54. 通过（A 社交网站 B 手机和电话 C 视频 D 飞机旅行）使人们可以保持和朋友、家人以及同事的联系，不管距离多远都可以维持感情。

百搭观点（社会）：

55. （A 做义工 B 社区组织社区活动和比赛 C 邻居交朋友 D 多推广社区的文化活动，如音乐表演）有助于促进人和人的交流，大家能相互帮助，关系也会更加密切，更有社区的感觉。

百搭观点（社会）：

56. （A 参加体育运动 B 关注时尚和服饰 C 阅读新闻 D 看体育比赛 E 发展一些兴趣和爱好 F 参加聚会 G 上网聊天和使用社交网站 H 用手机 APP 交友）可以增加和朋友的话题，丰富了社会活动，能认识更多朋友。

百搭观点（社会）：

57. 扩大朋友圈，可以（A 获得信息 B 获得朋友的建议 C 获得金钱的支持 D 获得工作或者生意的机会 E 和朋友一起消磨时间、解压）。

百搭观点（社会）：

58. 人们（A 购买昂贵的家具 B 购买复杂的电子产品 C 购买名牌衣服 D 购买昂贵的汽车 E 去海外旅游 F 甚至学外语）会觉得自己有面子，觉得能在社会上有地位，也就更加开心和满足。

百搭观点（科技）：

59. （A 坐飞机出行 B 开车上下班 C 坐地铁 D 使用 APP 叫车）让人们出行更加方便，提高了效率。

百搭观点（法律）：

60. （A 贫穷 B 缺乏教育 C 法律不够严厉 D 政府执法不严，警察人手不够 E 人们自私和贪婪 F 对政府政策不满 G 不同文化种族的人有矛盾）导致犯罪行为增加。

百搭观点（法律）：

61. （A 在公共地方遵守秩序 B 使用礼貌语言 C 在公共场合不抽烟 D 在公共场合遵守手机使用的社会规则 E 开会和赴约要准时 F 遵守穿衣的标准 G 诚实 H 平时尽量不要制造噪声 I 要遵守餐桌礼仪）属于社会规范和标准，体现了人们在意别人、体贴别人。

百搭观点（环境保护）：

62. （A 政府的宣传 B 提供设施 C 增加环保宣传 D 进行法律制裁 E 投资环保科技 F 补助使用环保科技的个人和公司）有助于提升人们和企业的环保意识。

百搭观点（环境保护）：

63. （A 汽车数量的增加 B 各种电器的使用 C 电能的消耗 D 不注意节约和回收 E 将机器用于农业和工业）都会让我们更加依赖化石资源，它们会增加温室气体的排放，污染环境，危害动植物和人的健康。

百搭观点（环境保护）：

64. （A 旅游业发展 B 城市发展）导致人口增加，带来很多环境后果，包括（A 垃圾增加 B 自然风景被破坏 C 汽车增加，空气污染和噪声污染）。

教育类话题讲解

百搭观点（道德、品质和行为）：

65. 学校通过（A 道德课 B 军训 C 阅读 D 实习 E 校外活动 F 树立模范）等来提高学生的品质，包括（A 责任感 B 勤奋好学 C 不放弃）等精神。

百搭观点（道德、品质和行为）：

66. 父母和老师可以通过[A 规则 B 惩罚（如罚站、留堂）C 减少一些福利（如看电视和打游戏）D 自身的榜样 E 书上的例子 F 奖励]等方式来影响小孩的是非感和行为，这些方式决定了是否喜欢学习、如何与人相处、生活的习惯等。

百搭观点（道德、品质和行为）：

67. 除了家长和老师之外，（A 名人 B 电影和电视里的角色 C 身边的小伙伴 D 邻居和亲戚 E 社区）都会影响小孩的想法和行为，小孩会模仿这些行为，因为他们觉得这些行为是好的或是值得推崇的。

百搭观点（智力）：

68. （A 上不同的课程 B 接触不同的文化 C 和不同阶层的人交流 D 通过各种渠道增加知识和见闻），人可以更加有创造能力，体现在（A 可以将不同学科的知识很好地利用起来，找到新的解决方法 B 能从各个角度想问题）。

百搭观点（智力）：

69. 通过（A 阅读书籍，包括电子书 B 看新闻 C 看教育类的电视节目和电影 D 看网络教育视频 E 和朋友、父母、老师交流 F 旅游 G 通过手机看信息）人们可以不断增加知识。

百搭观点（各方面的能力）：

70. （A 玩游戏 B 参加团队活动和团体运动项目 C 和邻居交往 D 参加社区活动 E 参加俱乐部和兴趣小组的活动）需要小孩和别人交流，倾听别人，从而提高交流能力。

百搭观点（各方面的能力）：

71. （A 团队运动项目 B 合作学习 C 义工 D 参加乐队和合唱团 E 玩一些团队游戏）可以提高小孩的团队合作能力。

百搭观点（各方面的能力）：

72. 读大学能够提高年轻人的（A 领导能力 B 组织能力（包括管理实践和资源的能力）C 解决问题的能力 D 找信息的能力 E 写作能力 F 使用电脑的能力 G 思辨能力和分析能力 H 实际工作能力的能力 I 团队能力和交流能力，包括演讲能力 J 情绪控制的能力）。

百搭观点（学习兴趣）：

73. （A 就业前景 B 专业是否符合自己的天赋 C 课程是否能提升实际能力 D 老师上课的方式是否有趣 E 老师是否注意和学生的互动）决定了某些学生对专业、学业的兴趣。

百搭观点（学习兴趣）：

74. （A 老师有针对性的指导 B 小班教学 C 父母在作业上提供帮助 D 有好的同学做榜样 E 从学龄前提高学习能力 F 在取得进步后给予学生一定奖励）都有助于增加学生的信心，克服困难，获得好成绩。

百搭观点（学习兴趣）：

75. （A 只关注考试，而且作业太多 B 死记硬背 C 缺乏课外活动 D 只关注理论知识，不注重实践 E 选课不符合自己的天赋）都会导致学生失去兴趣，没有学习的动力。

附录3：常用的口语100句

大家先看中文，使用句型，不看英文说一次，然后再对比英文，再说一次，练习口译能力。

表示“毫无疑问，坚定看法”

1. It is not surprising that...

毫无疑问，当经济受到影响的时候犯罪率会上升。

例句：It is not surprising that **the crime rate** will rise when the economy suffers.

2. There is a lot of evidence to suggest that...

证据表明，教育能减少不平等并解决贫困问题。

例句：There is a lot of evidence to suggest that education can **reduce inequality** and **fight poverty**.

3. It's well established that...

接触关于吸烟广告会让人过早开始抽烟，这是大家公认的。

例句：It's well established that people who are exposed to cigarette advertisements are likely to start smoking early.

4. It's true that...

确实，如今很多家庭成员之间关系不那么亲密。

例句：It's true that many families today are not very close.

表示否定的语气

5. It would be wrong to argue that...

认为金钱是获得幸福的唯一因素，这是不正确的。

例句：It would be wrong to argue that money is the only **ingredient of happiness**.

认为在学校学习艺术科目是浪费时间，这是不正确的。

例句：It would be wrong to argue that **studying the arts** at school is a waste of time.

6. It is a mistake to think that...

认为在外国住就能提高语言能力，这是错误的。

例句：It is a mistake to think that living in a foreign country can surely **improve one's language skills**.

认为修复历史建筑是浪费钱，这是错误的。

例句：It is a mistake to think that **the restoration of historic buildings** is a waste of money.

7. It would be unwise to...

强迫学校注重考试成绩是不明智的。

It would be unwise to push schools to focus on **exam grades**.

表示“第一次”

8. I first heard about...when...

当我想在网上买一些课本时，我第一次听说了这个网站。

例句：I first heard about this website when I wanted to buy some textbooks online.

9. I first saw...when...

当我和朋友一起看电视时，我第一次看了这部电影。

例句：I first saw this film when I watched TV with my friends.

10. I first met...when...

当我作为实习生在一家公司上班时，我第一次见到他。

例句：I first met him when I joined a company and worked as an intern.

当我报名参加一门叫《金融基础》的课时，我第一次见到她。

例句：I first met her when I **signed up for a course** called *Fundamental of Finance*.

表示“发现，察觉”

11. I notice that...

我发现男人喜欢发动机非常有劲的汽车。

例句：I notice that many men like big cars with **powerful engines**.

我注意到近几年有很多旧建筑被拆了。

例句：I notice that many **old buildings have been demolished** in recent years.

12. I discover that...

我很快发现通过在网上看视频学习一门技能很困难。

例句：I soon discovered that learning a skill by **watching a video** online was difficult.

13. I find that...

我发现有时团队合作没有单独工作有成效。

例句：I have found that working in a team is sometimes not as productive as working alone.

表示“学习，了解”

14. learn more about...

我对去国外旅游很感兴趣，因为我想了解更多不同的文化。

例句：I'm very interested in traveling abroad because I want to **learn more about different cultures**.

15. have a good/thorough understanding of...

外国公司对如何发展自己的生意以及营销有吸引力的产品有很好的了解。

例句：Foreign companies have a good understanding of how to grow their business and **market attractive products**.

16. gain an insight into...

通过学习历史，我们可以了解到历史上一些政治或经济危机的成因。

例句：By studying history, we can gain an insight into the causes of some political or **economic crises** in the past.

表示感受的句子

17. It is a great feeling to...

每天跑步很好，因为你能看到体育活动给健康带来的改变。

例句：It is a great feeling to **go for a run** every day because you can see how **physical activity** can make a difference to your health.

在假期参观一些文化景点是一种非常棒的体验。

例句：It is a great feeling to visit some **cultural attractions** on holiday.

18. It is enjoyable to...

学习一门乐器是很享受的事。

例句：It is enjoyable to learn how to play **a musical instrument**.

19. I was frustrated...

我很沮丧，因为我没办法入睡。

例句：I was frustrated because I was not able to **fall asleep**.

20. I was amazed at...

我很惊讶，一个大家庭是如何设法在这么小的公寓中生活的。

例句：I was amazed at how a big family could manage to live in such a small flat.

我很惊讶，这个小镇的人们对彼此是如此的友好。

例句：I was amazed at how friendly people living in that small town were to each other.

21. It was amazing to see...

看到这么多孩子一起看书、一起玩游戏，这是多么不可思议。

例句：It was amazing to see so many children reading books together and **playing games** together.

22. I was fascinated by...

我老师告诉我的关于海外留学的故事深深地吸引了我。

例句：I was fascinated by all the stories my teacher told me about **studying overseas**.

在太空旅行然后在月球着陆这个想法深深地吸引了我。

例句：I was fascinated by the idea of traveling in **outer space** and **landing on the moon**.

表示年龄的句子

23. When I was young,...

我年轻的时候和父母一起旅行，但现在我喜欢和同龄人去旅游。

例句：When I was young, I travelled with my parents, but now, I'd love to travel with friends **at my age**.

24. When I was younger, I remember that...

我记得小的时候我想当一名老师，但后来我改变了想法。

例句：When I was younger, I remember that I wanted to work as a teacher, but I **changed my mind** later.

25. When I was a kid,...

当我还是个小孩子的时候，我每天都和我爸爸一起做运动。

例句：When I was a kid, I **played sport** with my father every day.

26. when I was a teenager,...

我不记得我十几岁的时候自己参加了多少考试。

例句：I don't remember how many exams I took when I was a teenager.

27. For the majority of my life,...

我人生的大部分时间都生活在中国，所以我一直对去国外很感兴趣。

例句：For the majority of my life, I have been living in China. So I've been interested in studying in a foreign country.

28. ...since childhood.

从小时候开始，读书就是我最喜欢的爱好。

例句：Reading has been my **favourite hobby** since childhood.

29. ...since I was a child.

打小我就喜欢体育。

例句： I have been passionate about sport since I was a kid.

30. As I have grown older,...

当我长大一些以后，我发现金钱并不一定使人幸福，因为你有时可能会忽略家庭生活。

例句：As I have grown older, I have realised that money does not necessarily lead to happiness, because you may sometimes **ignore your family life**.

31. When I got a bit older,...

当我长大一点以后，我意识到快餐是有害的。

例句：When I got a bit older, I came to realise that **fast food** is harmful.

32. ...when I was growing up.

在我成长的过程中，我爸爸工作非常努力。

例句：My dad worked very hard when I was growing up.

在我长大的过程中，我的父母很注意健康的习惯。

例句：My parents paid a lot of attention to **healthy living** when I was growing up.

表示问题的句子

33. I don't really know much about...

我不太了解游泳。

例句：I don't really know much about swimming.

我不太清楚如何练习书法。

例句：I don't really know much about how to **improve handwriting**.

34. I'd love to learn more about...

我想多了解如何与父母相处。

例句：I'd love to learn more about how to **get along with my parents**.

我想多了解英语国家的风俗和传统。

例句：I'd love to learn more about **customs and traditions** of some English-speaking countries.

35. Of course, there are some small differences.

当然，一些小差别是存在的。如今，关于名人的新闻越来越多了。

例句：Of course, there are some small differences. News about celebrities has increased today.

36. I suppose one of the biggest problems that can occur/ happen is that...

我认为，会出现的一个大问题是有些儿童可能不再信任他们的父母了。

例句：I suppose one of the biggest problems that can occur is that some children may no longer trust their parents.

我认为，会出现的一个大问题是人们对手机的依赖越发严重，这导致他们记忆力下降。

例句：I suppose one of the biggest problems that can happen is that people **rely heavily on mobile phones** but they **have a poor memory**.

37. have difficulty in...

小孩很难耐心做事。

例句：Children have difficulty in doing something patiently.

许多家庭没办法挣足够的钱过幸福的生活。

例句：Many families have difficulty in earning sufficient money to **live a happy life**.

38. the main issue/problem is that...

如果你出名了，最主要的问题是你没有私生活了。

例句：If you become famous, the main problem is that you do not have your **private life**.

对于那些选择租房住的人来说，最主要的问题是他们不得不经常搬家。

例句：For those choosing to rent a flat, the main issue is that they have to move around a lot.

表示解决方法的句子

39. There are some measures/actions that could be taken to deal with...

有些方法可以用来解决交通堵塞。

例句：There are some measures that could be taken to deal with **traffic congestion**.

40. one solution/measure is to...

一种减少交通问题的方法是鼓励人们乘坐公共交通工具。

例句：To reduce traffic problems, one solution is to encourage people to **use public transport**.

41. A potential solution lies in...

一种可能的方法是少给学生留作业，所以他们可以花时间做体育运动以及追求个人爱好。

例句：A potential solution lies in **giving children less homework**, so they can spend more time **playing sports** and **pursuing hobbies**.

42. There are many ways to...

有很多方法可以缓解生活中的压力。

例句：There are many ways to **deal with pressure** in our lives.

43. One option is to...

一种选择是，倾听孩子的想法，试着去理解他们想要什么或是需要什么。

例句：One option is to listen to the kid, trying to understand what he wants or needs.

一种选择是早起，所以你可以避开交通高峰。

例句：One option is to get up early, so you can **avoid the traffic**.

44. A quick way to do this is to.../The easiest way to do this is to...

最便捷的方法是循环利用废品。

例句：A quick way to do this is to **recycle waste products**.

最简单的方法是征收燃油税。

例句：The easiest way to do this is to **impose a fuel tax**.

保持身材的一种方法是少吃快餐，多运动。

例句：A way to keep fit is to **eat less fast food** and **exercise more**.

45. One way of dealing with this is...

我认为解决年轻人失业问题的一种方法是为雇主提供奖励，鼓励他们雇用年轻人。

例句：I think one way of dealing with **youth unemployment** is to provide employers some **financial incentives** to encourage them to **recruit young people**.

表示不确定的句子

46. I'm not sure whether it's important/necessary to...

我不确定给每个大学毕业生买一间公寓是有必要的，这是个巨大的负担。

例句：I'm not sure whether it's necessary to **buy an apartment** for every university graduate. It is **a huge burden**.

我不确定让每个孩子都穿校服很重要，因为他们可能会丧失个性。

例句：I'm not sure whether it's important for all children to **wear uniforms** because they may lose individuality.

47. I couldn't really say for sure, but I suppose that...

我不敢确定，但我认为有些人在晚些时候成家是因为他们想专注于事业。

例句：I couldn't really say for sure, but I suppose that some people would love to **start a family** later in life because they want to concentrate on their careers.

48. I don't really know much about...

我不太了解如何解决全球变暖问题，我认为我们可能需要减少汽车尾气排放。

例句：I don't really know much about how to deal with global warming. I think possibly we need to reduce car emissions.

49. I'm not an expert on...

我不是建筑方面的专家，但我认为应该修复并保存旧建筑。它们是我们文化中的一部分。

例句：I'm not an expert on architecture, but I think some old buildings should be **restored and maintained**. They are **part of our culture**.

50. It depends on the situation.

视情况而定。如果你是在一次重要的会议上迟到，那么其他人不会原谅你。

例句：It depends on the situation. If you are late for an important meeting, other people won't forgive you.

51. It depends on whether...

这取决于你是给朋友买礼物还是为从来没见过的人准备礼物。

例句：It depends on whether you buy a present for your friends or whether you prepare a present for somebody you haven't seen before.

表示认同（觉得什么东西重要）的句子

52. That's probably a good idea...

通过看纪录片学习历史应该是一个好方法，因为这很有趣。

例句：That's probably a good idea to learn history by **watching documentaries**, because it is interesting.

53. I think it's important to...

我认为花时间和朋友在一起是很重要的，因为这可以维持良好的关系。

例句：I think it's important to spend more time with friends, because it can help **maintain a good relationship**.

54. What matters most is...

对很多老师来说，重要的是他们的学生能在考试中获得好成绩。

例句：What matters most for many teachers is that their students can **get a good grade** in the exam.

55. it is necessary...

我认为有必要教孩子如何做饭，这对他们的健康来说很重要。

例句：I think it is necessary to teach children about how to **cook a meal**, which is important to their health.

56. I think it's best to...

我认为最好上大学然后获得学位，否则你很难在当今的社会中成功。

例句：I think it's best to go to college and **complete a degree**; otherwise, you're unlikely to succeed in today's world.

57. It's better to...

最好给孩子们自由，让他们独自做决定，而不是让他们听从我们的指令。

例句：It's better to give children freedom to **make decisions** independently than require them to **follow our instructions**.

58. ...definitely has an important role to play in...

毫无疑问，在帮助孩子发展社交技能方面，父母扮演着重要的角色。

例句：Parents definitely have an important role to play in helping children **develop social skills**.

59. The role...should not be overlooked.

游客在发展可持续旅游业方面的作用不可被忽视。

例句：The role of tourists in **sustainable tourism** should not be overlooked.

60. have a huge/direct impact on...

是的，我同意互联网对我们的生活有很大的影响。

例句：Yes, I agree that the Internet has a huge impact on our lives.

61. have an effect on...

我们制造出来的垃圾会对动物产生影响。

例句：The waste we produce can have an effect on animals.

62. Without...I find it difficult to...

如果没有电脑，我很难完成我的工作。

例句：Without computers, I find it difficult to **complete my work**.

表示合理的句子

63. It is fair that...

顶尖的运动员能挣很多钱，这很公平。

例句：It is fair that top sportspeople can earn a lot of money.

表示喜好的句子

64. I like...

我喜欢读书，因为我可以丰富自己的知识。

例句：I like reading books because I can **increase my knowledge**.

65. I prefer to...

我喜欢自己一个人学习，因为我可以专注于书本。

例句：I prefer to study alone because I can concentrate on the book.

66. I enjoy...

是的，我一直很享受做运动，而不是在电视上看。

例句：Yes, I have been enjoying doing sports, rather than watching them on TV.

67. I'd love to...

如果我有足够的钱，以后我想买一辆宝马。

例句：I'd love to buy a BMW in the future, if I can afford it.

68. My favourite...is...

我最喜欢的爱好是读书，因为它能使我知识渊博。

例句：My favourite hobby is reading because it can make me more knowledgeable.

69. I don't dislike..., but I wouldn't say that...

我不讨厌游泳，但也不能说我喜欢这项运动。

例句：I don't dislike swimming, but I wouldn't say (that) I love this sport.

70. It's always interesting to...

是的，和朋友在周末喝杯咖啡总是很有趣的。

Yes, it's always interesting to have a coffee with your friends at weekends.

表示不同的句子

71. The main difference is that...

最大的区别是，许多男孩更愿意学习园艺和割草，然而女孩会选择学习厨艺。

例句：The main difference is that many boys prefer to learn **gardening and mowing lawns**, while girls would choose to learn cooking skills.

72. There are many striking/substantial differences between...

在如何度过闲暇时间方面，男人和女人有两个很大的不同。

例句：There are two striking differences between men and women in terms of the ways they spend free time.

表示原因的句子

73. The main reason why...is that...

例句：The main reason why people exchange gifts on some occasions is that it is **a marker of a strong relationship**.

人们会在某些场合交换礼物的主要原因是这种行为代表着牢固的人际关系。

74. This is because...

在某些城市中，提高汽油价格并不能让人们少驾车。这是因为他们乘坐不了公共交通工具，开车是唯一的选择。

例句：In some cities, **raising petrol prices** does not discourage people from driving cars. This is because they do not have access to **public transport** and driving is the only choice.

75. This is caused by...

我认为迟到是由较差的时间管理能力导致的。

例句：I think lateness is possibly caused by **poor time management skills**.

76. This is due to...the result of...

在某些地区，贫穷是由缺少发展经济的基础设施导致的。

例句：Poverty in some areas is possibly due to the lack of **facilities and infrastructures** for growing the economy.

77. It is understandable why...

我认为如今很多人吃快餐是可以理解的。他们太忙了，没办法自己做饭。

例句：I think it is understandable why many people today **eat fast food**. They are too busy to cook a meal.

78. a factor in...

我认为受教育是成功的重要因素。如果你想要成功，你需要上大学。

例句：I think education is an important factor in one's success. You need to **go to college** if you want to succeed.

79. the main cause of...

我认为，路面上车的数量越来越多是导致城市中交通堵塞的主要原因。

例句：I suppose the main cause of traffic congestion in cities is the **increase in the number of cars** on the roads.

80. Some people wrongly believe that...

有些人错误地认为，只要他们穿时尚的衣服，别人就会觉得他们有钱又有品位。

例句：Some people wrongly believe that as long as they wear fashionable clothes, they will be considered to be **wealthy and tasteful**.

有些人错误地认为，买房并不是一种冒险的投资，而且房价会继续上涨。

例句：Some people wrongly believe that buying a house is not **a risky investment** and **housing prices** will continue to rise.

表示地点的句子

81. It's where...

这是人们每天做户外活动的地方。

例句：It's where people choose to do outdoor activities every day.

表示时间和频率的句子

82. at weekends 在周末

83. during the week 在周中

我通常在周末去超市，因为平时我没有时间去。

例句：I normally go to the supermarket at weekends, because I have no time doing that during the week.

84. every day

我每天都和我的朋友打电话，因为这能帮助我们保持联系。

例句：I talk to my friends on the phone every day, because this can help us **keep in touch with each other**.

85. once a week/twice a week

如果天气好的话，我每周慢跑一两次。

例句：I **go for a jog** once or twice a week if the weather's nice.

86. hardly

不是的，我很少有时间看电影，因为我有时需要加班。

例句：No, I hardly have time to watch a film because I have to work overtime from time to time.

87. whenever I have free time

我一有空就去看我的家人，因为家庭活动能给我带来一种幸福感。

例句：I visit my family whenever I have free time because family activities can give me **a sense of happiness**.

88. I don't have time to do...

我没时间做运动，因为我的时间安排得很紧。

例句：I don't have time to do any sports because I **have a tight schedule**.

89. at this time of year

在每年的这个时候，很多家庭会花大量的钱给孩子买礼物。

例句：Many families at this time of year would spend a lot of money buying gifts for children.

表示过去时间的句子

90. ...in the last twenty years.

近二十年以来，我们度过闲暇时间的方式发生了很多变化。

例句：There have been many changes in the ways we spend our leisure time in the last twenty years.

91. That was the time when...

例句：That was the time when my father **took a walk** with me.

那是我父母和我一起散步的时候。

92. The last time...was...

我最后一次见到他是在一次晚宴上。

例句：The last time I saw him was at a dinner party.

我最后一次去图书馆是在大学。

例句：The last time I went to library was at college.

93. It was the first time...

那是我第一次来这座城市旅游。

例句：It was the first time I had travelled to this city.

表示将来时间的句子

94. someday

我希望有一天我能经营自己的事业。

例句：I hope, someday, I can **run my own business**.

95. At some point in the future,...

未来的某个时候，我想住在一个气候温和的地方。

例句：At some point in the future, I'd like to live in a place with a **mild climate**.

表示回忆的句子

96. I can't remember...

我想不起来小时候收的第一份礼物了。

例句：I can't remember the first gift I received as a child.

97. It was probably in my first year...

大概是在我大学一年级的时候，我在一家小餐馆打工挣钱。

例句：It was probably in my first year at university, when I chose to work for a small restaurant to **earn money**.

98. Looking back on...

回想起这些经历，我认为不应该害怕失败。失败促使你更加努力。

例句：Looking back on these experiences, I would argue that don't be afraid of failure. Failures can push you to work harder.

99. In retrospect,...

回想起来，我应该会做不同的决定，然后选择其他的做法。

例句：In retrospect, I would possibly make a different decision and choose alternative **courses of action**.

表示支持的句子

100. I'd say that...

我想说，如果人们想要成为好的沟通者，就应该学会倾听别人。

例句：I'd say that people should be able to listen to others, if they want to be good communicator.

附录 4：口语 9 分学生的备考心得

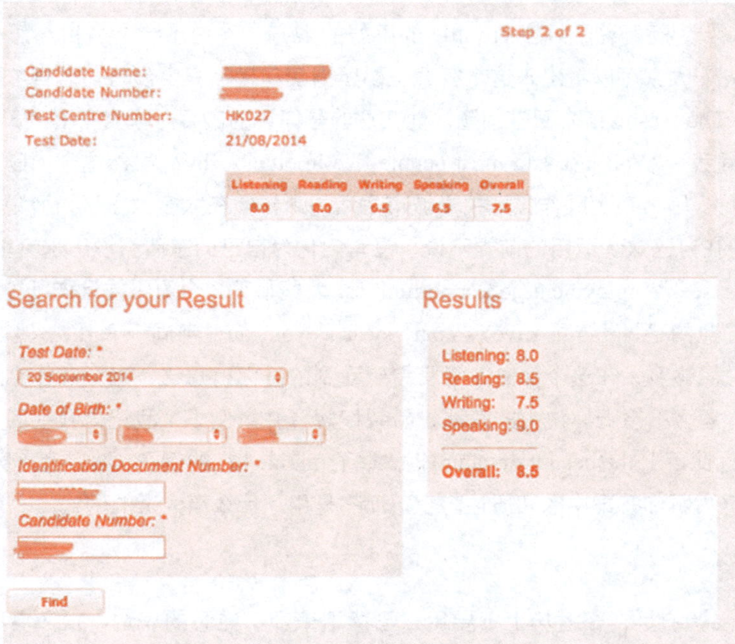

口语考试哪些方面比较重要 / 纠正口语误区

首先说明的是，我不是什么读外国语学校从小就跟外教练口语的孩子。我和大家一样接受中国式的哑巴教育，就是基础稍微好一些，语法比较清楚，口语之前唯一的优势就是发音比较好，因为没和外国人交流过，刚开始准备时连一句话都说不出来。8 月当我沉浸在复习口语的痛苦之中时，也想过考 9 分的人到底都说了些什么，然后现在回过头看，我觉得大家一定不要被很多中国所谓口语名师误导，很多人把口语神化了，觉得一定要说“特别地道的表达”，或背一大堆俚语和“变化的句式”，甚至觉得只有 native speaker 才能拿 9 分。其实很多 native speaker 也会拿 6 分。雅思口语考试一方面考查的是你是否 feel comfortable using English, 而另一方面考查的是你的思辨能力，就是你是否有很多 ideas，而 native speaker 不一定有很多 ideas。在走了很多弯路以后我发现，口语考试最重要的有以下几个方面。

1. 考官想听的首先是你的内容

这就是为何老顾强调用作文的观点和词伙准备如此重要的原因。这里顺便提醒大家一下练习 Part 3 的重要性。Part 3 往往是考查一个人真正语言水平和思辨能力的环节，考官尤其是大陆考官知道很多人准备过 Part 1 和 Part 2，所以他们会在 Part 3 问一些刁钻的问题来测试你的真实水平。很多人说我就想得 6 分，Part 3 跟我没关系 —— 但是如果你 Part 1 和 Part 2 说得很流利，Part 3 却突然结结巴巴，也会对你的分数有很大影响。我 9. 20 这场考试，虽然 Part 1 和 Part 2 说得很流利、很好，但我想能得高分是因为我在 Part 3 仍然表现很好，甚至更好。那天 Part 2 的题目是描述一个漂亮的人，我之前练习过这个 Topic 的 Part 3 是问关于人的相貌和品格以及明星之类的问题，没想到考官到 Part 3 直接说：“Let’s talk about the beauty of nature.” 我心里好无语，觉得这和 Part 2 根本没有关系嘛。第一个问题是 What do you think people love landscape? 我还疑惑了一下什么是 landscape，问他："You mean the natural scenery, like the lake, the great mountain?"他点点头。然后我大脑一片空白，我说："I think people love landscape because…"，然后迅速想了几秒，补充说："because most people live in cities"，接着说了好多 city life 的不好的地方，又说了一下大自然怎么好，最后说："So people love…"，大家可以看出来这个答案里面所谓套句模板完全没有，考官才不在意你用 That is because 还是用 The reason is 来回答问题，他在意的是你说的内容。考官在 Part 3 问的问题真的完全随机，他随后问我："You just said most people live in cities, why?"虽然这个问题在我意料之外，但我仍然胸有成竹，因为在老顾作文里关于城市生活的素材实在太多太多了，我说了一大堆观点和词伙（注意一定是在自己熟练运用的前提下说，没有内化为自己的东西强说出来会很 awkward），比如 leisure facilities, seek employment, job opportunities, 大概举了 3 个原因并且详细论述完才停下来。在 Part 3 我们要注意的是，一定要 give as many ideas as you can，不同于 Part 1 只需回答几句话，在 Part 3 你一定要说得够多，在这个部分，考官希望看到的是你有想法。老顾在作文里强调的拓展在 Part 3 同样重要，考官不想听你说虚的东西，希望你解释并举例子。我记得我在回答下一个问题为什么 cityscape 永远比不上 the beauty of nature 时，举了 marine life 的例子，然后考官笑着点了一下头，可以看出，他在努力听你答案中的实质性内容，而不是用了什么高大上的词汇。

2. 自然

首先一定要强调的是，在考场上不要用自己背下来却不熟悉的表达。很多老师在口语课上教了一堆俚语，然后让学生在考场上尽量去用这些东西，简直是误人子弟。当你在考场上刻意地去用一个表达时，只有一个结果，就是 sounds really really awkward, 而且考官一听就知道你是在刻意用这个词，分数并不会高。希望大家可以体会 speak spontaneously 是什么意思。但是不用不熟悉的表达不代表不能用好的表达，唯一的准则是，在平时练习中尽量去运用一些地道的口语表达，使之真正成为自己可以自然说出来的东西，而不只是记忆中的零星片段，然后在考试中，抛开一切杂念，focus on the question and speak as you think。

3. 不犯语法错误

和老顾在作文里强调的一样，语法是外国人很在意的东西，它在口语里同样重要。以前我觉得雅思口语至于吗，连时态、单复数这样的东西都在乎，口语谁会在意那么多。直到我有一天看一个中国明星的英文访谈，她在几个本该用过去时的句子里用了一般现在时，听起来真的非常尴尬。我体会到语法的准确对一个听者来说的重要性。经历了 8 月的口语复习挣扎之后，在最后备考的一周，我下决心在每个方面都做到完美，因此要求自己在口语中不犯任何语法错误，主要包括时态、单复数、人称，每天在练习中注意。最后的几天，我真的可以做到在无意识的状态下也能自然地转换时态和人称。考试那天，我从头到尾没有犯语法错误，除了有一次把 her 说成了 his，但我立刻纠正过来了。我想这会让考官对你的语言功底有一个非常良好的印象。

4. 流利

流利真的太重要了，其实应该是最重要的，但是把它列在第 4 是因为我觉得只要你做到了 1（有 ideas），你自然会流利。这里的流利不是指考官问一个问题你就可以立刻回答出来。正如 1 里所说，有时考官的问题是刁钻的，你肯定需要时间思考，哪怕你想几秒钟也不会有任何问题，但我在思考的几秒中时间里也没有慌张，而是非常淡定，也没有表现出对英语运用的不自信，而是专注于想这个问题。但是停顿太久也不行，你们之间需要有效的交流，停顿太久，考官只会认为你不知道该怎么回答这个问题。

如何准备

永远记住：Speaking is a habit. 上面所有强调的点都是基于每天的练习的，只能自己练口语的就自己练，可以和外国人练习的就多利用机会。不可能练一天就做到说得流利，不可能练一天就做到没有语法错误，不可能练一天就做到在 Part 3 抛一个问题脑子里就有一堆 ideas。但是 Practice makes perfect，不要纠结于为什么自己总是回答不好问题，just keep practising。

起初，我抱着把所有预测题都练习一下的想法，开始准备自己的口语稿子，因为 9 月遇上换题季，我准备了 5～8 月的 40 个 topic 的 Part 2 及 Part 3 相关问题，又准备了 9 月新题的 40 个 topic 的 Part 2 & 3，积累了整整 100 多页两万多字的 word 文档，每天练习说。后来其实考试里 Part 1 和 Part 3 并不是我准备过的问题，但是我仍然对答如流，我才真正明白准备这些材料的意义：准备的过程让我熟悉了所有主流的 topic，考场上即便考官随机抛出各种问题，我也能运用其他问题中的相关 ideas 和词伙去说。所以想要背现成素材的同学们醒醒吧，重要的其实是你自己准备素材的那个消化过程，而不是素材本身，你说再平常的词汇也没关系，有关系的是你在准备过程中针对每一个话题积累的 ideas，和逐渐学会的熟练地组织语言的能力。

考试过程中应注意的问题

1. 放松

你可以在平时的练习中注意这个注意那个（比如语法错误、用词），但进入考场，一定告诉自己 relax，唯一需要做的就是专心听考官的问题，专心思考怎么回答。其他什么有没有用地道口语表达、有没有用变化的句式统统抛到脑后。你放松的状态会给考官一个积极的暗示：He/she feels comfortable when he/she speaks English.

2. 自信其实和放松没有明确的界限

我想说的是最后一次考试，坐在门口等考官出来的时候，我紧张得要死，因为最后一次机会对我实在太重要，我心都快跳到嗓子眼了，但我不停地告诉自己 relax and be confident。从见到考官开始的整个过程，我一直保持着微笑，假装自己是一个口语高手、对自己的口语有十足信心的样子。整个过程，虽然我遇到了各种各样想都没想过的问题，但因为我心里只有一点：Focus on the question and speak as you think. 所以我可以集中注意力思考每一个问题然后给出很多观点。

3. Part 1

这一部分很重要，考官会对你的表达能力有一个初步的印象。唯一的要点是 Answer the question directly, 别说其他花里胡哨的东西。考官问什么就答什么，多则多说，少则少说，一般是 2～4 句，我这次考试个别问题也说得比较多。但不要说和问题无关的东西。

4. Part 2

这一部分同样很重要，会加深考官对你语言能力的印象。要点是要像讲故事一样去说。一定要有一个自然的开头，比如这次考试的 Part 2，假如我说 Here I would describe XXX. She is a really beautiful person，虽然没有错，但是考官也是人，他每天听那么多考生说，这样的开头很难吸引他的注意力。我一般会像跟朋友聊天一样去描述 Part 2，比如这次我准备说我喜欢的一个歌星，开头是 When I was a child, one day I was watching TV and saw a girl singing in a talent show. I was attracted by her voice... 这样，考官的注意力很容易被吸引过来，考官乐于继续听你接下来的故事。另外就是可以在 Part 2 答案里加一些有趣的东西，一点点就好，比如我说："At first I was just fascinated by her powerful voice. Soon I found she was really beautiful. I mean she doesn't have standard beautiful looks, but there is something really special in her eyes, and she looks gorgeous when she is on stage. "考官点了点头，我想如果我只是描述了她的五官怎么好看，一定会和很多人重复。然而，就是这样一点点不一样让 Part 2 的答案好了很多。看到这里你会发现，要点仍然不是使用多么高大上的词汇，而是你的内容。

5. Part 3

不好意思，这一部分同样非常重要，甚至比前面更重要，在口试中没有任何一个部分是你可以疏于练习的。Part 3 为什么重要以及哪些地方比较重要已经在前面口语应该注意的问题里的第 1 点详细阐述过了。

我觉得虽然只准备了 2 个月，但这 2 个月似乎过得异常漫长，我经历了很多痛苦之后才有了这么多深刻的体会。最后告诉大家，不要纠结于还有一个月或还有一个星期、口语是不是没有希望提高了这样的问题。我在最后一个星期被逼得没办法的时候，告诉自己，不要想别的，就想怎样考一场完美的雅思考试，每天都要有提高、有顿悟。事实上真的是，因为那段时间在上老顾的课，我在写作和口语上每天都有新的领悟。

附录 5：如何保证在雅思作文和口语考试中使用正确的时态

雅思口语和书信写作一样，时态变化非常大。对比而言，雅思大作文的时态比较简单（基本上就是一般现在时、现在完成时和一般将来时），而图表作文用一般过去时居多。

在口语考试中，或参加 G 类考试时，在考场上主要是通过句子的谓语和时间状语来确定时态。

一旦确定时态，在回答中或者写作中就要保持时态的一致。正如下面很多题目的回答所示，谓语动词和题目的时态保持一致。如果谓语动词是过去时，回答一般就要用过去时；如果是现在时，回答就要用现在时。

- 一般过去时的谓语动词和时间状语。

例题：In your country, did people in the past keep in contact in the same ways as they do today?

谓语动词总结：出现 did 等助动词或者是系动词时使用一般过去时。

时间状语总结：in the past, when you were a child, when you were younger, 10 years ago...

回答：Many people in China in the past **contacted each other** by mail or by making phone calls, but now they write email.

- 一般现在时的谓语动词和时间状语。

例题：How easy is it to travel around the country?

例题：What kind of people become famous people these days?

例题：Should individuals or governments be responsible for making people's lifestyle healthy?

谓语动词总结：出现 does, do, is, am, are 这些助动词或者是系动词时使用一般现在时。

出现 should, could, can 这些情态动词也用一般现在时。

时间状语总结：these days, today, now, in today's society, every day, usually, always, nowadays...

回答：**It is** very convenient to travel throughout the country because we **have** high speed train services between major cities.

回答：Every ordinary people **can rise to fame** overnight. Some people, for example, **put** funny videos online, which **can make** them famous easily.

回答：I think government policy **can promote** healthy living and **it is** the government's responsibility to help the public live a healthy life.

- 现在完成时的谓语动词和时间状语。

例题：Has your country changed much since you were a child?

例题：Have relationships with neighbours where you live changed in recent years?

谓语动词总结：如果出现 has/have + 过去分词，就用完成时态。

时间状语总结：...since you were a child, in recent years...

回答：Yes, **there have been** many significant changes in my country over the few decades. The economy **has been expanding** rapidly and many people **have been lifted** out of poverty.

回答：Yes, I **have seen** some changes. We **do not socialise** with neighbours as much as we did before.

• 一般将来时的谓语动词和时间状语。

例题：Do you think all new homes will be equipped with household machines in the future?

例题：Would you prefer to live in a hot place or a cold place? Why?

谓语动词总结：如果出现 will, would，用将来时态。

时间状语总结：in the future...

回答：I think people in the future **would buy** many household appliances because they **won't have** a lot of time cooking a meal, doing laundry and tidying the room. They need efficient machines to do household chores.

回答：**I'd like to** live in a place with a mild climate.

• 让学生展望未来的问题一般出现在口语 Part 3。

将来时态的表现比较多样，除了常用的"will do"之外，还有"would like to""be likely to"等。当表示不是很确定的情况时，可以使用"might""would"这样的表达。

我们看看下面的例子：

例题：Do you think hobbies people have will be different in the future?

回答：Yes, there **will be** some changes, I think. More hobbies **will involve** web-based technology. People **are likely to** stay at home to play video games and online games. Instead of visiting friends and going out for social life, they **might spend** more time chatting online.

• 注意，有些问题涉及不同时态的使用。这种题目往往涉及过去和现在的对比。

例题：Is this different from the kind of achievement that made people famous in the past?

回答：Today, some television shows **can make** people famous very easily, but in the past, only talented politicians, writers or scientists **could become** reputable.

例题：Do you like the same colours now as you did when you were younger?

回答：No, when I was a kid, **I loved** bright colours, but now, **I prefer** dark colours.

上面这些题目主要出现在口语的 Part 1 和 Part 3 中，在 Part 2 中，时态也可以从题目中看出。

像下面这题，题目里出现了一般现在时、一般过去时、现在完成时等时态。学生在回答的时候，都要对时态做出相应的变化。

Describe a piece of electronic equipment that you find useful.

You should say:

what it is

how you learned to use it

how long you have had it

and explain why you find this piece of electronic equipment useful.

简单的回答：

(The electronic appliance I'd like to talk about **is** a microwave oven.)

I **bought it** last year, and I **followed** the manual to learn how to use it.

I **have used** it since then, because it **has been** very useful.

Whenever I **want to** have a quick meal, I **put** packaged food in it and it'll be ready in five minutes.

下面我们说说虚拟语气的应用。虚拟语气在口语中是一种凑时间的方法。

学习点 1：虚拟语气简单来说，就是阐述一种不可能发生的条件下，可能产生的结果。看看下面这些例子。

例 1：

If he studied harder, he might pass the exam.

大意：如果他学习勤奋，他可能通过考试。（他没有勤奋学习）

例 2：

If I were you, I would take an umbrella.

大意：如果我是你的话，我就带伞。（我根本不可能是你）

例 3：

If he had taken my advice, he would not have made such a mistake.

大意：如果他采纳了我的建议，就不会犯这种错误了。（他没有采纳）

学习点 2：虚拟语气的动词变化主要取决于所描述事情是发生在过去、现在还是将来。我们主要介绍过去和现在，因为在雅思考试中这两者使用的比较多。

	正常语气 indicative mood	虚拟语气 subjunctive mood
过去	I did not have money, so I could not enroll on the course. （我没有钱，所以我不能注册） 描述的是一个过去发生的事实	If I **had** money, I **would/could/might have** enrolled on the course. （如果我有钱的话，我就注册那个课程了） 描述的是一个和过去事实相反的假设
现在	I do not have money, so I cannot enroll. （我没有钱，所以我不能注册） 描述的是一个现在的事实	If I **had** money, I **would/could/might** enroll on the course. （如果我有钱的话，我就注册那个课程了） 描述的是一个和现在事实相反的假设

学习点 3：虚拟语气在写作和口语中都有很重要的应用，是一种凑字数的好办法。

以这篇作文为例，首先我写了科学对保护环境的重要性，举例说明如何有助于节省资源：

Scientific research also makes it possible for us to **preserve the environment** for future generations. A large proportion of these projects aim to improve the efficiency of using natural resources. For example, the research on **alternative energy sources** can help find replacements of **fossil fuels** and slow down the destruction of the **natural landscape** for oil drilling or mining.

但是我发现字数不是很够，但是考场时间不足，又想不到其他拓展方法，怎么办？可以用虚拟语气阐述一个和前面的描述相反的事情。如：

If financial resources were spread thinly, scientists would not be able to make breakthroughs in these areas of study.

段落最后一句话事实上是通过虚拟语气去强调“要把财政资源投入到科学调查上”，意思是“如果资源分布太窄，那么科学家很难有什么突破性的进展”。

我们看看口语的例子。

Part 3 有这么一个题目：

Do you think technology has made our lives simpler?

你在考场上忧心忡忡，不知道怎么回答，这时候突然想到说电脑：

Yes, I do, computers enable us to get whatever information we want easily.

We can even work or study at home with computers.

这个时候，你大脑里又开始闹水灾，不知道说什么，其实你可以用虚拟语气。比如说假设没有电脑了，生活会有什么变化。

If we did not have computers, we would have to go to school or travel to the office every day. This could be a big challenge.

附录 6：口语 Part 2 标准化问题回答的一些思路

大家可以参考这些关于回答 Part 2 who, when, where, how 的问题的思路。为了避免和其他考生重复，你可以进行一定程度的改动和丰富。

例如，如果题目需要你描写你的一个朋友，那么你可以说 he is very strong, passionate about sport, 然后加入例子，如 He goes to the gym regularly and also plays soccer. He also watches live games on TV. 这样就不会重复。

描述人 who（每句话可以作为描述人的一种可能回答）

思考方向	可能的回答
外貌和外形	高大 tall and strong，非常喜欢体育，love sport，精力充沛 full of energy
	漂亮，去哪里都是关注的重点 centre of attention
性格	很有礼貌 polite and friendly，很有人缘 get pretty well with others
	外向 an outgoing personality，和朋友出去玩 hang out with friends，很多朋友
	内向 reserved，not very sociable 喜欢一个人在家里 stay at home
素质	乐于助人 be ready to help others，心肠很好 a man who has a big heart
	热情好客 show hospitality, 和朋友一起吃饭 eat outside
	责任感强 have a strong sense of responsibility
生活习惯	办公室工作 work in the office，很少运动 lead an inactive life
爱好	热爱音乐 passion for music，喜欢唱歌、听音乐等 be obsessed with music
	爱阅读，坚持每天阅读 love reading, 爱学习 enjoy learning something new
工作	职业女性 working mum，同时需要照顾家人 raise a family
	管理非常忙 run a company，到处飞 fly frequently to different places
年龄	年轻人，有很多梦想 realise their dreams，希望成功 achieve success
	老人，有经验 life experience, be experienced in，给我很多的建议 give some useful advice，非常有智慧 wise
经济情况	出身贫寒 from a poor family，生活拮据 live on a tight budget
	比较富裕，衣食无忧 live a comfortable life

描述时间 when（每句话可以作为描述时间的一种可能回答）

思考方向	可能的回答
周	工作日，很忙 busy with work，很累，没时间放松 no time to relaxed 工作压力大，没有时间去
	周末，不用上课 attend lectures，可以和朋友一起 meet up with my friends
日	上午，容易专注学习和工作 concentrate on work，想东西很快 have a sharp mind
	晚上，在家里看电视，和家人去散步运动 go for a walk

季节	春天，花开 flowers in bloom，树木变绿，适合去远足 go for a hike，爬山 hill walking
	夏天，国外旅游 travel abroad，海边度假 get a sun tan on the beach
	秋天，成熟的季节 harvest season, 天气凉爽，秋游 autumn outing
	冬天，比较寒冷，在家里 stay indoors 过传统的节日 celebrate traditional festivals
大学	大一，学习勤奋，需要适应大学的生活 adapt to university life
	大二，学习专业课 specialist courses，提高自己的专业能力 specialist knowledge
	大三，考各种考试 take exams，希望可以找到工作 find good jobs
	大四，实习 work as an intern，需要对未来有一个明确规划 a defined career path
人生的阶段	小学，有春游 school trips，课外活动 extracurricular activities，很高兴
	中学，每天备考 prepare for exams，很累
	工作，每天要培训 receive training，要完成工作，压力很大 experience stress

描述地点 where（每句话可以作为描述地点的一种可能回答）

思考方向	可能的回答
家	在家里，比较轻松 feel relaxed
大学	图书馆，很多学生复习备考 revise for exams
	书店，可以挑选喜欢的书籍，增加知识 read for pleasure
城内设施	咖啡吧，环境比较好 inviting ambience，有好听的背景音乐 background music
	健身房，有很多的设备 exercise equipment，很多训练的课程 training sessions
	公园，当地的重要景点 a major attraction，可以运动和骑车
	购物中心，有很多喜欢的品牌店 chain stores，周围有很多饭馆、电影院，KTV，娱乐设施丰富 recreational facilities
城市中心	CBD，有很多商业街 shopping streets，办公大楼 office blocks
住宅区	residential areas, 空间比较大，下班后可以运动，环境比较好
乡村	环境比较好，空气很好，食品新鲜 fresh ingredients
富人区	affluent suburb 环境好，有很多好的学校 prestigious schools
风景区	scenic sports, 吸引很多的游客 receive visitors
林区	forested areas, 很多人爬山、远足等
城市的种类	大都市 metropolitan areas, 非常拥挤，熙熙攘攘 hustle and bustle
	小城市 small town, 生活节奏比较慢 life is slow，人们很淳朴 unsophisticated
	科技城市，有很多高科技公司 technology companies，经济发展很快

国家	文化遗产很多的国家，有很多历史建筑 historic buildings
	经济发达的国家 affluent country，有很多就业机会 job opportunities
	英语国家，提升英语，感受外国文化 English-speaking country

描述方式 how（每句话可以作为描述方式的一种可能回答）

思考方向	可能的回答
媒体	网络，看新闻 read news，看视频 watch videos
	手机，看 mobile phone apps 去增加知识，还有看社交媒体 social media
	电视，访谈节目 talk shows，电视新闻 television news，纪录片 TV documentaries
	报纸，专栏作家分析，增加了解 written by columnists
	书籍，权威人士写的 written by experts，有数据支持 backed up by statistics
身边的人	朋友，有相关经验，给了一些建议 give advice
	老师，有很多知识，传授很多知识给我 impart knowledge to
	同学，学习成绩很好 excellent student，和我分享很多知识
	父母，有很多生活经验 life experience，给我建议
	上司，很强的领导能力 leadership skills，给我很多指点 give me guidance

图书在版编目（C I P）数据

顾家北手把手教你雅思词伙：2.0版 / 顾家北编著. —北京：中国人民大学出版社，2017.6
ISBN 978-7-300-24521-8

Ⅰ.①顾…　Ⅱ.①顾…　Ⅲ.①IELTS-词汇-自学参考资料　Ⅳ.①H313

中国版本图书馆CIP数据核字（2017）第123484号

顾家北手把手教你雅思词伙（2.0版）

顾家北　编著

Gu Jiabei Shoubashou Jiaoni Yasi Cihuo（2.0 Ban）

出版发行	中国人民大学出版社		
社　　址	北京中关村大街31号	邮政编码	100080
电　　话	010-62511242（总编室）		010-62511770（质管部）
	010-82501766（邮购部）		010-62514148（门市部）
	010-62515195（发行公司）		010-62515275（盗版举报）
网　　址	http://www.crup.com.cn		
	http://www.1kao.com.cn（中国1考网）		
经　　销	新华书店		
印　　刷	北京玺诚印务有限公司		
规　　格	185mm×260mm　16开本	版　　次	2016年8月第1版
			2017年6月第2版
印　　张	16.75	印　　次	2018年7月第10次印刷
字　　数	388 000	定　　价	46.00元